LANDSCAPES

History of the British Landscape

General editor: MICHAEL REED

The Fairy Glen, Bettws.

Frontispiece   The Fairy Glen, Bettws, signed Myrbach, used as an illustration to P. Villars, 'A foreign artist and author in England', *Art Journal* 1887, p. 273 (Courtesy University of Exeter Library). With thanks to the artist who, unusually, included all the other artists in the picture.

LANDSCAPES

The Artists' Vision

Peter Howard

London and New York

First published 1991
by Routledge
11 New Fetter Lane, London EC4P 4EE

Simultaneously published in the USA and Canada by Routledge
a division of Routledge, Chapman, and Hall, Inc.
29 West 35th Street, New York, NY 10001

Set in 10/12 pt Times, Linotron 202
Disc conversion by Columns Ltd, Reading
Printed in England by T.J. Press (Padstow), Cornwall

British Library Cataloguing in Publication Data
Howard, Peter
Landscapes: the artists' vision.
1.   English landscape paintings, history
I.   Title
758.10942

Library of Congress Cataloging in Publication Data
Howard, Peter
Landscapes: the artists' vision / Peter Howard.
p.   cm.
Includes bibliographical references.
1.   Landscape painting, British. I.   Title.
ND1354.H79   1991
758'.141'0941—dc20   90–8178

ISBN 0–415–00775–5

For Margery, Jay and Ben

Contents

List of figures

Acknowledgements

For a geographer to write a book concerning painting is a daunting task. It would not have been attempted without the support of Roger Kain of the University of Exeter, nor achieved without the critiques of art historian colleagues, Michael Pidgley and Sam Smiles. In addition, many of the causes for the changes in taste uncovered in the work are the result of conversations with scholars in many disciplines, especially members of the Landscape Research Group.

Those who have allowed their pictures to be reproduced here are acknowledged in the appropriate place. The library staff at the Royal Academy of Arts deserve special mention for their tolerating someone spending many weeks poring over their catalogues with a calculator. Similarly the staff of the West Country Studies section of Devon County Libraries, and of the Royal Albert Memorial Museum, Exeter, must often have been perplexed by the strange collection of material demanded of them.

Finally my thanks to my wife, Margery, and children, Catherine, Philip and Rebecca, for having survived the experience.

Peter Howard
10 October 1989

1

Why study pictures?

This is a book about pictures. That a series of volumes on the History of the British Landscape should include one about pictures should cause no surprise, for the word 'landscape' continued to refer only to pictures for many years after its introduction into English from the Dutch 'landskap'. J.B. Jackson has studied the derivation in some detail in *Landscape Meanings and Values*,[1] although that study deals with its usage in America with some marked differences from British usage. In America the landscape is frequently imagined as a plan view, and the word often seems synonymous with the geographer's 'region', although one retaining a strong visual cohesion. In Britain landscapes are almost invariably imagined in elevation, a concept much closer to the word's artistic origins.

Of course, studies of pictures usually emerge from the discipline of Art History and concentrate on the artists and their work. This study derives from the geographical discipline, and is concerned not with the pictures themselves but what they can tell us about landscape in reality. Pictures, even photographs, do not always tell the truth about the appearance of the landscape. Only by examining a very large number of pictures of a particular view, as is being done by Farmer,[2] can the truth of appearance be gauged with any accuracy. No single picture is reliable evidence even for the existence let alone the appearance of any object in it.

If pictures are not sound evidence of the appearance of places, they are excellent clues to the ways in which places were perceived, and who considered which places to be attractive at what time. Meinig has suggested that 'landscape images have an objective content as 1) they can be attributed to someone who 2) created, obtained or conveyed in a context which 3) is shared with others'.[3] Heathcote has made the most direct appeal for the use of pictures: 'Research into man's perception of his environment both past and present . . . would gain much from a study of landscape painting.'[4] By examining the landscape pictures produced over a long period an accurate account of the ebb and flow of popularity of certain locations and certain subjects can be derived. The map of historical landscape taste produced by such a method is one that shows very dramatic fluctuations over short periods of time. The fact that landscape taste is not static has been known for a long time, though far too frequently ignored. Several writers have shown the comparative modernity of the preference for mountain scenery, for example, which was considered unattractive until the eighteenth century. M. Hope Nicholson demonstrated this in 1959,[5] and later an article by Ronald Rees uses works of art for the same purpose.[6]

Keith Thomas[7] has shown, by a detailed and fascinating study of writings which reveal man's attitudes to animals and plants, how over three centuries an almost total transformation was wrought in the perception of nature. However, the speed of change which the evidence of pictures reveals is much faster than he suggested for an earlier period, and its consequences for the planning of attractive places very considerable.

Nevertheless his work is unusual and outstanding in exploring the territory on which a serious study of landscape attitudes might be based. There have been numerous theories expounded in recent years which attempt to explain why certain people have certain perceptions of their surroundings. These theories have emerged from various disciplines, and the need for a cross-disciplinary approach is now well established. This work is discussed in Chapter 2. Inevitably there has been a tendency for theoretical speculation to run ahead of the exploration of the territory. Thomas's work is exceptional, in being primarily a work of survey. This book, perhaps presumptuously, has a similar aim, still in Britain, but studying the period succeeding Thomas's interest, and using surviving pictures rather than writings. Some discussion concerning the possible causes and processes of changing tastes is attempted, but this is secondary to the drawing of the map of artists' landscape perception.

For practical purposes landscape tastes are often considered static. The conservation of specific tracts of land as National Parks or Areas of Outstanding Natural Beauty, or the listing of historic buildings, quite often for aesthetic reasons, all presuppose that notions of what constitutes attractive landscape are known, commonly held and unlikely to change in the short term. The evidence adduced here will deny at least the latter. For example, the attractiveness of moorland, such as in the Pennines or Dartmoor, dates only from the last quarter of the nineteenth century, and developed very rapidly.

The remainder of this chapter falls into two parts. First some account is given of the kind of techniques which are employed to produce the diagrams and maps which form the results of the exploration, though much detail is left to Appendix 1. This is followed by a rather speculative attempt to put English landscape preferences within a broader European context. The sources of many of the ideas which surface throughout the book are given in Chapter 2, before proceeding to draw the map of English artists' tastes in Chapters 3 to 8 and to speculate on causes and the future in Chapter 9.

The evidence from the Royal Academy

Landscape painting appears in this country in the seventeenth century; Martin Hardie is more precise: 'It would not be unreasonable to say that landscape painting "soe new in England" was brought to London when Pieter Paul Rubens came to the Court of Charles I in 1629.'[8] Rosenthal dates it later, but even more bluntly, claiming that 'British landscape painting was a product of the Restoration.'[9] Itinerant painters, often Dutch, were for many years important in disseminating landscape as a genre, and the Ogdens have studied its rise during the seventeenth century.[10] Thereafter, it began its period of dominance as the major subject in art, and the evidence used in this book dates as a continuous thread from the founding of the Royal Academy of Arts in 1768 and its first Summer Exhibition the following May. Since then a similar exhibition has been held every summer to the present, and a full catalogue has always been published. From time to time the rules governing the exhibition have been changed but such changes, listed at Appendix 2, have never been of a kind greatly to alter the flow of evidence. By the simple process of examining all the titles of landscape pictures exhibited from the first, 1769, exhibition until 1980, locating and mapping the places depicted, and noting the subjects of the pictures, a very large body of evidence can be accumulated, running to 75,000 titles.

There are other long running exhibitions of work. The Society of Artists (1760–91) and Free Society of Artists (1761–83) were significant in the eighteenth century, the British Institution (1806–67) in the nineteenth and the New English Art Club (1886–present) in the twentieth. None of these even approaches the longevity of the Royal Academy exhibition. The Old and New Watercolour Societies have done better (starting in 1805 and 1832 respectively and both continuing to the present) but they are restricted to one medium of picture, and there is plenty of evidence to suggest that each medium tends to be biased towards certain subjects.[11] Nevertheless the existence of these other annual shows can be used as a control, and Table 1 compares the figures obtained from the Royal Academy and the British Institution for the 1850s. The similarity is

Table 1 A comparison of landscape exhibits at the British Institution with those at the Royal Academy, 1850–9.

British Institution			Royal Academy		
County	No.	%	County	No.	%
Kent	155	7.5	Kent	159	6.8
Devon	123	6.0	Devon	148	6.3
Sussex	88	4.3	Surrey	124	5.3
Surrey	84	4.1	Sussex	89	3.8
Yorkshire	62	3.0 ⎫	Cumbria	82	3.5
Middlesex	62	3.0 ⎭	Yorkshire	70	3.0
Cumbria	59	2.9	Middlesex	64	2.7
Berkshire	50	2.4	Berkshire	60	2.6
Norfolk	42	2.0	Essex	39	1.7
London	30	1.5 ⎫	Isle of Wight	33	1.4
Essex	30	1.5 ⎭	London	27	1.2
Warwickshire	28	1.4	Warwickshire	26	1.1
Channel Isles	26	1.3	Norfolk	25	1.1
Isle of Wight	23	1.2	Channel Isles	24	1.0
Buckinghamshire	21	1.0 ⎫	Cornwall	23	1.0 ⎫
Oxfordshire	21	1.0 ⎭	Hampshire	23	1.0 ⎭
Northumberland	17	0.8 ⎫	Buckinghamshire	20	0.9
Gloucestershire	17	0.8 ⎭	Durham	19	0.8
Derbyshire	16	0.8	Cheshire	16	0.7
Cornwall	15	0.8	Oxfordshire	14	0.6

Numbers are total numbers of landscapes locatable to the county exhibited in the ten exhibitions. Percentages are numbers expressed as a proportion of the total number of locatable landscapes of England.

outstanding; of the top ten areas in the Royal Academy statistics the top eight are the same as the top eight for the British Institution. Numbers 9 and 10 (RA) rank as 12 and 14 in the BI, but the percentage differences are only between 1.41 for the Isle of Wight in the RA as against 1.16 in the BI.

A slightly more worrying aspect of the validity of the data obtained from the Royal Academy source is that the Academy has seen major changes in its status over its lifetime. In the eighteenth century most major artists were members. This position has slowly declined until for much of the twentieth century membership of the Academy has acted as the 'negative of ambition' for many significant artists.[12] However, the Academicians have always been professional artists of some stature, if not always so regarded by the avant-garde of the day. Also, despite the lowering of its status there has been no diminution in the number of pictures submitted to the Academy from which the Academicians could select those to hang. Table 2 indicates, on the contrary, that the odds against being selected have grown continually longer. Pictures hung at the

Academy exhibition are at least selected by artists of undoubted professional status, whatever the status of the painters themselves. The proportion of the selected pictures depicting landscape has inevitably varied. Although an average figure is about 30 per cent (of the pictures only, i.e. after the sculpture and architecture have been omitted), Figure 1 shows distinct variations. These fluctuations may have been due to prejudice on the part of the artistic establishment against landscape as a genre at various times. Certainly Reynolds's views about the inferiority of landscape painting were well known,[13] and there seems to have been continued prejudice in the late nineteenth century. This is suggested in Collier's presidential address to the Devonshire Association in 1879 when he claimed that landscape was still inferior: 'the Royal Academicians would seem so to regard it, if we may judge by the extent to which it is represented among them.'[14] His complaint, however, is hardly borne out by the figures. Obviously the fluctuations have necessitated the use of figures based on the proportion of landscape works in any one year which represented a particular place or subject.

The greatest problem in the use of the Academy catalogues is that the evidence is only that of the catalogue entries and not that of the pictures themselves. Two serious shortcomings follow from this. First, given catalogue entries alone there is more doubt as to whether a picture is a landscape than if the pictures themselves could be consulted. Even then the landscape genre fades off into other types in all directions. The distinction between seascapes (which are here included as landscape) and marine pictures is often imprecise, while portraits, and especially genre scenes, often have significant landscape backgrounds. The term landscape is interpreted throughout this book in its wider context, commonly used when referring to real landscape, thus including townscape and almost all outside views in which people or animals do not dominate. Artists usually differentiate between landscape and townscape, and Inglis has supported

Table 2 Submissions and exhibits at the Royal Academy Summer Exhibition.

Date	Submissions	No. hung	Ratio
1860–9	n.a.	n.a.	2.5 : 1[*]
1869	4,500	1,284	3.5 : 1
1896–1914	12,000	1,900	6.3 : 1
1929–39	11,000	1,500	7.3 : 1
1968	10,000	1,200	8.5 : 1

[*] In 1860–9 the ratio is for those selected, not all of which were hung.

Source: extracted from S.C. Hutchinson, *The History of the Royal Academy, 1768–1968*, London, Chapman & Hall, 1968.

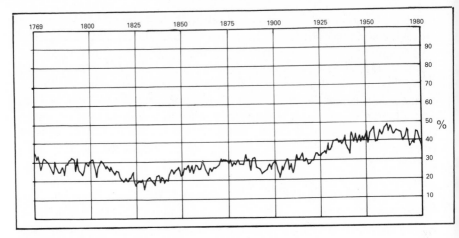

Figure 1   Proportion of pictures at Royal Academy Summer Exhibition classified as landscapes (Source: RA catalogues).

their position, suggesting that townscape has a political component not possessed by the more innocent, rural landscape picture.[15]

When only written entries are available there is the danger of including works which are not landscape at all. For example, the picture title *Clare* could refer either to the place in Suffolk, and be a landscape, or to a girl's name and be a portrait. Luckily the catalogue by Algernon Graves[16] can be consulted, which lists all the works by an artist exhibited at the Royal Academy, and clues can be found in the context of the artist's other work. The general rule used has been that the picture is normally considered to be a landscape if a place-name is included in the title, unless there are convincing reasons for not doing so. There is no common pattern in the titling of work. Hence the degree of geographical accuracy which can be obtained varies widely. Over 60 per cent of the titles can be located to a county but only half give sufficient information to be capable of being mapped (see Figure 2). One artist's *Autumn Landscape* might be another's *View in Wales* and another's *View from Llyn Gwynant looking west, noon, September*. Some place-names are ambiguous because of the number of places having the same name. Usually the artist's address can be used, if near to one of the possibilities. Great care has to be taken not to assume without good cause that a work represents a known popular location of that name.

Perhaps the most intractable problem of this kind arose with the earlier pictures of Wales. English artists touring a Welsh-speaking area, in the days before the Ordnance Survey helped to codify and ossify place-names, would listen to the name and scribble this on their work. Two hundred years after the Royal Academy's editor had attempted to transfer this to a catalogue, the modern researcher must attempt to discover the original location. Doubtless some are wrong, but hopefully enough are correct to give a fair idea of the popular locations.

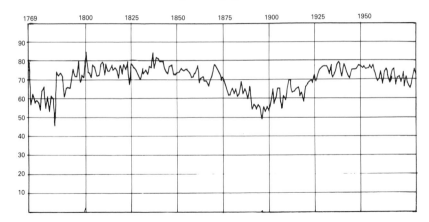

Figure 2 Proportion of landscapes at Royal Academy Summer Exhibition which can be located (Source: RA catalogues).

The Devonshire pictures

The second problem which arises from the use of titles is that the subject matter of the picture is not usually very obvious. Thus although Lynton can be found to be a popular locale at a certain time, evidence is frequently absent to determine whether it was the town itself, the seaside, the cliffs or nearby streams which were the attraction. To overcome this a large sample of pictures has been studied all depicting the county of Devon, and from these it has been possible to add some idea of subject matter to the bones of the locale information. As a result, many of the actual examples here quoted, and sometimes illustrated, derive from that county. No doubt differences would have occurred if another county had been taken but there is no reason to suppose them to be substantial. Unfortunately there is nothing which could act as a sample of landscape pictures from the entire country in the randomness of which one could have any confidence. Perhaps the closest are the works of J.R. Abbey, but these are restricted to aquatint and lithography.[17] Finding a sample with not only a proper representation of all media but also of all geographical areas, all landscape subjects and all periods of history, would be a very major task. The Devonian pictures have deliberately included a substantial number of photographs, to make some amends for the fact that photographs are not admitted to the Royal Academy Exhibitions.[18]

The quantitative nature of the evidence produced makes no allowance whatever for the importance or otherwise of the artists concerned. This is very different from most of the output of art historians which has had the effect of creating hierarchies of artists, though these undergo continual revision. Both Constable and Palmer, for example, are artists whose place in the upper reaches of the hierarchy was long delayed. The

Devonian artist Frederick Lee can stand for the reverse: much revered in his lifetime[19] but largely ignored since. Generally an artist's importance, seen in retrospect, is largely dependent on the degree of innovation adopted, a quality of little value to the present purpose. Once artists have achieved the distinction of being selected for the Exhibition, any further interest in their artistic status is useless to this study. Of course the shifting background of artistic landscape taste which this study surveys can be used to put major artists into another context. For example, of the two greatest English landscape painters Constable seems the more revolutionary in terms of the places and subjects depicted. Turner, on the other hand, seems to follow the crowd in terms at least of locale. Stillman has eloquently pointed out the limitations of quantification, writing about physical landscapes, but equally applicable to art:

> Of one thing I am sure: the great living values of 'nature' transcend the potentials of university-based scholars to define, measure and analyse. This is a life that is within all of us, gloriously so: all that scholars can do is peer, criticize, and now and then peek at a morsel of something quantitative.[20]

At least this 'peek' makes no claim to comprehend the values of nature, merely to map where others have attempted to.

In the same way as artistic quality is ignored, so is the topographic accuracy of the depiction. No doubt a few paintings are as accurate as any photograph, though we have unfortunately no way of recognizing which they are; rather more will have been selective in their subject matter, and a few, such as the work of Peter Lanyon, may be more or less completely abstracted, despite having a locatable title. Nevertheless they all can act as statements that an artist has viewed a certain place sufficiently favourably to depict it.

The illustrations are intended solely as exemplars of common types. They are not included for their artistic significance; indeed some are the clichés which developed after artists of greater stature had discovered and popularized a new landscape fashion. The value of such clichés lies in their didactic strength – they are so obvious that they lead the way to an understanding and classification of much more subtle pictures.

Causes of change

While the major aim of the book is to produce a picture of the changes in the perceived attractiveness of particular places and landscape types over two centuries, to do so without speculating on the possible causes of the changes being unearthed would be absurd. However, the degree of certainty which can be attributed to these causes is inevitably of a different order. The study of Devon leads to the conclusion that some

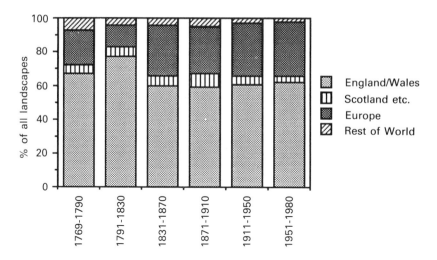

Figure 3 World distribution of landscapes at the Royal Academy (Source: RA catalogues).

causes are of quite a local nature, and there are obvious limitations on knowledge. For example the importance of the publication of *Childe Harold* as a possible stimulus to the great fashion for the Rhine Tour in the nineteenth century had escaped the author until a casual conversation brought it to light.[21] There must be many similar omissions which will doubtless irk readers having local knowledge.

In addition to causes of change there are also distinctive processes which emerge, though of too speculative a nature to be dignified as laws. One such is the principle of the continually increasing number of attractive features. While a taste for a particular place or landscape feature often arises suddenly, it very rarely disappears completely; although it may decline in importance it remains within the portfolio of attractiveness as a place or subject to be reworked at will. The number of places perceived as attractive therefore tends continually to increase.

One further drawback of the Royal Academy figures should be mentioned. The existence of prestigious Academies in Scotland and Ireland means that Scottish and Irish artists only rarely exhibit at the RA. They have been free to submit, as have been foreigners; indeed Monet and Pissarro once submitted but 'naturally we were rejected'.[22] In general, however, the picture of taste here described is that of English and Welsh artists. Of course they frequently exhibited pictures of Scotland and Ireland, and these are here examined, but there can be no guarantee that the Scottish view of Scotland has been similar to the English view. The kind of work done by William MacTaggart on Macrihanish Bay rarely occurs by Englishmen, nor is the Irish penchant for far western, Celtic fringe landscapes in the 1920s always echoed.

The English artist's view of foreign countries is not closely examined here, but it cannot be completely omitted. Very commonly a new landscape subject has first been found abroad and subsequently similar views were depicted nearer home. The fashions for the Alps were mirrored in the English and Welsh mountains, and the beauty of certain English rivers was commonly legitimated by reference to the Rhine. At any one period, therefore, the preferences of artists working overseas were an important part of understanding tastes at home (see Figure 3).

Some attention must now be given to the problems of using art as a surrogate for landscape. This book shows the changes which affected the location and subject matter of the pictures of ordinary, that is not particularly outstanding or avant-garde English artists. Did those artists depict all the kinds of landscape which they found attractive? Indeed did these artists find these places attractive in the broad sense, or merely paintable? Did these tastes represent their own preferences or the tastes, or what the artist thought were the tastes, of their patrons? To what extent do these tastes also represent those of the general public? Is there a trickle-down effect of taste, and if so how are artists' tastes mediated to those who do not look at art?

Serious discussion of these important questions is left to the final chapter, though much more study needs to be given to many of them, especially the mediation of elitist tastes to the general public and how it is achieved. To summarize that discussion at this point may, however, enable the reader to understand some of the assumptions being made. Certainly there are some types of view in which artists delighted but which seemed to be largely unpaintable. The wide panoramic prospect is the most obvious example. Nevertheless artists' writings leave one in no doubt that most of them loved the places they depicted, and frequently regarded landscape painting as relaxation. No doubt some artists' idiosyncratic ideas of what constituted attractive landscape failed to sell, as George Morland discovered,[23] so the perceptions of patrons were clearly important. Certainly the perceptions here mapped are those of a very narrow and elite band of the population; whether it was an artistic or wealthy elite is arguable. The perceptions of this elite are certainly not those of the general public, but there seems good evidence to suggest that they affect and precede general preferences, that artists (though doubtless not artists alone) discover new tastes which are mediated by many means, including guidebooks, to the travelling public.

English and European tastes

Before looking in some detail at the sources of the ideas for this book, a short and speculative attempt is made to put English attitudes to landscape within the context of the rest of Europe. Within the realm of cultural geography one might expect a serious study of the differences between national schools of art. After all, painting and other arts show a marked degree of spatial differentiation, but in fact such work is almost completely lacking. Not only is art not a commonly accepted cognate discipline for geographers, but such studies are fraught with difficulties, the most important being the danger of determinism, of attributing highly complex effects to simple causes. One of the very few attempts has been that by Nicholas Pevsner in *The Englishness of English Art*, which understandably if not very helpfully avoided the problem by making little attempt to explain the differences noted.[24]

An examination of European art as a whole does seem to suggest a division between southern and northern attitudes to the environment, the boundary between the two running along the Alps and Pyrenees, thus leaving France as the only major country with a foot in both camps.

In the south the landscape has been seen by Edward Hyams in *Soil and Civilization* as having largely been denuded of forest during classical times.[25] In addition the environment was easily viewed as more of a challenge or threat than an opportunity or a comfort. The presence of earthquakes and volcanoes, of long summer droughts and flash floods is bound to have left its mark. That environmental attitudes stem partly from the nature of the landscape itself can surely be seen in Japan where the threat is so severe as to leave the only response to nature one of reverence, as seen at its most obvious in Hokusai's images of Fuji, and Hiroshige's masterpiece *The Great Wave*.[26] Throughout Mediterranean Europe the environment might similarly be regarded, not as infertile or inimical to man, but as frequently uncomfortable and even dangerous. The result has not been to revere nature but rather either to ignore or to idealize it. There is little pure landscape work in Italian art, and generally landscape is seen either as a backdrop to human activities or as predominantly man-made, and frequently as both. Man is seen as urban, with the city as his creation and one of the main sources of his inspiration.

An alternative response is to observe and depict nature, and the natural man, but so gracious a nature and so graceful a man that both remain highly idealized and unreal. Southern art usually stresses the creations of the human mind, cerebral and usually formal. This same cerebral response leads to man or land, when depicted, being infused with an idealism, and an elegance or gracefulness which seems to be eternally optimistic of the perfectibility of man. Futurism, as much as high Renaissance art, seems a movement absolutely within the expectations of Italy – the optimistic belief in man's ability to save himself and a lack of interest in nature except as a resource.

When landscape is much used, albeit as a backdrop to human activity, as in most of the work of Nicolas Poussin, it is frequently highly composed and constructed. Not only is the picture itself a carefully composed object but also there is much more emphasis in southern

European painting on the structure, the landform and geology of the landscape, as Ewart Johns has pointed out.[27]

Hence south of the Alps, landscape is a quite different concept to that with which the English are familiar. Ben Wheeler has made a distinction between the arts of the flesh and those of the brain, and frequently sees the practice of art as the attempt by people to bring the animal and intellectual parts of their nature into some cohesion.[28] Clearly southern Europe is largely concerned with the latter. Where landscape is deployed three main features distinguish it: (a) it is constructed by man, leaving this in no doubt by the use of geometry. The evidence here comes mainly from garden design, but is seen also in painting; (b) the interest in the appearance of the land is largely structural – either in its actual geology, or in the way it can be organized to form a geometrical, and therefore logical, basis for depiction; (c) where landscape does not appear to be man-made it becomes idealized, a garden of Arcadia the cultivation of which requires no effort, and which can be inhabited by people as graceful, ordered and ideal as the land itself. It is landscape as backdrop, even when no figures are seen they are expected. The *memento mori* of Poussin's much copied *Et in Arcadia Ego* is perhaps the archetype of such painting, with its symbolic use of man's works.[29]

Italian and Spanish garden design also demonstrates the same characteristics. The much greater use made of the sound and sight of running water, and of dense shade, is an obvious adaptation to environmental circumstances, but such gardens are nearly always highly architectural. They contain a much greater percentage of stonework than their equivalents further north, and the few plants used are usually heavily sculpted and arranged in geometric shapes. The control of man over the environment is highly manifest.

North of the Alps the attitude to landscape is quite different and we seem to be looking at the art of a people who carved their space out of the forest. Altdorfer's early landscapes, some of the earliest where the landscape is more than a backcloth, have humans, even saints,[30] almost completely dominated by the trees around them. In England this attachment to the forest long outlasted the removal of most of it. The fear coupled with the fascination of the forest is still sufficiently potent in the twentieth century for Kenneth Grahame to write that most resonant chapter of *The Wind in the Willows* when the mole experiences the wild wood![31] Nursery rhymes and fairy stories continue to confirm this interest. The forest represents the most powerful symbol of refuge, as put forward by Appleton,[32] but it is also crawling with hazards. The symbolism of the forest can be controlled by building great replicate arcades of stone as cathedral naves, or by exposing the post and pan on the sides of Essex buildings. Conquering nature in the north may be hard work but it doesn't overwhelm us with earthquake, drought or volcano.

There does seem some reason to be optimistic about agriculture! Landscape as a whole is much more popular. After the beginning of the agrarian revolution people, or perhaps one should say some men, the owners of the land, felt able to control nature sufficiently to be able to admire it. Even then for many years well-farmed land was the epitome of attraction while woodland was the fascinating but dark side of the landscape.

The painting by Douanier Rousseau in the National Gallery is perhaps the supreme example of this.[33] The lady is so secure from prying eyes in the forest that she is able to stretch langorously naked on the nearest convenient *chaise-longue*, but surrounded by a wealth of hazards, human, animal and serpentine. The group of painters who put this forest symbolism in the forefront are the nineteenth-century German Romantics, led by Caspar David Friedrich. However, German, Swiss and Scandinavian forest worship is almost invariably concerned with conifer forest, while in Britain it is reserved for deciduous trees, most particularly oaks. Today this preference is rationalized by reference to native species, although the French share the reverence for the oak, though they add the chestnut, and in both countries the beech and the ash are also important.

The beginnings of English interest in landscape art stem from these two major roots. The southern was represented in Britain by the popularity of the Roman school of Claude, Poussin and Salvator Rosa, and also, somewhat later, Canaletto. The northern tradition came from the Dutch. Hobbema, van Goyen and Ruysdael were among those who gave us some very significant symbols including the coast scene, the cottage in a wood, the panorama, and the windmill.[34]

In the north the accent is on realism and on appearances rather than composition and structure; the involvement with realism extends to an interest in atmospherics, which may be evanescent to a planner's view of landscape but are at the core of the painter's interest. Constable thought the 'sky the chief organ of sentiment'.[35] Not only are English watercolours typically northern, but so is impressionism, always interested in the look of things, rather than how they work. Similarly there is a fascination for ordinary people, not at all idealized and rarely graceful, most famously in Breughel's work, but very much alive in the Barbizon school's interest in real peasants, or the Newlyn painters' depictions of fishermen and later photographic interest in miners. Even the landowners, in portraits they have themselves commissioned, are often replete with warts. An earthy, even bawdy, sense of humour is often present, with Hogarth's and Rowlandson's work far from untypical. Even children, while often over-sentimentalized, were rarely idealized. The emphasis tends to the fleshly, the real or, where there is fantasy, to the phantasmagorical or macabre. However, the North admires the South to a much greater extent than the feeling is reciprocated and Italian models were frequently imported into Britain.

Lowenthal and Prince in a much-cited article have attempted to describe English landscape tastes, which they describe as deciduous, tidy and with a preference for façades or the keeping up of appearances.[36] This represents, of course, the preferences of the upper classes, those most likely to buy pictures and whose ideal of the decent life was based more on Italian models. Many of that class had indeed visited Italy on The Grand Tour, and regarded it as the epitome of good taste. The preferred landscape was tidy, unchaotic, able to be comprehended and well tended. Such a preference for tidiness may well be the result of English 'landedness'; the English gentry, the greatest patrons of the arts, not only owned much of the land, they also lived on it for much of the year. Many understood it, worked it and played on it. As the Agrarian Revolution gathered pace they were able to afford to take sizeable parts of it out of cultivation and create English landscape gardens. These bore more than a passing resemblance to the deer parks which had been around for centuries. Indeed perhaps the first way of understanding a type of garden design is to comprehend its purpose. The Japanese is for contemplation, the French to be seen in, but the English is there to do things in – and things included not only the gentle art of bowls but also hunting.

Here then is an attempt to map the rapidly changing perceptions of a group of elitist English artists over two centuries. Their very Englishness, and their elitism, are such that they cannot be used as a surrogate for anyone else's perceptions. Because their attitudes have been influential a study of them may tell us much about the origins of our own attitudes, if we are English and part of the elite which might actually influence the future of the landscape. In any case the sheer speed with which their concepts of the attractive have changed may give pause when next we try to conserve some present preference in legislative concrete. The other conclusion must be that in situations where current notions of aesthetic pleasure are opposed to a proposed landscape modification, the notions of attractiveness are as capable of manipulation and change as the proposed modification.

The basis of the account which follows is chronological. After examining sources of ideas there follow six chapters each devoted to a period of landscape aesthetic perception, though some of these periods are more clearly defined and convincing than others. This diachronic structure inevitably breaks down, and includes within it frequent digressions to trace the development of particular fashions, either for places or for landscape features, in more detail. The final chapter, reverting to an even more speculative mode than that just established, examines some of the causes and processes which appear to be at work in explaining the pattern uncovered.

2

Landscape studies:
a new field

The development of a recognizable field of landscape studies has been a remarkable feature of the academic scene in the last two decades. Sponsored by the journals *Landscape* in the United States and by *Landscape Research* in Britain, a remarkable series of books and articles has arisen from various disciplines which had not always recognized their cognate common field. These include geography, landscape architecture, aesthetics and psychology, though many others have also become involved.

Geographers had been urged in an address by the President of the Royal Geographical Society, Sir Francis Younghusband, in 1920 to regard the 'beauty of the earth's features as within the purview of geographers'.[1] This call went largely unheeded at first, partly because the discipline was establishing itself within the sciences, and, later, in the quantitative revolution of the 1960s in the social sciences. The isolation of art education largely outside the universities did nothing to promote the aesthetic education of geographers, especially at a time when modern art practice was little concerned with iconography, symbolism or subject matter. Vaughan Cornish, therefore, remained an isolated figure with his concept of aesthetic geography in the 1930s,[2] although many regional geographical texts of the period were liberally sprinkled with aesthetic adjectives, few of them clearly defined.[3]

More generally geographers contented themselves with suggesting art as a possibility. As long ago as 1937 Leighly suggested that 'the key to the historical understanding of the cultural elements of the landscape is . . . to be found in the methods and results of investigating the material products of artistic creation', and he wondered if it were 'possible that a science can be founded by taking for its field so heterogenous phenomena as arbitrarily selected fragments of the land'.[4] Artists' selections of fragments of the land appear to be far from arbitrary, so perhaps a science can indeed be founded.

Since 1970, however, the discipline has also encompassed a considerable revival in its humanistic side,[5] and the development of perception studies showed the chink which would allow the discipline access to an area as much dependent on attitude and prejudice as fact. This may have been a reaction to the considerable amount of work on evaluating landscapes by numeric means which many saw as inflexible and restrictive.[6]

The main body of recent work has examined attitudes to landscape at a variety of levels. Though to produce any schema suggests a unity of purpose that is not always evident, the scale from the universal to the personal is one into which much work can be usefully fitted. Some perceptions of landscape are claimed to be applicable to all of mankind. No writer, however, would deny that there are also obvious differences between the perceptions of various members of the species. These have been ascribed to macro-cultural features, such as religion, to national attitudes and habits, to the prejudices deriving from age, class, profession, sub-group, education, or residence, and finally to individual predilections, which themselves vary according to the activity being carried out. The artists studied in this work must, therefore, be seen as predominantly Christian, English, adult artists, usually male, usually from the middle class, and trained in a way which largely distinguished them from their fellows.

Universal theories

In 1975 Jay Appleton published *The Experience of Landscape*[7] which attempted a universal explanation for landscape preferences. William Gilpin and others had attempted to codify the attractive without explaining it, Appleton attempted an explanation without becoming embroiled in a classification. The concept that preferences may be based on the primitive hunter's wish to see without being seen, to find good prospects and effective refuges, whilst avoiding hazards, has undoubtedly stimulated much other work, a great deal of which has been directed to demonstrating the existence of major differences at a less than universal level. However, Gordon Orians, working from the standpoint of environmental biology, has also proposed a universal theory, based on the origin of *Homo sapiens* in the savannahs and the consequent desire to find, or create, landscapes which resemble this original habitat.[8] Such a theory seems eminently reasonable if regarding an English landscape park, but less so when surveying Versailles. Shepard's attempt to bring Freudian analysis into an explanation of landscape symbols must also rank as a universal theory, although there may be gender implications.[9]

Cultural theories

At the same time as Appleton was writing, Yi Fu Tuan was surveying the range of responses to places exhibited in different cultures, inevitably noting the wide differences between, for example, the United States and China.[10] This provided the basis for a second string of ideas which were concerned with cultural attitudes to landscape, while a third thread derived, at least in part, from the work of the urban sociologist Kevin Lynch, and his *The Image of the City*.[11] This thread was concerned with the direct investigation of the attitudes of individuals, in this case into their understanding of a town plan. Such ideas were influential in the work of Brian Goodey and many other writers concerned with mental mapping, and were closely connected with the work of the environmental psychologists.[12]

There has been surprisingly little work after Tuan on the differences between groups of people on such a large scale. The effect of religion on perception has, for example, been scarcely examined except for a short article on the landscape symbolism of the Koran.[13] Keith Thomas clearly points out the influence of religion on attitudes to nature in early modern times.[14] The differences between Catholic and Protestant ideas, which can be seen to persist in present-day European attitudes to environmental problems, may well be connected with the north/south division already noted. Whether Catholic attitudes have reinforced southern, Mediterranean ones, or been reinforced by them, is perhaps of less account. Certainly the idea that modern, largely northern, eco-consciousness is a revival of the Puritan spirit in a secular world is a tempting one.

Perhaps the change which Thomas notes between 1500 and 1800 in Britain can be summed up by seeing the earlier viewpoint as an alliance between Man and God against Nature. Slowly this changed until Nature was seen to be a manifestation of God, sometimes even opposed by Man. The rapidly developing attitude today would see Nature as God, with Man largely in opposition to it, except for the new priesthood of environmentalists. The new ecumenical movement forging an alliance between the twin sects of art and environment may be one key to a rapid change in perception taking place today.

Nationality

Differences in attitude between national groups have received rather more attention. Lowenthal and Prince long ago attempted to define peculiarly English landscape tastes,[15] and the differences between American and English perceptions have informed much of Lowenthal's more recent work also.[16] Ervin Zube and others have demonstrated that there are significant differences between American and Australian attitudes.[17] Within a single country the techniques of small-group research used by Jacquie Burgess have been most successful in teasing out the deeply held if often illogical feelings inherent in different ethnic and class groups in Britain.[18]

Art has been discovered to be valuable evidence particularly in this field of national identity. The value of artworks in showing the change from colonial to independent national perceptions has been fruitful, including the work by Ronald Rees and Brian Osborne in Canada, and that by Jonathan Watkins and Val Vallis in Australia,[19] all of whom also acknowledge the role of art in moulding that change. Gussow's study of American painting has also identified the role of art in shaping national consciousness, and there are hints that the same may be true in Wales and Scotland.[20]

Politics and class

Within the perceptions of one nation J.B. Jackson has argued that there are two distinct attitudes to, and indeed types of landscape which are based on differences of power and class.[21] Almost all designed landscapes, buildings, communications, towns, gardens, and much farmland, especially in the United States about which he was writing, are political in nature, and are counterposed by the vernacular – landscapes made by ordinary people, without professional input, and without much consciously aesthetic motivation. In America he finds these in the urban strip and the trailer park and makes out a powerful case for taking them seriously.

In England the present author has suggested the same might apply to our suburbs, allotments, and to that farmland not taken over by large estates, or by incomers from town.[22] Fred Inglis has argued that the English rural landscape has always acted as an innocent, naïve location, free of the political loadings of the city, a foreign country to which the urbanite can escape whether in reality or through the frames of pictures on the dining room wall.[23]

There may be a process at work whereby the vernacular landscape becomes appropriated by the powerful class, and thereby turned into political landscape. This can be seen in many English National Parks where an obsolescent vernacular architecture has become the very symbol of the appropriation of the area by a rich and powerful immigrant group.

Art history

These differences between class groupings also informed the new art historical approach, argued by Michael Rosenthal, which began to examine the iconography of pictures, and uncover the political and

power-based codes which informed the reading of such work.[24] The
publication of *The Country and the City* by Raymond Williams, together
with ideas coming from media studies, were influential in helping John
Barrell to move across the boundary from literary to art criticism and
throw light on the necessity of the artist's vision being seen as related to
the political needs of the class which formed the patrons and purchasers
of the work.[25] Such work owed much to the semiological ideas coming
into art from literature via photography, which enabled art to be
considered as a coded language which could be unpacked. Such studies
took some time to cross the boundary from the meanings of the figures in
the artwork to the meanings of the landscape itself. However, the
catalogue to the exhibition of Richard Wilson's work,[26] and recent work
by Denis Cosgrove and Steven Daniels, have clearly made this jump.[27]

This has become not only the most controversial arena in which the
perceptions of different groups have been examined, but also that where
the study of art and that of landscape have been most firmly allied. That
art represents the view of an elite seems to be a concept that has
surprised and angered some critics. Art has traditionally served the
powerful, whether the church, the Whig aristocracy, the Fascist cause or
Stalinism. If it had not done so in modern, western art it would be indeed
surprising. The scholarship which distinguishes this area of work will
undoubtedly create a much more informed reading of art, but has on
occasion been used merely to attempt to deduce an artist's political stance
from his work, which can scarcely be its full potential.

Insiders and outsiders

Another factor which has shown itself to be a fruitful area of research has
been the examination of significant variations in the perceptions of locals
and visitors. Relph has categorized several types of insiders and outsiders,
with quite different attitudes to place.[28] In general the insider is too
concerned with social relations to be particularly interested in the
appearance of objects – including landscape. The wish of the National
Trust for Australia to conserve various old buildings in the town of
Beechworth, Victoria, is observed with little interest by the local
residents, just as keen to expound on their past, but seeing it as
populated by people, not enshrined in buildings.[29]

Many have recently suggested that the distinction between the
professional, architect, planner or designer, and the amateur, is akin to
this insider/outsider antithesis. Artists, therefore, have usually been
outsiders, either physically because they were on tour, or because their
training distanced them from the attitudes of their neighbours. When out
of their artistic role, of course, they could revert to being insiders again.

The problem of training professional architects, landscape designers and others fully to comprehend the perceptions of the insiders on whose behalf they are usually working has highlighted this problem recently, and such organizations as Common Ground have recognized the difficulty in the field of art and conservation.[30]

The tourist, by definition an outsider, and one usually particularly keen to seek visual experience, has been taken as a figure of great importance by John Jakle,[31] and the tourist view may be one particularly influenced by art. In stressing the significance of tourism, not only as an industry but as the activity by which perceptions are formed, he discovered the frequency with which the tourist seeks framable views, following their understanding of aesthetic composition.

There are, however, degrees of outsideness, noted by Relph,[32] and distinctive differences occasionally occur between locally resident artists and those on tour. Similarly there seem to be genres of landscape art which were provided primarily for insiders, such as many townscape views in print form, rarely occurring at national exhibitions but freely available locally.

Environmental psychology

Environmental psychologists have been at the forefront of the work which examines individuals' perceptions of places. Work by Kenneth Craik, Stephen and Rachel Kaplan and Jack Nasar[33] has rarely used art in the attempt to measure perception, but nevertheless has done much to highlight the nature of individual preferences, as well as measuring differences between national and other groups. Brian Goodey's work has also tried to unpack the meanings inherent in places to individuals performing different tasks and functions, and Meinig has shown the importance of activity and profession in perceiving the value of landscape.[34] His short paper is a timely reminder that the aesthetic is only one of many sets of meaning which landscape gives to the viewer, one of great importance to the artist, and, as Jakle suggests, to the tourist, but by no means the normal way of observing place. Indeed Denis Cosgrove's work makes it clear that the very concept of landscape itself is one very closely tied to western ideas over the last few centuries.[35]

That attitudes to nature and to landscape are rooted in past controversies and cosmologies is now well understood. Graham Cox has traced the peculiarly English split in attitudes between those wishing to conserve the landscape (represented by the Countryside Commission) and those concerned to protect nature (represented by the Nature Conservancy) to a long, politically loaded tradition closely connected with poetry and painting.[36]

Self-consciousness

Of course, not all the work done on landscape perception can be fitted neatly into this schema of descending orders of universality. Some, such as Keith Thomas's work, and this one, deal with the process of historical change, a feature markedly absent from much of the geographical and psychological work.[37] Before concluding this survey the work of Relph should again be mentioned. Apart from his study of insideness he has also noted characteristics of places which have much to do with their attractiveness.[38] He sees two antitheses. In one of these he distinguishes between authentic and inauthentic places. While Disneyland and the film set may lie at one extreme of this antithesis, and the Cotswold cottage at the other, they are not absolute and static categories. The comparatively inauthentic, the Palladian mansion set on an English hillside, can be authenticated by the passage of time and by that process of Anglicization to which all immigrant styles are eventually subjected. Conversely the authentic may become so vulgarized by constant exposure that it becomes a mere cliché. This process leads to his second antithesis, his distinction between self-conscious and unselfconscious places. Over time places which attracted at least partly because of their unselfconscious and naïve appeal begin to discover their own attractiveness and become an image of themselves. He regards this as a major factor in the changing fashions for places. One of the main agents in increasing self-consciousness is the artist. There are many places which have become the victim of publicity, and artists were among the first discoverers of them. St Ives could perhaps be regarded as the outstanding example of this artistic pollution.

Changing tastes

Many writers have been aware that attitudes and time are closely related. Some have shown how place and time are woven together such that one can ask 'What time is this place?'[39] or that the perceptions of history can transform our understanding of places such that the past becomes a foreign country to be visited.[40] Historians of literature and art have often shown the vision of places by artists and writers to be quite different to present perceptions, though the place is often changed by them. The discovery of Scotland and of the Lake District have been studied in this way, and Esther Moir regards the late eighteenth century as the discovery of Britain itself. Both Ronald Rees and Jane Zaring have shown the preference for mountains as comparatively new.[41]

Keith Thomas has given the most detailed account of the changes between 1500 and 1800 in man's attitudes to nature, using mainly literary sources.[42] During this period the confident assertion of man's authority over and difference from other forms of nature was gradually undermined.

Of course, attitudes to nature and to landscape are not synonymous, especially when so many attractive landscapes included the works of men as a major feature, but there are many characteristics of the landscapes artists preferred before 1800 which are closely related to the ideas which Thomas claims as indicative of the earlier situation.

The techniques used by Thomas lack the accuracy of dating changes in taste which the quantitative study of painting can give, and many studies based on literature seem to place changes in attitude earlier than is found in this study. Two possible reasons suggest themselves for this. The first lies in the historian's natural wish to seek for the causes of events, which desire contains the obvious danger of perceiving changes as having taken place earlier than was the case. More importantly this study is unusual in looking at very ordinary, though professional, art, not that produced by the avant-garde, and a study of these latter, together with many writers, might well produce dates markedly earlier than those given here.

Art and location

Enough has been said to demonstrate that the use of art in this book is different from traditional art history. Indeed as the final aim is not to throw light on art or artists it cannot be compared with any art historical writing. However there has been considerable study of English landscape painting, and in many cases such work has been most valuable. Grigson's study *Britain Observed*[43] and the volume by Jacobs and Warner[44] are valuable for topographic information. Work by Michael Rosenthal has also begun what is now a common and most welcome re-emphasis on the subject matter of landscapes.[45] Similarly exhibitions of British landscape art have produced fine catalogues often highlighting particular locations.[46]

Very few works look in detail at particular iconographic elements, however. Links's study of townscape painting does not attempt to unravel the meanings of the city, nor does the substantial work on country house depictions.[47] Holcomb has looked at the role of bridges,[48] and Grigson at church towers.[49] Stafford has discussed archaeological remains and similar objects and more work is forthcoming on that subject.[50] There has been work on the importance of the rainbow, an important symbolic feature in Victorian art.[51] Trees and woodland have been given some attention by Douglas Davies and Stephen Daniels respectively.[52]

Literature

There has been rather more study of landscape in literature than in art, even at a purely local level. In 1931, for example, Gilbert Sheldon wrote on 'Devonshire scenery as depicted in English prose literature'.[53] The work by Pocock has drawn inferences from literature to explain the particular preferences of the writers, and of others.[54] Margaret Drabble, and Eagles and Carnell, have made more popular forays into the field.[55] That literature should have received more interest than art is scarcely surprising given the comparative educational isolation of art from the academic disciplines. However valuable these insights from literature may be, there is little chance of their being useful for a quantitative analysis, because of the sheer paucity of numbers. Hence exactitude is missing. Also there is little way of discriminating between authors such as Hardy or Scott, who were instrumental in provoking a liking for certain landscapes, and those such as Wordsworth and Blackmore, who while undoubtedly promoting the popularity of certain places, must be seen as part of a fashion, rather than the instigators of it.

On the other hand literature can move about the landscape in a way which art cannot. Paintings suggest a static view, while the writer may not only progress through a landscape but jump from one to another with great ease. This might make the quantitative study of literature more difficult, but it can promote the feeling of being in a landscape much more than a picture can, and only be rivalled by film, which itself has recently come under scrutiny.[56] Hepburn, in looking at the difference between art and nature, pointed out that in reality 'His [the observer's] motion may be an important part in his aesthetic experience.'[57] Indeed Relph even claims that literature can produce a feeling of 'vicarious insideness' with a place.[58] Quite frequently literary references are valuable in confirming preferences found in art, or even suggesting them. Typical of such references is Jerome K. Jerome's *Three Men in a Boat*, published in 1889, at the time when the Thames between Oxford and London was immensely popular with artists. They were not unnoticed, for 'the neighbourhood of Pangbourne . . . must be as familiar to the habitués of Art exhibitions as it is to its own inhabitants'.[59]

Music

With the publication of John Burke's *Musical Landscapes* and a series of programmes with Richard Baker on landscapes in music on Radio 4 has come some interest in the relationship between music and landscape.[60] This has not yet reached major proportions, and is largely concerned with the inspiration of particular places on certain compositions. The problems of studying literature surely also apply to music, made more severe by music's abstract nature. All too often the assumption that a certain piece was inspired by a particular landscape is based only on anecdotal evidence.

Music, though, does serve to remind us that landscape attractiveness is not exclusively a visual phenomenon. Both sound and smell are significant parts of the landscape experience which are completely missed in any study of pictures. Whether there are places which attract largely by sound or smell is a question worth study. Certainly Vaughan Cornish thought he detected three zones of fragrance in his native area around Sidmouth.[61] Artists of course are also attracted by their other senses, and the fact that a considerable part of the experience of both the seaside and the river bank must surely be aural has not apparently reduced their popularity to artists.

Quantification in art

The possibility of studying art in a quantitative manner has also not gone completely unremarked. In *The Art Journal* of 1883 the increase in numbers of Cornish scenes at the Royal Academy was noted.[62] The Ogdens' major study of seventeenth-century landscape painting also used quantitative evidence to demonstrate the growing importance of landscape as a genre, taking their figures from major collections.[63] Both John Barrell and Michael Rosenthal have used numerical evidence from the Royal Academy exhibitions, and Alison Martin has used figures derived from the Victoria and Albert Museum's collection.[64]

The role of the present work differs markedly from many of these others. We can now imagine a very large field of knowledge, so far largely unexplored. That field consists of all the perceptions of the landscape which are held or have been held by all groups of people, some being professional groups, some national groups, some much smaller. The work reviewed in this chapter has given us several theoretical ideas regarding the formation of these perceptions, without knowing much about what those perceptions actually have been. This book at least tries to discover what the perceptions of one small, but perhaps influential group, British landscape painters, have been. It is, therefore, primarily a work of survey rather than of theory, with all the problems of presenting a considerable body of data in a coherent form that that implies. When the space of this new territory has been surveyed and mapped we may be in a better position to discover which of the available theories, like lists of conventional signs, is the best fitted to the map.

Landscape perceptions in 1769

For the period before the Royal Academy can be used as evidence, Keith Thomas's work coupled with some art historical studies can give some clue to prevailing perceptions. Apart from surviving pictures and documents there are also the buildings, and more especially the gardens, which can stand witness to the thinking of their creators. For the seventeenth century the genres and popularity of landscape in painting have been carefully noted by the Ogdens.[65] Nor should the possibilities of cartography be ignored, as Harley has pointed out, but the decoding of the iconography of maps is in an early stage.[66]

Certainly the early tourists, up to 1700, had little interest in the visual, the concept of landscape scarcely having arrived, and this lack of interest was shared even by Defoe and Fiennes. Tristram Risdon, surveying Devonshire in the 1620s, placed his emphasis squarely on the genealogical. He is much concerned with land, scarcely at all with landscape, except for some antiquarian interest. The few comments in which he uses a visual, and favourable, adjective almost always concern built objects – Bideford's fair bridge, or the wide streets of Exeter.[67] By the time of Celia Fiennes's visit, fifty years later, but by someone of much more metropolitan outlook, the number of aesthetic comments had increased but little, although she certainly found much pleasure in well-farmed landscapes. Indeed the view most favoured would comprehend the greatest possible extent of well-farmed, neatly hedged, enclosed land. Some views from the ridges of East Devon clearly approached this ideal, the most noted being that from Fairmile, on the Great West Road near Honiton.[68]

As ever, English attitudes to their own land were much influenced by their attitudes to overseas, and especially to the classical landscapes and architecture of Italy. The south always tended to be seen as a superior culture by northerners, perhaps because of its more cerebral nature.[69] The reverse is much less true. In the Age of Reason, this preference is entirely understandable. As a result there was a continuous series of irruptions of southern foreignness into the north, in all the arts and typified by the use of classical models for building, and in garden design. Post-Impressionism represents another such irruption at a much later date, and the Greek and Egyptian revivals are also part of the same process. These are not matched by similar irruptions of northern ideas into the south on anything like the same scale, at least since the Barbarian invasions. Classicism possesses the typical features of the south – logic, rules, and form.

By 1769 the Agrarian Revolution, and the development of the distinctively English landscape garden, were well established. Landowners, who formed the largest group of patrons of the arts, had both time and money to indulge in the arts, often personally, and it was their patronage and perceptions which created the set of preferred subjects and places with which this chronology can now begin.

3

Classical landscape 1770–1790

In the later part of the eighteenth century landscape attitudes become decipherable through painting as well as the arts of gardening and architecture, in which previous attitudes had largely been encoded. Although landscape had been a significant part of the totality of painting since the mid-seventeenth century, only a hundred years later is there a sufficiently large output to be capable of being measured. The Ogdens attempted measurement, but only to discover the proportion of landscapes, as compared with other genres.[1] Before 1769 the landscape pictures available can tell us something of the favourite subjects, and their manner of treatment, but to attempt statistical analysis of the places depicted would be unwise.[2]

The founding of the Royal Academy in 1768 with the first annual exhibition in the following spring allows the techniques described in Chapter 1 to be exploited. There were other annual exhibitions as well; the Society of Artists ran from 1760 to 1791 and the Free Society of Artists from 1761 to 1783.[3]

The period under consideration in this chapter may well have begun substantially before the first Summer Exhibition in 1769, and the closing date is taken as 1790. The term 'Classical' is appropriate for many, though not all, of the major subjects at this period. The love of Classical buildings, most of them only recently built, both in town and country, underlay many favoured scenes. The preference for marine scenes and the antiquarian interest in major ancient buildings, monuments and piles of masonry, were also greatly influenced by the Roman school of painting, and most importantly Claude Lorrain.[4] The same general ideas seem to support the fascination for the well-farmed landscape and for the urban panorama. In both, the evident pride in the works of man was a

Figure 4 J.M.W. Turner, *Crossing the Brook*, oil, *c.* 1815, 193 × 164 cm (Courtesy The Tate Gallery, London). Apart from the added Italianate features and style, the picture contains at least three actual views melded into a single scene.

natural consequence of the Augustan ideals of the Age of Reason. However, the interest in the scenery of both North Wales and the Lake District indicates that such Classical ideology was being challenged by a new set of interests long before the end of the period in 1790. To expect precise dates in a history of taste would be quite unrealistic, and just as Picturesque subjects and locations can be found before 1790, so did the attraction of some Classical subjects continue well into the nineteenth century. Even within the mountainous districts, however, there were changing preferences for individual motifs which reflect the shift from a set of ideas here labelled Classical to a new set much more confidently labelled Picturesque.

Garden design, which underwent a revolution in the eighteenth century, and architecture remain available as evidence, and have been much studied. Reference will be made where appropriate, but usually in the existing histories of those arts the social factors influencing their development have been well argued.[5] The importance of the Agrarian Revolution, and the significance of the landed aristocracy, enabled great schemes to be laid out, and the Classical Period must be seen against that background. Painting (or rather picture making, as prints, drawings, and, later, photographs, are also discussed) has not previously been analysed for the evidence it can give of recurring locales and popular themes.

Many artists were much influenced during the period, as were their patrons, by the Grand Tour.[6] The Tour served many purposes other than art for the young gentry, but the study of art was frequently a significant element. Italy was by far the most important destination of the tour, and the familiarity with Italian landscape and art led to a constant search for Italianate objects in this country. Such a search continued well into the nineteenth century, and Turner's painting *Crossing the Brook* (1813) can serve as a typical example. In many cases such pictures made no attempt to depict actual landscape and the pictures were merely compositions of Italianate elements, but here Turner is known to have declared Gunnislake Bridge to be Italian,[7] and the downstream view clearly suggests this by the use of the tree. In fact there are at least three views in the picture, one from Blanchdown wood, one from the top of Hingston Down, and the close foreground of the mouth of the canal tunnel just opened.[8] Such disregard of topographical accuracy is very much part of the Classical tradition and follows the practices of Claude Lorrain and Nicholas Poussin. The latter, in particular, is noted for the careful structure and composition of his paintings. The use of overhanging trees, notably umbrella-shaped pines, and the conscious use of *coulisses* and *repoussoir*[9] tend to make this influence manifest.[10] When John Swete toured Devon in the late eighteenth century, in praise of some scenes he referred not only to Claude (for example in praising the view of Axmouth from Seaton church) but also to Salvator Rosa, the Neapolitan painter most renowned for his brigands set in fanciful and romantic landscape. At Watcombe, for example, Swete found that it reminded him of a Rosa, 'it was a spot where Nature seem'd to have suffer'd some mighty concussion'.[11]

Landscape painting in the Classical tradition is usually explained by art historians by reference to exclusively painterly concerns, especially as regards the distribution of the objects on the canvas. However, Jay Appleton's work *The Experience of Landscape*[12] has provided an alternative way of seeing. Instead of seeing an arrangement of shapes for reasons which lie within aesthetics, we are invited to envisage the viewer as part of the scene. Thus where the trees, so common on one or both sides of the picture, were seen only as frames, they can now be seen also as hints that the viewer cannot be seen. Appleton's Prospect/Refuge theory refers aesthetics back to environmental psychology, and suggests that the balanced landscape composition, including a dark side of the landscape, may be rooted much more firmly in man's way of seeing than merely a compositional rule.

Italy forms such an important focus in this period that the particular locations are significant. Italy, to all intents and purposes, was equated with Rome, and the surrounding Campagna, plus Naples for a shorter visit. People may have visited Venice, but paintings of it are rare, and Florence was also out of favour. Perhaps the existence of a major school of *Vedusti* painters at Venice did not encourage English artists to attempt their own depictions.[13] The most popular sites, apart from the great architecture of Rome itself, lay in the Alban hills, especially Lakes Albano and Nemi, but the great gardens at Tivoli were also much depicted, though jokes about the nature of Italian gardens were commonplace.[14] The formality and symmetry of Italianate garden design were totally out of favour with English garden designers, but the painters still found them attractive. The Royal Academy gave scholarships for travel to Italy: 'The goal was usually the same – Rome, possibly Naples and a short visit to Florence, Milan or Venice.'[15] The tour was so popular that the Royal Academy regarded their successful representations to the government against charging artists customs duties on their own paintings brought back from Italy by students as a major achievement.[16]

The route to Italy varied a little. Some, such as Reynolds, went by sea,[17] though more frequently tourists went through, but largely ignored, the Alps.[18] Francis Towne and J.R. Cozens were among the first influential painters to bring back depictions of the mountains and glaciers, usually those around Mont Blanc and Chamonix. Cozens has been called 'the first interpreter of the organ of the mountains'.[19] Long before 1800 depictions of the Alps and lakes, especially Lake Geneva, were commonplace, and such scenes had significant impact on the landscapes sought at home.

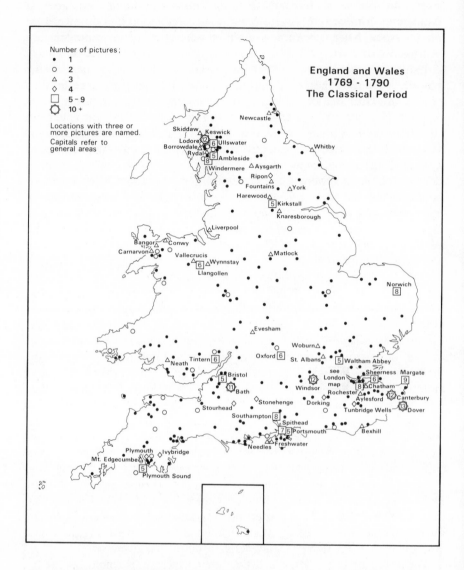

Figure 5 Map of Landscapes depicted in Classical Period, 1769–90, England and Wales (Source: RA catalogues). For details of the sample used, see Appendix 1.

By far the most outstanding fact when looking at the titles of landscapes exhibited at the Academy in these early years is the paucity of place-names. Most landscapes were compositions. John Rothenstein's remark, 'a special aim of landscape painting is the reduction of the disorder of nature to an orderly design' is most obviously true in this period.[20] Many artists saw no reason for this design to relate to a particular place, and frequently even to guess the subject matter with any confidence is difficult. Many paintings strive to be a pleasing arrangement of motifs – landscape compositions, which term is frequently used in the title. Such landscapes were constructed from a kit of parts, sometimes including sketches done on the spot, but quite often the entire picture is a product of the imagination or achieved by using models. Gainsborough, for example, is recorded as having used table-top arrangements of vegetables and coal.[21]

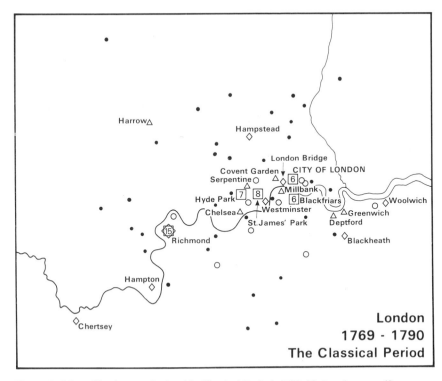

Figure 6 Map of landscapes depicted in Classical Period, 1769–90, London area (Source: RA catalogues).

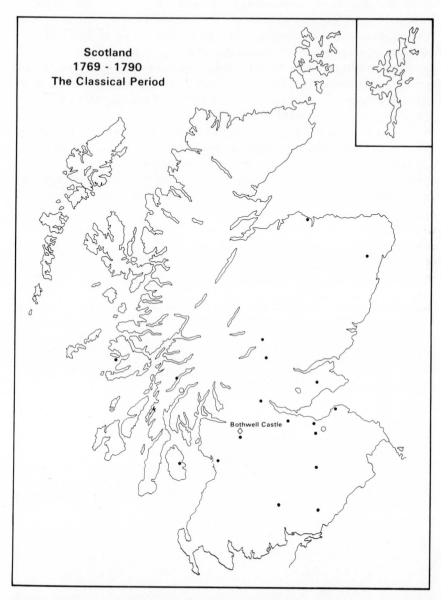

Scotland
1769 - 1790
The Classical Period

Bothwell Castle

Figure 7 Map of Landscapes depicted in Classical Period, 1769–90, Scotland (Source: RA catalogues).

Travel

Travel within Britain during the period was largely by horse and there were constant comments on the state of the roads. In Devon, for example, John Swete thought they were 'execrable' at Fremington,[22] and throughout the clay regions and backward areas of the west conditions were very poor. No wonder there was a strong tendency to find subject matter within a short distance of civilization, which latter term included only London, a few spas and very few provincial cities. No doubt some artists used the canal system, but there is little evidence of it in their work or writings. Coastal sailing packets were, however, often the fastest and most comfortable means of transport. Towards the end of the period the rapid building of an effective turnpike system was among the most important factors ushering in the new period of Picturesque travelling, with long tours being taken to remote parts of the country. The appalling conditions of travel may well have been the principal reason why the view of England at this time was essentially a summer view, though late rather than early summer was favoured. Generally the pictorial sky was fairly innocuous, except in those Sublime works where nature had to be seen as inimical.

Status of landscape painting

The artistic establishment generally took a dim view of the importance of landscape painting. Sir Joshua Reynolds in his discourses ranks it very low on his hierarchical list of genres,[23] and even Gainsborough making his living in Bath by painting portraits of the wealthy tended to regard his fondness for landscape as a self-indulgence.[24] However, the foundation of the Academy and other societies at least gave respectability to the artistic profession, a respectability made obvious in the catalogues by the number of paintings, especially landscapes, submitted by the gentry. Many, however, preferred to remain anonymous, especially the ladies. The attribution 'By a lady of quality' is frequent.

Locations and subjects in the Classical Period.

The overwhelming feature of the maps (Figures 5, 6 and 7) is the dominance of London which, with Middlesex, accounted for 15 per cent of the landscapes of England exhibited during this period, a figure not to be exceeded until the twentieth century. The pictures of London tended to be of major, modern, and usually Classical buildings, and this feature was shared with the numerous views of Bath, which was by far the most important place for the gentry to forgather, although Richmond was most important for day visits and short trips. Most artists lived close to their

Figure 8 Hastings from the Sea, steel engraving after Clarkson Stanfield, from *Stanfield's Coast Scenery* 1836 (Courtesy M.R. Pidgley). The newly developed resorts were popular in print form, especially views of the promenades, either from the sea, as here, or overlooking the resort from a hill. Hastings has been attractive to artists over an unusually long period, though the subjects have changed. This classical type of view lasted, in print form at least, until the 1850s.

customers, travel being so difficult, and usually did not travel far to find their subject matter. At Richmond the view from the hill was particularly favoured and was clearly a place for the gentry to be seen.[25] Oxford, St Albans and Norwich were also sufficiently genteel to attract painters and some resorts were becoming fashionable, the most important being Margate, though Brighton was also frequently depicted. Hastings probably represents an unusual case of a town which has always remained acceptable pictorial material, though doubtless the subjects changed in detail. There can be no doubt that acceptability by the small, purchasing public, namely the gentry, was essential to the artist of the day. John Barrell suggests that George Morland represents one painter who failed to achieve this and suffered accordingly.[26] This acceptance could only be achieved by depicting the gentry's favoured views in a way which flattered them. Whether having to make oneself acceptable to the gentry was any more arduous or odious than having to do the same to an even smaller group of gallery owners and directors in the present day is, of course, a matter of opinion. Luke Herrman and John Hayes have both provided studies of the relationship between the artist and his patron in the eighteenth century.[27]

Some idea of how the aesthetic qualities of towns were perceived in this period can be gained by referring to the comments of famous tourists. Celia Fiennes, for example, passed very few comments on the appearance

of things, but she is moved to exclaim that Exeter 'is a town very well
built, the streets are well pitched, spacious noble streets'. Defoe regarded
Barnstaple as a 'large, spacious, well built town'.[28] Of course, rebuilding
was very common at the time, and new streets were everywhere being
added, especially terraces and circuses, and many country towns were
completely rebuilt after disastrous fires.[29] Within the favoured towns,
which only rarely included the smaller market towns, these street scenes
and pictures of important buildings were the dominant genre. In London
such scenes were found in Covent Garden and the West End, but both
Hyde Park and St James's provided other views of a gracious townscape,
often including gentry as staffage.

Urban panoramas

One major kind of urban scene, other than the view of a building or
street, was the urban panorama. Many of the earliest panoramas were
done by itinerant Dutch artists as early as the seventeenth century, and
occasionally, as with the views from the sea of Plymouth and other
maritime cities done by Van de Velde in the 1660s, one may suspect an
ulterior motive of espionage.[30] Often such panoramas were taken from a
position across the river as with the well-known view of Henley by Jan
Siberechts.[31] Apart from these, Hendrik Dankerts, Francis Place, and
Wenceslaus Hollar (a Bohemian) deserve mention.[32] Some towns were
usually seen from across the river, especially where there was an
impressive skyline, as with the view of London from Southwark or
Millbank. Many of these panoramas were produced in print form, which
suggests that wider sales were expected than might be the case for
paintings which could always represent an idiosyncratic taste (either of
the artist or the patron). Presumably the purchasers were citizens of the
cities depicted, and thus these panoramas can be seen as indicative of
civic pride. Noticeably they were confined to the larger and more
traditional cities, not to the country towns, although these developed civic
pride some years later, about 1850.

The points from which each city was viewed became quite standardized.
In the case of Exeter the two viewpoints were from Trew's Weir, giving
an upriver view, favoured most famously by Turner,[33] or from the hill
above Exwick (Figure 9), here shown by Copplestone Warre Bampfylde,
a local dilettante, but also depicted by Towne and others. The panoramic
view over a city from an elevated viewpoint is probably most famous in
the view of London from Hampstead Heath, but most cities had a similar
point. The format of such work was often markedly horizontal, the width
often being three times the height, and the links between these pictures
and early cartography are quite evident, and have been studied by
Rees.[34] Often one has to do little more than imagine the viewpoint to be
at a rather steeper angle to produce a map. Discovering and visiting these

A North West View of EXETER from a hill behind Exwick 1750

Figure 9 C.W. Bampfylde, *Exeter from Exwick*, watercolour, 1750, 26 × 43 cm (Courtesy Royal Albert Memorial Museum, Exeter). A view, here by a member of a local landed family, overlooking a town from a high vantage point. Most cities had a viewpoint from which they could be most flatteringly seen, a symbol of urban pride.

famous viewpoints today is a rather depressing pastime. All too often the view is as impressive as ever, or would be had it not been completely ignored by development, or privatized, so that the view is now only obtainable from a boardroom. Such interruptions to great views are as likely to be the result of tree planting as of more concrete forms of development.

This genre was completely unsuitable to be made into a composition, being of the wrong dimensions and having a completely different purpose. This is confirmed by the paucity of such views at the Royal Academy, compared with their popularity in print form. Though it is difficult to judge by titles alone, such views were probably considered too topographic.[35] During the succeeding Picturesque period, with its concern for a carefully composed landscape, though usually based on reality, this type largely disappeared. Gilpin thought the view of Barnstaple to be grand but 'too great a subject for the pencil'.[36] Somewhat later in the nineteenth century the genre was almost totally eclipsed by the attraction of quaint, often half-timbered buildings, although it did survive in some smaller market towns where it had not previously occurred. These Picturesque buildings needed to be seen from close to, and usually in portrait format to match the Gothick architecture. Sometimes local artists discovered views other than the standard; Swete for example said that he knew 'a spot from whence Exeter is seen to greater advantage'[37] than from the favourite site on Exwick Hill.[38]

Somerset

The enormous importance of Bath, and the numerous views of its modern streets, especially the Queens Square, made this period Somerset's artistic heyday, accounting for 5 per cent of English landscapes in the 1770s (Figure 10). Towards the end of the century Glastonbury Abbey became a favourite, along with many other ruined abbeys, but Wells never ranked very high on the list of popular cathedrals. Overall the county only ranks 24th by area (Appendix 3). Apart from that the county had little to offer the Picturesque and Romantic traveller, even Cheddar Gorge proving insufficient to tempt artists from the more convenient Avon Gorge at Bristol.

In 1869 *Lorna Doone* was published, and its influence is attested by the monotonously regular title *The Doone Valley*. Nevertheless the fascination for Exmoor, including Minehead and Porlock, in the last thirty years of the nineteenth century was repeated on all other moorlands, so Blackmore must be seen as part of the genre, not the instigator of it. During the twentieth century a few pictures of Sedgemoor and the Mendips have been seen, but until very recently the vernacular architecture of the county has not been much admired. Altogether, of 105

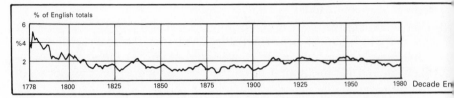

Figure 10   Graph for Somerset (Source: RA catalogues). For detailed explanation see
Appendix 1. The early vogue was mainly at Bath, plus other 'lions' at Wells and
Glastonbury. Only after 1860 did Exmoor become important.

pictures of Somerset in the mapped sample, 23 represent Bath, mainly
eighteenth-century, and 25 Exmoor, mainly late nineteenth-century.

Buildings of antiquarian interest

Apart from the panoramas there were two other major genres of
townscape painting in the period before 1790. First there was much
antiquarian interest in the depiction of great buildings of the usually
distant past. Foremost among these were the medieval cathedrals, though
castles and abbeys were also favoured. The most popular cathedrals for
artistic purposes were already becoming defined, and included Canterbury
(the cathedral accounting for the great majority of views of that popular
location), Westminster, Durham, Lincoln and Ely. Such views became
even more popular in the Picturesque Period, and are discussed in detail
in Chapter 4. The attitude to such buildings is cynically described by
Defoe when he visited Exeter in 1724 and remarked 'The cathedral
church of this city is an ancient beauty, or, as it may be said, it is
beautiful for its antiquity.'[39] Such antiquarianism, most manifest in
Stukeley's guides, was also responsible for the numerous depictions of
major archaeological sites, although these were often hopelessly inaccurate,
not only in their depiction but also in the purposes supposed for them.[40]
Of these, Stonehenge was by far the most important.

   The importance of the wide streets of recent Georgian buildings in
Bath has already been mentioned and several other towns were depicted
for the same reason, e.g. Devonport and Brighton, the latter as much for
the promenade as the inland streets. The importance of cleanliness,
modernity and functionalism is stressed by visitors. Canaletto was widely
regarded as the perfectionist in these matters and visited England in 1746-
55, though largely confining himself to London.[41] Samuel Scott was
another for whom London provided most of his subject matter.[42] In
general terms the depicted buildings of the eighteenth century were
classical, modern and functional, except where the age and sheer scale of
the building justified its interest on an antiquarian basis. Into this latter
category came most of the abbeys, notably Glastonbury, as well as the
cathedrals. In the case of the abbeys, to draw a distinction between the
urban and rural would be rather pointless. The ruins of Tintern were

Figure 11 A mezzotint after Thomas Girtin, *Kirkstall Abbey on the River Aire*, from *The Rivers of England*, 1824. (Courtesy M.R. Pidgley). The ruined abbey was a major attraction for the antiquarian, usually depicted from a low angle, with a river and as little modern housing as possible. Kirkstall was not quite as popular as Fountains and Rievaulx.

famous, though usually visited as part of the fast developing tour of the Wye and South Wales. Valle Crucis was similarly part of the North Wales tour, but Kirkstall (Figure 11) and Fountains were major sites in the north. In general a good ruin had to be impressive, forming a silhouette against the sky, the arcades should be standing, and sheer scale was also an advantage.

The castle

Castles were also often depicted, but there seems to have been a decided preference for those in the country rather than the town. Of them all Windsor was by far the most popular, although perhaps strictly in a class of its own. For one thing it was not a ruin, so perhaps might fit more easily into the group of country houses, as would Warwick, another favourite. Also, Windsor being the royal residence, artists may have had an eye on royal patronage. Paul and Thomas Sandby were both employed there, for example, not only for their painting but also in the design of the grounds.[43] Whether ruined or not, one of the most obvious features is the pronounced vertical extent of the most favoured castles, at least in their representations, and the lack of clutter of other buildings around them.

The country house

The country house was, however, probably the most numerous subject during the Classical era, together with views of their grounds, many of them newly landscaped by Lancelot Brown or other garden designers. The scatter of dots over the maps (Figures 5–7) is largely the result of this particular genre, and such a scatter is not to reappear until the twentieth century when it is brought about by the ubiquity of the motor vehicle. Most of the depicted houses were comparatively new, being either built in the century or given new façades. Most are classical, many Palladian, and there was considerable discussion concerning the architectural style and the building materials, with white stucco being preferred certainly to brick, and concerning the situation. Houses were frequently rebuilt to give them a commanding position, whereas the old house had often sheltered in a valley. There were few depictions of those houses which had remained largely unaltered in the eighteenth century and were medieval, Tudor or Stuart in general appearance. In Devon places such as Dartington Hall were largely ignored, though there were exceptions where the aristocracy in residence were of great significance or were major patrons. Powderham Castle, though largely medieval, and in a low-lying situation, was quite favoured; it was, after all the home of the Courtenays, Earls of Devon. Charlecote in Warwickshire was another exception, possibly because of its Shakespearean connections,[44] although Shakespeare was not to be a major associational attraction until about 1850.

Patronage was often extended to artists by commissioning pictures of the house and grounds, and by employing them as drawing masters to teach the children, especially the daughters. John Cotman worked in this way.[45] At Ugbrooke House for example, the Cliffords employed both John Varley and Francis Towne as drawing masters.[46] Where major houses were not much depicted in this period patronage was probably little extended.

Much of this work can most correctly be called Landscape Portraiture, with Richard Wilson's depictions of Croome Court and Gainsborough's famous picture of Mr and Mrs Andrews as noteworthy examples.[47] Some artists toured around the great houses, though whether always by invitation is not clear. Many of them were open to the public in any case, at least to the respectable public, as most tourists' diaries make clear.[48] In one year, 1784, John Feary depicted Castle Hill, Haunton Court, Stevenstone and Beam, exhibiting all these at the Royal Academy. William Tomkins, whose work at Saltram is well known, also painted Mamhead, Ugbrooke and Tapley in a single year (1773).

Many of these patrons were themselves painters, or had a deep interest in the arts, as did the members of the Society of Dilettanti[49] for example. Such country houses were important in employing artists in the provinces, giving them some sort of income. Inevitably the artists' perceptions of rural landscape were influenced by their residence and employment, as is probably the case also with those employed by the provincial colleges and departments of art today, which have taken over the role of provincial employers of artists. Although many of the pictures required by the family were portraits, the wish to have one's property on canvas, be it house, park or livestock, was responsible for many depictions.

The houses most commonly depicted by artists were, therefore, the result of several factors. Certainly accessibility was of significance, for in Devonshire, for example, even the greater houses in the north and west of the county did not score very highly. The rank of the owner may not have been as significant as the amount of patronage extended by the house, and the building materials seem to have been of little significance, despite arguments about the aesthetic qualities of various materials.[50] Some, such as Ugbrooke, were clearly preferred for their grounds (designed by Brown) rather than for the house (designed by Adam but in a decidedly unusual vein).

The East Midlands

One group of counties in the East Midlands owes most of its artistic importance to its country houses, and hence is comparatively popular in this period. Northamptonshire, Leicestershire, Rutland and Bedfordshire (Figure 12) have been consistently among the least attractive counties to artists (ranking 40th–43rd out of 45 in the total number of Royal Academy depictions per square mile of area (Appendix 3)). Of course, what proportion of the unlocatable pictures actually depicted scenes in these shires cannot be known, though there is some reason for supposing that the number may be quite high. Several unlocatable pictures were sporting scenes, and these counties are famous for their hunting. Nevertheless this region has scored consistently poorly. The landscape may be undulating but is not perhaps remarkable. The type of views which could be obtained there could also be found in the Home Counties closer to the metropolis, and the region tends, therefore, to lie in 'perceptual shadow'. Such shadows occur frequently, and the concept is discussed in Chapter 9.[51] Not only the rural landscape is ignored. The larger towns of the region, such as Leicester or Northampton, have only rarely been exhibited nationally, Peterborough Cathedral being the sole major building to make a regular appearance at the Academy, apart from the great country houses such as Canons Ashby, Burghley, Woburn and Ampthill, often the centres of very considerable estates.

After the fashion for country house views declined, these counties had little left to offer. There were a few pastoral river scenes on the Great Ouse or the Nene, and a few glimpses of Charnwood Forest. In the twentieth century they have provided views of stone villages and farms, as have all other parts of the country, but the consistent unfashionableness of the whole area remains the outstanding feature.

42

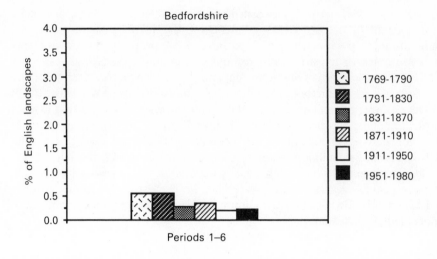

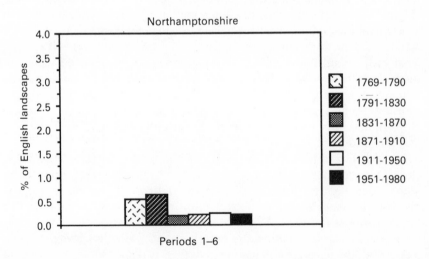

Figure 12 Histograms for the counties of the East Midlands: (a) Bedfordshire, (b) North-amptonshire, (c) Leicestershire, (d) Rutland (Source: Royal Academy catalogues). For detailed explanation see Appendix 1. One of the few attractive features for artists were the country houses.

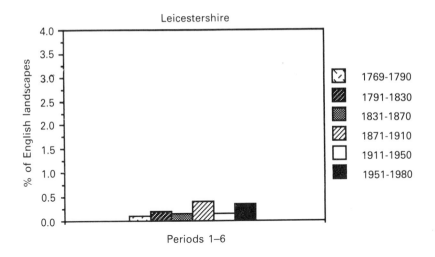

Leicestershire

Periods 1–6

1769-1790
1791-1830
1831-1870
1871-1910
1911-1950
1951-1980

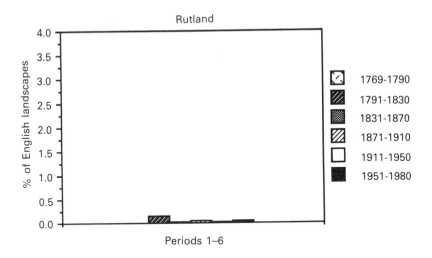

Rutland

Periods 1–6

1769-1790
1791-1830
1831-1870
1871-1910
1911-1950
1951-1980

Landscape parks

During the eighteenth century the English landscape park broke away
from being an English version of a European model and became
something quite distinctive, though rapidly copied on the continent.
These newly laid-out gardens and parks, by Kent, Bridgeman, Brown and
their imitators, soon became popular subjects themselves, long before
they had matured, partly perhaps because they were by far the most
convenient outdoor scene to a painter resident in a country house.
Several parks made regular appearances at the Academy, as did
Charlecote in Warwickshire,[52] normally depicted with deer, and often
employing some imagination as to the eventual size of the trees.
Unfortunately views of the grounds are often difficult to distinguish from
views of the house by title alone.

The still waters of the newly constructed serpentine lakes were put to
use as middle ground, enabling the eye to move smoothly from
foreground to background.[53] Similar uses of water are found in marine
painting, and in the very popular views of Alpine and other lakes and
estuarine scenes. Henry Hoare's great garden at Stourhead regularly
adorned the Academy's walls, although the house did not appear. The
vogue for such parkland scenes lasted about a decade longer than that for
country houses, only declining significantly in the 1840s. This may reflect
the growing to maturity of the parks, and throughout the Picturesque
Period, as the gardens in actuality became rougher in texture, so too did
the preferred scene.

Slowly the preference for symmetrical, Palladian mansions declined and,
as Gothick became the preferred style for new houses, most notably
Fonthill Abbey built by the notorious William Beckford and illustrated at
the Academy several times annually in the 1800s,[54] so too did the older
medieval houses come into favour for the artist. Locally, houses such as
Dartington Hall suddenly came to prominence again, ivy-encrusted
Gothick piles, situated in low-lying, well-sheltered hollows. These
landscape portraits became much rarer after 1830 at least in their painted
form, though prints, presumably more in tune with more popular taste,
remained common for some years after.

Mount Edgcumbe, on the Cornish side of the Tamar but then in
Devon, was probably the most favoured house of the West Country in the
eighteenth century, and its decline in fortune may be typical of many.
Celia Fiennes, usually loath to allow sentiment to enter her account,
referred to it as 'bedecked with woods . . . the finest seat I have seen'.[55]
Pococke called it 'by far the finest situation I ever saw, exceeding
everything in the beauty of the near prospects'.[56] A movable camera
obscura had been installed to make the landscape even more of a picture,
and no doubt to be used for drawing.[57] Its fame certainly lasted until 1812
when Turner gave a picnic there.[58] Ayton thought that 'among all the

Figure 13   William Daniell, *Mount Edgecumbe from the Citadel, Plymouth*, acquatint, 1825, 17 × 24 cm (Courtesy Devon Library Services). One of the greatest country houses, for views both towards and away from its grounds. Such views continue in print form well into the nineteenth century but largely died out in painting before 1825.

scenes that memory could recall none could be paralleled with this'.[59] Before that, however, Gilpin had thought it 'a mere map of the country, and has little picturesque beauty'.[60] Shaven lawns running down to wide prospects over the Hamoaze, usually lacustrine at full tide, did not appeal to him and the site ceased to be a major location for art shortly after 1800.

Marines

The coast was considered less attractive than the river scene during the eighteenth century, judging by the numbers of views, and was to remain so until the mid-nineteenth. There were three main categories of coastal views, one of which, the estuarine scene, may perhaps not be strictly coastal, and another, the marine scene, not strictly landscape.

The view across an estuary, done usually in watercolour, with the water at flood tide, was very popular. Such views have much in common with the preferred views of lakes which were then so common from Alpine journeys, and perhaps the insistence that they were beautiful 'at full tide only' helped to reinforce this lacustrine vision. Along with other genres which were usually in watercolour these views reached their zenith in the succeeding Picturesque period, and are therefore discussed in more detail in the next chapter.[61] They were frequently combined with country house views, looking from, or towards, a major riparian seat, and often looking from one to another.

The main genre of truly coastal landscapes, before 1800, was the sublime coast. Aesthetic theory of the time postulated that the opposite of beauty was sublimity which attracted by fear and awe.[62] The sea fulfilled these characteristics admirably, either as a storm scene, where the awe derived from the manifest power of the elements, or from the wide panoramic seascape, where the sheer expanse was awesome. The Eddystone lighthouse was only one popular location for storm scenes, where often the picture is so full of water that the term landscape seems hardly appropriate. Elsewhere Nicholas Pococke specialized in such views, usually long-shore scenes full of wrecked or struggling vessels. Sublimity is a diminishing asset of any scene. Awesomeness is inevitably lessened with familiarity, and in any case few British scenes could rival foreign scenes, especially those in America which were to become well known as the nineteenth century progressed. When John Swete, the local Picturesque traveller, visited the highest waterfall in Devon, in the Lydford gorge, he found it a 'prospect of the tremendous nature', and the 'blood froze in veins'.[63] However, the better-travelled Joseph Farington was less impressed:

> though a pretty scene for ladies to visit in fine weather there is nothing about it that can justly be called very interesting, nothing magnificent, no rocks, no grandeur, a scene not to be spoken of by those who have been in Wales.[64]

In visiting the Valley of the Rocks, near Lynton, one can find little in common with someone who was 'imprest with dread'[65] there, or understand the gross vertical exaggeration given to prints of the place, not only because the site is now tamed by tourism, but also because our experience, even vicariously, of other countries cannot allow us to be frightened by a few tors and boulders.

Sheer expanse could also be sublime, for which the words 'grand', 'terrific' and 'solemn' were commonly synonyms. Stukeley called the view from Stockland Hill 'a most solemn view, a boundless extent of water thrown into a mighty horizontal curve'.[66] Such a taste for the huge and unusual lasted a long time but finally faded in the mid-nineteenth century.[67] One theory goes so far as to suggest that the Sublime as an aesthetic concept crossed the Atlantic to the USA in the mid-nineteenth century, there to become a firm characteristic of American painting from the Luminists to the Abstract Expressionism of Rothko and De Kooning.[68]

Marine pictures

The third main group of coastal works comprises the marine pictures. These are included here because they are not easy to distinguish from

Figure 14   George Rowe, *Valley of Rocks, Linton, Devon*, lithograph, *c*. 1835, 16 × 21 cm
(Courtesy Devon Library Services). The outrageous vertical exaggeration used to heighten
feelings of sublimity also continued longer in print form than in painting.

landscape work, even when seen, let alone when working solely from
catalogue entries. Marine art is a major subject in its own right and has
had considerable attention paid to it.[69] Many pictures were made by
naval officers, for whom drawing was an essential skill, especially for
those engaged in hydrographic survey. Such work may not have graced
the Academy's walls, but it is frequently found in local collections. Many
of the professional artists involved worked exclusively on marine pictures.
The distinction between marines and estuarial views is sometimes
unclear, although much marine work was in oil, most estuarines in
watercolour. The amount of careful detail given to the ships is usually
indicative of the marine interest. Most marine paintings at this time and
right through the Napoleonic wars depicted warships and the naval
dockyards.

The importance of this branch of art accounts for the concentrations
shown on the map (Figure 5) in the Medway estuary, at Plymouth, in the
Solent and much of the work at Dover and Liverpool.

Through the Classical and well into the Picturesque Period the
principal marine genre was in the harbour, or not far outside it. There is
usually plenty of activity, and the details of the shoreline vie with the
ships for importance. As systematic tours along the coast became
popular, such as Turner's series of prints along the south coast of

England, such work merged with coastal and industrial work, as at
Teignmouth. At Plymouth the ships used as prison hulks during the wars
were a particular favourite, adding a *frisson* of Romantic significance to
the marine interest. Another popular view was of ships careened on the
mud, for work on their keels. This produced powerful diagonals in the
picture. That the navy had a significance beyond the aesthetic is suggested
by Samuel Johnson on his visit to Plymouth when 'The magnificence of
the navy, the shipbuilding and all its circumstances afforded him a grand
subject of contemplation.'[70] Overseas the connection between the
presence of the navy and the popular locations for British artists is very
obvious, Gibraltar and the West Indies being particular examples. Art
follows the flag, and the intrinsic patriotism of artists became obvious
again in the twentieth century.

Many coastal areas had their own marine painter, such as Thomas
Luny at Teignmouth or J.W. Carmichael at Newcastle. They concentrated
as much on shipbuilding as shipping and this became one of the
established aesthetic industries. After 1815 marine art became quantitat-
ively much less important, this coinciding with the period when sail gave
way to steam, the subject of Turner's *The Fighting Téméraire*. Only in the
late nineteenth century did the genre revive with artists such as Wyllie.
Even then modern ships were by no means universally admired.[71] By
then the merchant navy was the more common subject, except during
wartime.

Hampshire and the Isle of Wight

The graph for Hampshire (Figure 15) demonstrates the county's
popularity at this time. The county contained a reasonable crop of
country houses, though none was of outstanding importance. Two great
buildings of antiquarian interest were Winchester Cathedral and the

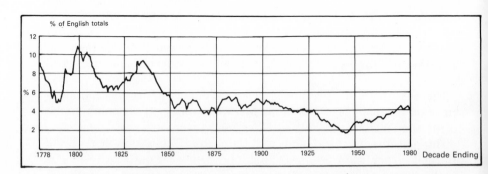

Figure 15   Graph for Hampshire, not including the Isle of Wight (Source: RA catalogues).
The marine interest is largely responsible for the vogue in the early nineteenth century.

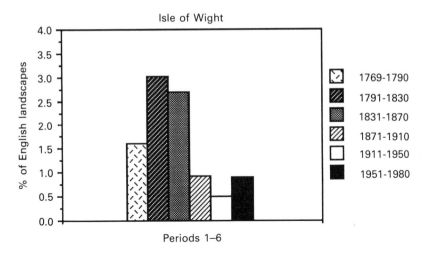

Figure 16 Histogram for the Isle of Wight (Source: RA catalogues). Although the marine interest was strong, the island's coasts remained a firm favourite until well into Victoria's reign.

ruined abbey at Netley, both of which appeared regularly at the Academy. The main bulk of work, however, was marine or at least estuarine and centred on Portsmouth, the Solent and Southampton. William Gilpin was doubtless responsible for giving the New Forest some favour in the early nineteenth century, living at Boldre, but the Forest only really became fashionable at the end of the century along with other heathlands. As antiquarian interest declined, later followed by marine work, Hampshire lost a lot of its interest, as apart from Christchurch there were few places to fulfil the need for the fishing village in the twentieth century.

The Isle of Wight was close enough to the mainland not to have to wait for steam packets to become available before it gained favourable notice. With the undoubted cachet enjoyed by islands it has ranked 2nd in pictures per unit area, only overtaken by London with Middlesex (Appendix 3). Marine scenes in the eighteenth century may have given it its greatest popularity, with ships seen off the Needles as the regular stereotype, but the view from Steep Hill, and Carisbrook Castle, provided much inland interest well into the nineteenth century. So did the eastern resorts, especially Ryde, Shanklin and Ventnor. After mid-century, however, the island lost favour markedly, and there was a shift to the small harbours of Bonchurch, Yarmouth and Freshwater.[71]

Industrial subjects

Studies, especially by Klingender on the depiction of industries in art, suggest that this is a major feature in the eighteenth century.[73] This is not borne out by the Royal Academy catalogues. The best that can be said is that industry is less unattractive in the eighteenth than the nineteenth century. Despite the examples of Joseph Wright and Philip de Loutherbourg there are very few titles of paintings exhibited there which clearly relate to industrial sites. The quality of a few major works of art should not be read as widespread aesthetic attraction. Nevertheless there does not seem to be the widespread avoidance of modern industrial processes which characterized the period after 1850. There were many pictures of rural industry, mainly windmills and watermills, though these were to increase markedly later as a whole catalogue of 'acceptable' industrial processes developed in the Picturesque Period. Only Coleorton colliery in Leicestershire, of the unacceptable processes, occurred more than once in the Royal Academy catalogues, and this was probably due to the considerable artistic patronage of the owner.[74] Shipbuilding was certainly found attractive, but usually must be seen as part of marine painting.

The appearance of many industrial sites depicted in print form may suggest that they were more acceptable to a bourgeois taste than that of the buyers of paintings, and those who selected works for the Academy. Wright's *View of Cromford* was legitimated by reference to marine work: [the windows] 'remind me of a first rate man of war; and when they are lighted up on a dark night look most luminously beautiful'.[75] Klingender suggests that industry could be seen as a part of the Sublime:

> The iron industry had not yet lost its picturesque character. Still surrounded by romantic scenery, the great ironworks, with their smouldering lime kilns and coke ovens, blazing furnaces and noisy forges, had a special attraction for eighteenth century admirers of the sublime.[76]

In sheer numbers the Industrial Sublime was overwhelmed by other genres, and urban industry was not to become a significant taste until the twentieth century – and only then when the industry depicted had become safely moribund.

Tours

Towards the end of the period, and perhaps one of the causes of the demise of the Classical concepts, was the development of touring within the British Isles as well as the established Grand Tour to Italy. The Lake District, North Wales and the Wye valley were the most favoured tours,

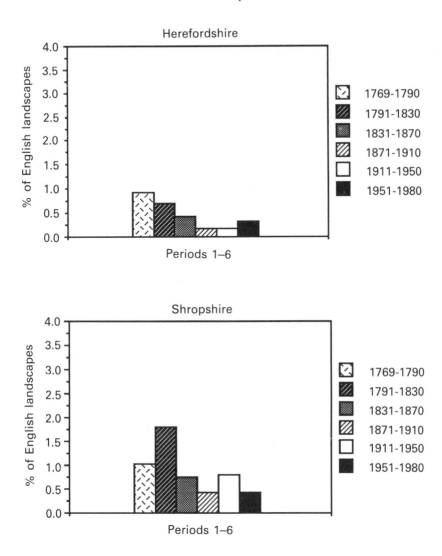

Figure 17 Histograms for (a) Herefordshire and (b) Shropshire (Source: RA catalogues). Both counties show a marked lack of attractiveness, probably a result of the proximity of Wales.

typically taking place in the late summer and early autumn. Mountains became fashionable, and the development of the turnpike system extended the possibilities markedly. Frequently sights seen abroad encouraged the seeking of equivalents at home. North Wales was often compared with the Alps, and the view of a castle overlooking a lake, the Alpine favourite being Chillon on Lake Geneva, became a Welsh cliché also, especially at Dolbadern, Carnarvon and Conwy, the sea often acting as a surrogate lake. Travelling to North Wales must have been almost as tedious as to the Alps, but artists managed it in large numbers. Their interest lay primarily in the coastal castle towns of Carnarvon, Conwy and Bangor, but also in the Snowdonian valleys and lakes, with Llangollen, and Valle Crucis, being a secondary area no doubt visited *en route*. The mountains themselves remained usually as a backdrop.

The Welsh Marches

The popularity of the North Wales tour may explain the comparative favour of the Marches, the counties of Shropshire and Herefordshire, which have their peak at this time or a little later (Figure 17). The interest lay mainly in the valley of the Severn, notably at Buildwas Priory and Wenlock Abbey, and also the Teme. For two counties with such a variety of landscape their comparative lack of popularity (ranking 34th and 38th by area (Appendix 3)) is somewhat surprising. This is despite two major writers on Picturesque theory residing in the area, Richard Payne Knight at Downton and Uvedale Price a near neighbour. Their houses, with those at Hadley Park and Hawkstone, were sometimes depicted, and some Wye tourists worked at Goodrich Castle and Ross on Wye. After about 1840 only Ludlow was consistently attractive, as much for its vernacular buildings as for its castle. Much Wenlock also appeared. These two counties surely represent a case of perceptual shadow, being ignored on the way to more exciting or spectacular landscape just beyond. The views they could offer were available nearer to London. The same may be true of the Southern Uplands of Scotland which, after Walter Scott's popularity had declined, failed to achieve the favour which their physiography might lead one to expect.

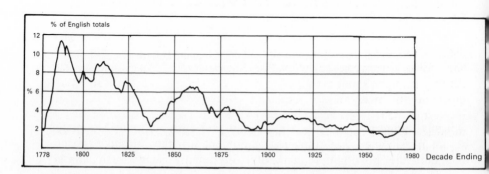

Figure 18 Graph for Cumbria (Source: RA catalogues). The great vogue for the Lakes was well on the wane before 1800. Later the rivers became more popular.

Figure 19　Aquatint after William Green, *Man Mountain on Coniston Water*, 1815 (Courtesy M.R. Pidgley). A carefully composed view using the lake to link foreground and distance, with appropriate sidescreens.

Cumbria

The Lake District was the other mountainous tour, markedly more popular before 1800 than after (Figure 18). Wordsworth must, therefore, be seen as a follower of fashion, rather than an instigator of it, at least in purely locational terms. The central valley, from Windermere, through Ambleside, Rydal, Lodore, Borrowdale to Keswick and Skiddaw was overwhelmingly the focus of attention, though Ullswater and Coniston both had visitors. As in North Wales the interest was largely confined to the valleys, waterfalls, and especially the lakes rather than the mountains, though the area lacked the major ruins which so often formed features in Welsh pictures.

After its great period, when it accounted for 11 per cent of the English landscapes exhibited, Cumbrian output declined to just over 2 per cent in the 1830s. However, the interest in the Romantic river scene in mid-century brought about a revival to 6 per cent in the 1850s centred much more on the river valleys, especially Borrowdale and the Esk. Later interest in the fells, especially around Kirkby Lonsdale, was comparatively minor, and the recent revival has been as much centred on the coast, especially around Morecambe Bay and the Solway Firth, as in the Lake District itself. Barrow's crane-scape has appeared occasionally in recent times.

South Wales

At this period South Wales was almost as popular as the north, and while much of this favour was the result of the rapidly developing tour to the Wye valley, there was also much interest further west. Visits to the castles there, Manorbier and Pembroke, Cilgerran, Carreg Kennon and Caerleon, were popular, and the Neath valley was also favoured. The well-documented tour of Paul Sandby in 1771 was thus only one of many.[77] Thereafter, there was little further interest until the coasts of the Gower and Pembrokeshire became popular in the late nineteenth century, and the rise in favour of the mining landscape of the valleys after the Second World War.

Other areas were also visited, no doubt often depending on personal circumstances and recommendation, as Gainsborough visited Devon to see his friend William Jackson, the cathedral organist: 'I hope to see you in about a fortnight (late July), as I purpose spending a month or six weeks at Tingmouth (*sic*) or other places round Exeter', and asking Jackson, on behalf of Edmund Garvey, to 'get him a sight of whatever is worth seeing in Exeter'.[78] Frequently artists travelling on the turnpikes would make sketches during stopovers and these account for the numerous pictures of places on the main routes. In Devon such pictures depict Honiton, Chudleigh, and most importantly, Ivybridge, a village that owes its perception to artists during coach stops.

Figure 20   P. Sandby, *Ivy Bridge near Plymouth*, copper engraving, 1780, 13 × 18 cm (Courtesy Devon Library Services). A well-frequented stop on the coaching run to Plymouth, Ivybridge took its name from the perfect assemblage of Picturesque elements close to the road.

Throughout this chapter there has been little mention of what many would assume by the word 'landscape', i.e. views of rural England and more rarely, Scotland and Wales. In general the rural landscape was not much painted, except as foreground in other sorts of pictures. Great panoramic views over new enclosures were as popular with artists as with other travellers, judging from their written accounts, but they were not often sketched. There may have been little market for such scenes, regarded perhaps as admirable rather than beautiful. Gilpin thought one such view was 'too great a subject for a painting'.[79] Swete in East Devon noted 'from every eminence pleasing views [of] inclos'd meadows', and at Maiden Down, 'I had pleasure in seeing the wild unproductive common converted into inclosures.' He did not paint them, however.[80] Fiennes thought the view from Blackdown was 'full of enclosures, good grass and corn' and Defoe saw from Honiton Hill 'the most beautiful landscape in the world – a mere picture – and I do not remember the like in any one place in England'. Shaw in 1788 described Haldon as 'a barren flinty common, but one of the noblest prospects in the kingdom', while from Fairmile there was a 'fine amphitheatre of meadow and arable enclosure'.[81] Pictures of such prospects were not to find favour as art, however, until the twentieth century.

Although many pictures of woods and cottages on the Dutch model were exhibited they were rarely located. Many were obviously compositions, frequently acknowledging their debt to Ruysdael and others, as Gainsborough felt 'such a fondness for my first imitations of little Dutch landskips'.[82] The range of landscape genres quoted by Stechow was not well represented, and rarely gave rise to fashions for particular locations.[83] In an age when Italy and Holland were the epitome of everything desirable in landscape, most English painters were faced with three choices, to travel abroad, to produce landscape compositions or to descend to mere topography. The most common compromise was to depict the British landscape through rose-coloured Claude glasses, as Wilson saw Wales.[84] Only with the rise of Picturesque theory did English landscape artists learn to select the paintable without reference to foreign examples, though even then with much reference to theoretical considerations. Several hints of this major change have been detected before 1790. We can now turn to its heyday.

4

The Picturesque Period 1790–1830

The period under consideration in this chapter almost exactly coincides with that often regarded as the golden age of British landscape painting, a period which included Turner, Constable and the Norwich school, and which saw landscape become established as a major area of artistic endeavour. Not surprisingly the number of books available reflects the importance given to these artists, with Hussey's study of the Picturesque still retaining its importance as a seminal work.[1]

Picturesque theory

The strangest feature of the period was the enormous importance given to landscape aesthetic theory, and the transfer of that theory to actual landscape, much of it with no pretensions to having been designed. Although Burke had provided a theoretical construct for the ideas of the Classical Period these had remained largely in the realm of art, including gardens.[2] Gilpin, acknowledged at the time as the chief polemicist of the Picturesque, applied his theory to everyday agricultural and semi-natural landscapes as well.[3] There was little evidence to support the assertions of what constituted the Picturesque, which concentrated on the aesthetic pleasure to be gained from roughness, from a lack of symmetry, from antiquarian, preferably ivy-clad ruins, from bridges and the pleasing juxtaposition of related objects. In the broadest terms a Picturesque landscape on a scale of roughness lay between the beautiful and the sublime, the Romantic lying further towards the sublime, or grand. The most distinctive feature of Picturesque ideas was that all exterior objects were to be judged by whether they contributed or not to a verisimilitude with a fine picture. Nature, and the whole of man's works, were to imitate art. Appleton, in recognizing Gilpin's importance, said,

> Whether Gilpin could be said to have directed public taste in landscape
> or whether he merely displayed a susceptibility to the kind of visual
> environment in which the public was increasingly discovering aesthetic
> pleasure may be questioned.[4]

Such an aesthetic system obviously poses the question whether it is
proper to judge a functional object such as a barn by its aesthetic
qualities, and the paradox between practicalities and appearance was
recognized at the time,

> What is the reason that those objects which displease us . . . in nature
> please us most in painting? A deep road, a puddle of water, a bank
> covered with docks and briars and an old tree or two are all the
> circumstances in many a fine landscape.[5]

The writer suggests that the pleasure lay in 'la difficulté vaincue'. The
conquest of nature by the simple process of hanging it on the wall, or
painting it, may explain much of the love of many landscapes, from the
merely picturesque to the fully sublime.[6]

The language of Picturesque theory, when describing actual landscape,
continually deploys phraseology which emanates from painting and
drawing, 'We had hills but they were tame and uniform, following each
other in such quick succession, that we rarely found either a foreground
or a distance'[7] was one of Gilpin's complaints. 'It is not sufficiently
divided into portions adapted to the pencil'[8] was another.

Kenneth Clark in 1935 suggested that by 1792 the Picturesque cult was
'allied to antiquarianism'[9] which was certainly older, but the adhesion of
Picturesque ideas also altered the way in which antiquarian artefacts were
considered. Ivy became essential. Clark also suggested that 'The
picturesque was a tyranny as severe as was the heroic couplet to the
poet.'[10] Certainly most tourists of the time, and those artists who left
extensive writings, seemed to be more concerned with whether some
scene could be fitted into Picturesque ideas than whether they liked it,
sometimes apologizing for liking something that didn't fit. Personal
preferences were often seen as merely an extension of the rules.

Because most significant Picturesque views are still considered
attractive today, if often too pretty, it may be useful to describe what was
not Picturesque but has acquired attractiveness since. The South Hams of
Devon near Slapton were 'not picturesque – the general flatness of the
country around it, and the deficiency of woodland embellishment barred
all pretensions'.[11] Gilpin called it 'a country, however, in which the
farmer glories, though the painter treats it with neglect',[12] so other ways
of seeing could be recognized as existing. The emphasis on woodland,
which became even more important after 1830, certainly occurs in almost

all accounts. Among other items which were not accepted were moors and heaths, villages and farms, though cottages were accepted by some, Classical buildings and formal gardens, long sweeping bays and violent coasts.

Travel

Until 1815 much of the continent was barred to English travellers for long periods due to war. Simultaneously the turnpike road system was being rapidly developed, and these two events led to the Discovery of Britain. Quite frequently these new roads were depicted by local artists as they were built, or shortly after. Doubtless this was not unconnected with the involvement of the local gentry in promoting such roads and their patronage of art. Bastard's road at Ashburton was depicted as was the 'Alpine Way' along the Exe valley,[13] typically taking a longer and better graded route along the river valley and replacing a ridgeway road. The turnpike stopping-places, most notably Ivybridge, remained firm favourites; 'the bridge, the high grounds beyond it, the rocks and the foaming current assume the most picturesque relations', declared Maton.[14] Indeed Ivybridge may well represent a place, now a rapidly growing suburb of Plymouth, which owes its development to the turnpike trade and to Picturesque theory. Away from the main roads, however, the horse remained the main means of travel. John Swete, who was Devon's own travelling expert on Picturesque matters, typically toured in the late summer, starting each day at dawn. Rowlandson's creation, Dr Syntax, travelled similarly and was able to lampoon the main routes of the day.

Figure 21   Thomas Rowlandson, *Dr. Syntax Sketching the Lake*, watercolour from *The Tours of Dr. Syntax* (Courtesy M.R. Pidgley.) The satirical account of the Picturesque tour by Rowlandson was not far removed from reality.

As so often happens cartoons provide the quickest and most precise pictures of current concerns even where these are quite hard to find in the serious literature (Figure 21). The state of the hotels may have either attracted or deterred visitors. Dibdin complained that, 'In short the most filthy cottage upon Derbyshire's peak is a palace in comparison with the Hotel between Holsworthy and Tavistock.'[15] The Peak District was, after all, a major tourist area, which could scarcely be said of north-west Devon.

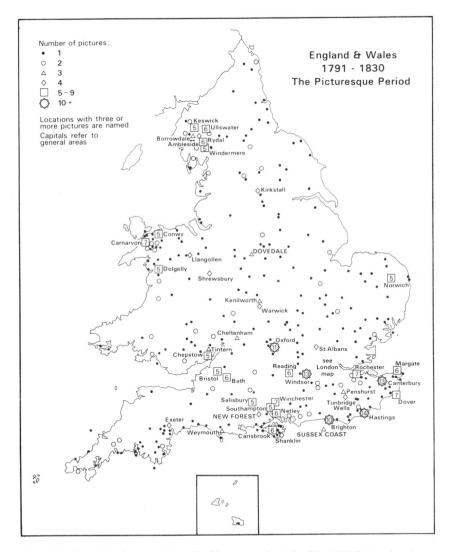

Figure 22 Map of landscapes depicted in Picturesque Period, 1791–1830, England and Wales (Source: RA catalogues).

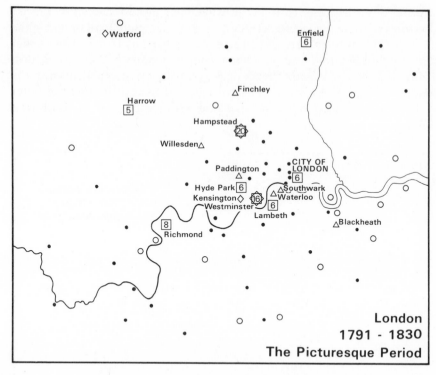

Figure 23   Map of landscapes depicted in Picturesque Period, 1791–1830, London area
(Source: RA catalogues).

Foreign travel

The year of Waterloo, 1815, marks a distinct watershed in the art of the
period, as immediately the wars were over artists started to invade the
continent again and in much increased numbers. Italy still remained the
firm foreign favourite, but with considerable changes in preferred areas.
There was more interest outside Rome, in Naples and in Tuscany. The
northern parts of France, especially the coastal towns, plus Rouen and
Paris, became much more visited than before the wars, showing no sign
of the abhorrence of the landscapes of a former enemy as occurred after
the wars of the twentieth century. The interest in mountains which was
noted towards the end of the Classical Period continued, in the Alps and
especially the Swiss lakes. Chillon Castle on Lake Geneva was to become
perhaps the most important stereotype of all.[16] The Rhine for a short
period around 1800 also rose to prominence, but this ended with the end
of the wars. Rather later Greece became a particular focus of interest, no
doubt due partly to the Greek struggle for independence, as well as
Byron's popularity.

Outside Europe many ideas were also being brought back from India,

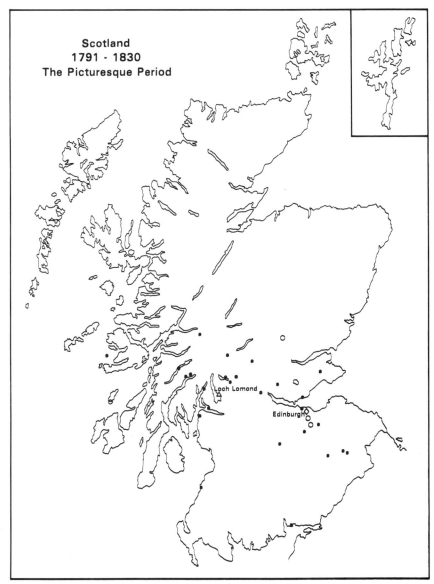

Figure 24   Map of landscapes depicted in Picturesque Period, 1791–1830, Scotland (Source: RA catalogues).

not least by the highly prolific Daniell brothers, who rarely failed to exhibit their full quota of pictures, though these pictures did not greatly influence English scenes. Swiss lake scenes, Italian scenery and Rhine analogies, however, had profound influence on how English scenes might be legitimated.

Media

The print market greatly developed during the period. When the invention of lithography occurred[17] it had marginal effect in Britain compared with the sudden growth in steel line engraving which, by greatly increasing the life of a plate, allowed for the possibility of wide sales of prints. These could now become souvenirs, fulfilling much the same function as the modern picture postcard, albeit to a wealthier and more restricted travelling public. The popularity of a subject matter in print form can be taken as indicative of a greater spread of public approbation than an oil painting indicates, and with several types of picture, e.g. panoramic views of towns and views of country houses and parks, popularity survived much longer in print form than in paintings. The wider public held on to their preferences longer than artists; thus preference or taste may well trickle down through a hierarchy, though that hierarchy is not necessarily the same as the social one.

Different printing techniques were used for different kinds of subject matter (see Figure 107). The aquatint was particularly useful for Picturesque subjects and has a subject profile very similar to that of the watercolour. The line engraving was the obvious choice for buildings, and the discovery of new techniques may itself have encouraged the growth of different preferences.

The artist

Artistic practice also underwent significant change in the period. As Fawcett makes clear, this is the time when provincial art schools began to be an important part of town life. The Norwich school had achieved greater distinction than the others, but by 1824 there were already seven artists' materials suppliers in Liverpool.[18] Many larger centres had flourishing artistic communities by 1830, although most artists still regarded London as the only chance of major success, and had to concentrate very largely on portraits to survive outside it.[19]

The profession of drawing master to the big country houses and patrons continued. The systematic tour was, however, comparatively new. This consisted of a tour which systematically traced a river, coastline or similar route, followed by the publication of a book, liberally illustrated with prints. Views on the south coast of England provided Turner with much employment,[20] and William Daniell accompanied Ayton on his tour round the coasts of Britain, later illustrating the book.[21] Similarly Frederick Christian Lewis gave series of views down the Exe, the Dart and the Tamar and Tavy, always remembering to include among his significant views all the great riparian houses.

Touring

Artists toured their own country in numbers much greater than in the preceding period, doubtless due to the improving travel conditions. The most usual time of year was summer, later rather than earlier, tending to start in August and finish in October. This no doubt partly accounts for the paucity of wintry landscape views until much later in the century. Tours undertaken by Joseph Farington and exhaustively described in his diaries are typical. He visited North Wales in 1800, Central Scotland and the Borders in the following year and Paris in 1802. The next year he followed the very common tour of the Wye valley. In 1805 he visited East Anglia, and Lancashire in 1808, neither very popular tours. In 1810 he toured Devon, and the following year Cornwall.[22] Quite commonly he would obtain advice about the places to be seen from friends and patrons, as he did from Bishop Fisher of Salisbury, who specially recommended him to see Stourhead and Land's End whilst in the West Country.[23] At a more local level he would visit locally renowned experts, and in Devon he met with John Swete, who had, during the previous two decades, toured most of the county seeking Picturesque sites.[24] The important role played by these local travelling gentlemen in creating the mental map of the places worth seeing in their areas as judged by Picturesque theory, or their own interpretation of it, needs to be studied in more depth.[25]

Rivers

River scenes were more predominant at this period than at any other. Rocky streams and waterfalls were much admired wherever they could be found, inevitably more commonly in the Highland zone. In counties where there were few falls the expectations were less, and John Swete gives a detailed account of the differences between five falls in Devon.[26] However, even the grandest of them, Whitelady waterfall in Lydford Gorge, did not impress Farington.[27]

The Wye tour

There can be no doubt which river was the favourite. Gilpin had written extensively about the River Wye in the 1780s[28] and the great sites there were the subjects of innumerable pictures. Tintern was the focal point, as it was for Wordsworth, but the Wynn Cliff, Ross and Goodrich Castles and Symond's Yat were all much depicted.[29] Generally the river was seen from the water, as Farington took boat from Monmouth to Tintern.[30] This was still a standardized trip for tourists long after artists had generally abandoned the Wye.[31] For many years the Wye, and especially the view at Tintern, remained an archetype with which other places had to be compared.[32]

Incised valleys seem to have most exactly suited the Picturesque taste. The Rhine was an important overseas visit for at least a short period around 1800, and the incised stretch of the Rhine Gorge was particularly favoured. The Bristol Avon was frequently depicted at the Clifton Gorge, and the lower tidal reaches of the Tamar were another favourite. Perhaps the continuous presence of a deflected vista[33] in the valley bottom, with the ubiquitous woods on the slopes, made these rivers peculiarly suited to art.

Dovedale and Derbyshire

The most popular river scenery not in an incised valley was Dovedale, which was the focus of a tour which included visits to the important houses at Chatsworth and Haddon, Derwentdale and the caves of the Peak District, although the moorlands were avoided or denounced.[34] Derbyshire ranks 22nd by area (Appendix 3) among the English counties with a distinct peak of favour in the first half of the nineteenth century (Figure 25). Despite the famous industrial views by Joseph Wright, it has been the river valleys and the country houses which have been its pictorial highlights. As interest waned in both river scenes and country house views in mid-century so was Derbyshire comparatively abandoned, providing only about 1 per cent of the English landscapes since then. As

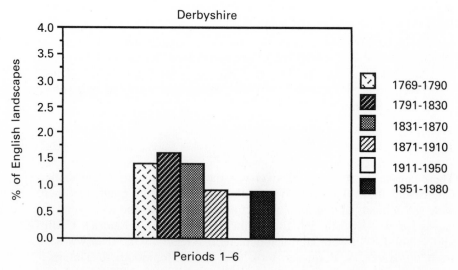

Figure 25   Histogram for Derbyshire (Source: RA catalogues). Dovedale and Derwentdale with visits to the great houses formed the attractions.

late as 1852, however, Mrs S.C. Hall could write 'the hills . . . mimic Alpine scenery to perfection' and she could recommend including 'the troops of miners with their safety lamps and quaint costume'.[35] A quarter century later the area had become over-popular, the very tone of some writing confirming a clichéd view. Of the Dove, Bradbury writes, 'With what "poetry of motion" does this wild and winsome water-girl dance along', though even in 1878 he never pays Haddon Hall a visit, 'but some artists are breathing the ancient air of the place'.[36] By then things Elizabethan were fashionable. Many of the recent pictures have been village views from the Peak District, notably of Eyam, but oddly the Dark Peak does not seem to share in the common approbation of moorland in the later nineteenth century.

Further north both Wharfedale and Wensleydale were favoured, with the chief attraction being around Bolton Abbey and Woods on the upper Wharfe, where 'the ruined portions of the priory offer several good subjects', and by the 1870s there were seats at all the points of view along the Strid.[37]

Evidence that this penchant for the larger, upland rivers was well established occurs in the many volumes of prints produced by the 'systematic tourists' such as F.C. Lewis, already mentioned. Such books were intended for sale, though to a restricted elite market partly composed of the country gentlemen whose houses figured so prominently in the subject matter.

The preferred rivers have a lot in common. Usually they were of moderate size, between 10 and 20 yards across, and with rocky beds, neither mountain streams nor lowland pastoral mature streams. They meandered within very defined valleys, sometimes incised, and with sides at least 100 feet high, usually wooded. On the Tamar for example Swete thought that the river became too wide below Calstock to be reckoned Romantic.[38] Some rivers were popular because of special features, notably waterfalls, as on the Greta, the Dee, or at the Falls of Clyde. Most pictures included a bridge, usually seen from downstream, and the Picturesque nature of an ivy-mantled bridge was asserted by Swete, at Baples Bridge, a very small example over a stream near his home: 'a bridge, stream and trees when tolerably group'd are generally picturesque'.[39] At Whiddon Park, on the Teign below Chagford, the view from the meadow

hath something in it, pleasingly wild and picturesque – in the more distant ground craggy rocks protrude their pointed surfaces through the heath beneath which the river runs. In the middle scene rise part of the woodland honours of the Park, rich thick and finely coloured by autumnal tints and in the nearer ground is seen the extremity of an old wooden channel for the conducting [of] water.[40]

Figure 26   F.C. Lewis, *Okeford Bridge*, etching, 18 × 13 cm, *c.* 1831, from *The Scenery of the River Exe* (author's collection). Most of Lewis's systematic accounts of river valleys were illustrated with gentlemen's seats and dangerous bridges.

Many of these bridges were being replaced as part of the road improvements, which did not always improve their Picturesque qualities. At Oakford Bridge, Swete thought the 'planks and wooden rails, very picturesque but insecure and disgraceful'.[41] Obviously aesthetic appreciation did not extend so far as to threaten life and limb! This is the bridge depicted by Lewis in Figure 26. As was an almost invariable rule the bridge's function is emphasized by the presence of a traveller on it. In the hand-coloured version of this print in the possession of the author he wears a red coat. The peasant in a red coat becomes a regular motif, though more, one suspects, because of the aesthetic need for complementary colour than any truthful comment on the common garb.

If most tours were focused on mountainous regions, or famous rivers, there was one which focused on a writer's landscape. This was the tour of central Scotland, which to a large extent was concerned with the places frequented and described by Sir Walter Scott, who stands as one of only two writers, the other being Thomas Hardy, who had unquestionable influence on the perception of their own contemporaries. The tour visited Dryburgh and Jedburgh, Lanark, and the two castles of Bothwell and Roslin.[42] The latter managed to satisfy not only through its associations but also because it fitted perfectly into the continued taste for castles.

Figure 27 A steel engraving after David Roberts, *Melrose Abbey, Roxburghshire*, from *The Gallery of Modern British Artists*, 1835 (Courtesy M.R. Pidgley). Abbeys remained a favourite, Melrose's popularity being enhanced by being in Walter Scott country.

Figure 28 David Cox, *Kenilworth and Dolbadarn Castles*, soft ground etching, 1813. (Courtesy M.R. Pidgley). These occur in *A Treatise on Landscape Painting and Effect* by Cox, and such books must have further enhanced the popularity of two such major sites as Kenilworth (left) and Dolbadarn.

Castles

Castles had been popular for some time, but the emphasis shifted slightly from mere antiquarian grandeur to large, ruinous, ivy-mantled buildings in a rural setting. The use of ivy was to become a metaphor for women,[43] but at this time there is little in the pictures to argue that it did any more than emphasize a building's ruinous condition, thereby giving it status as a *memento mori*. The ivy usually adorned, or hid, a building which had once been a centre of authority and power, either lay, in the castles and occasional ruined country houses, or ecclesiastical in the case of the abbeys. In most of these studies, such as those of the immensely popular Berry Pomeroy Castle, the notion of 'how the mighty are fallen' is very close to the surface. In Devon the two most favoured castles, Berry Pomeroy and Okehampton, were both rurally located, on a mound rising high above a river, well wooded, and, at Okehampton, beside the main road. The urban castles, such as Exeter, Totnes and Tiverton were scarcely represented.

Warwick, Kenilworth, Dudley and Chepstow were the outstandingly popular castles, but there were many others, including Goodrich and Berry Pomeroy. Maton, describing the latter in 1796, gave a clear account of the preference in saying that the buildings were

> beautifully mantled with ivy and so richly incrusted with moss that they constitute the most picturesque objects that can be imagined . . . the noble mass of wood fronting the gate, the bold ridges rising in the horizon and the fertile valley opening to the east.[44]

Okehampton, on the main road to Cornwall, was also much visited, and described by Southey as a 'ruined castle on its hill, beautifully ivied and standing above a delightful stream'.[45] Many major Welsh castles were essential calls on the tour of the Principality. Other castles remained largely undepicted, however. These included those made of brick such as Tattershall, those closely hemmed in by buildings, such as Totnes, and those without the elevated site which seems to have been an aesthetic requirement, such as Porchester.

Worcestershire

Dudley Castle in Worcestershire was so popular that the county as a whole reached its summit of favour in the first quarter of the nineteenth century (Figure 29) largely through its depiction. Like all the west Midland counties, Worcester has been more visible than the eastern Midlands, but still only ranks 27th in pictures per unit area (Appendix 3). There were also a few views of Evesham Abbey, but few country houses. Later in the century the interest in castles dropped dramatically, and the

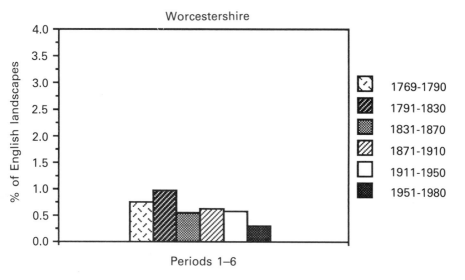

Figure 29   Histogram for Worcestershire (Source: RA catalogues). The county's popularity rested heavily on Dudley Castle until the vogue for half-timber later in the nineteenth century.

discovery of the Malverns and the orchards around Evesham were insufficient to compensate for the loss of Dudley, no doubt suffering from the expansion of the Black Country as well as the loss of Picturesque concepts.

Cathedrals, churches and abbeys

Cathedrals remained a common subject, without much change in the preferred examples. These have remained remarkably constant: Westminster, St Paul's, Canterbury, York, Durham, Lincoln and Ely. The first four represent those of greatest architectural or associational importance. The remaining three were able to produce the most imposing pictures, because of the ability to see them from below and at a reasonable distance. One writer, praising Canterbury, admitted that it lacked 'the exceptional advantages of situation possessed by Durham . . . by Lincoln . . . and by Ely'.[46] The least depicted have been Chichester, Hereford, Worcester and Lichfield, not so easy to see at a range sufficient to appear imposing.

Parish churches were still comparatively rare subjects. They were 'but rarely objects of beauty'.[47]

Abbeys were much more popular, probably because they were mostly ruined. Fountains, Tintern, Strata Florida and Valle Crucis head a long list, with the ruined Cistercian abbeys set in upland scenery most

favoured, the desolation of their surroundings exaggerating the effect of
the ruins. Crowland was an exception to the upland preference, towering
upwards against the sky, like so many castles. Girtin's pictures of the
Yorkshire abbeys are particularly well known, though their popularity
had waned when Lefroy wrote in the 1880s.[48] Some such as Bolton and
Tintern combined both abbey and river. At Tavistock the abbey buildings
had been converted to fulfil market functions for the town, and Gilpin
found this quite unacceptable, not stirring the heart with memories of
former greatness. 'The picturesque eye is so far from looking at these
deeds of economy under the idea of pleasure that it passes by them with
disdain, as heterogenous absurdities.'[49]

Fonthill Abbey, a new Gothick construction by the very wealthy
Romantic, William Beckford, was excessively popular during its construction around 1800, but should perhaps be classed as a country house, with
its attraction surely more to do with patronage than aesthetic theory.[50]

John Swete, the Devon Picturesque enthusiast, made the distinction
with previous tastes clear when visiting Newenham Abbey, never a major
site. After referring to it being a 'jumble of ruins', he continued, 'which,
if there be a distinction between Beauty and Picturesque according to the
idea of Mr. Price, has none of the former but is abundant in the latter.'[51]

Figure 30   An anonymous drawing of Dartington Hall, pen and wash, dated 1827,
14 × 22 cm (Courtesy Devon Library Services). The Picturesque ideals allowed the older,
medieval houses to become attractive even when inhabited.

Country houses

Swete's comments are also useful in explaining the preferences for country houses, which undoubtedly suffered some decline in favour during the period, but remained significant. At Eggesford he explained that 'brick houses are always offensive when situate among fields and Woods' – and he recommended Portland stone or stucco. Later he clarified this at Ebford where he objected to the current fashion for brick. He liked 'white cottages, grey churches, buff seats, and local stone for Gothick piles'.[52]

One kind of country house which increased in favour at the time was the older Gothic pile. Of Powderham Castle, for example, Swete exclaimed, 'no style whatever can be so adapted to the pencil as one of these old Gothic Edifices.'[53]

Cottages

The village and cottage were generally ignored but there was some disagreement whether inhabited small homes could be attractive, within the terms of Picturesque theory. Shaw as early as 1788 thought Bradninch 'a very picturesque village of moss-clad houses',[54] but the more normal view was that cottages were 'mean and dirty' as Swete described those at Moretonhampstead, while Chagford's buildings were 'mean and irregular'.[55] When depicted they were frequently ruinous, as were those by Samuel Prout, and sometimes described as hovels. The inhabitants were, however, usually healthy and rubicund, if farm workers, though gypsies were allowed to be scruffier, and were seen as valuable additions to the scene.[56]

The coast

Along the coast there were major developments at many resorts which have been attributed to the Napoleonic wars and the consequent closure of much of the continent to English visitors.[57] Very many resorts became popular haunts for artists, no doubt tempted there partly by the market provided by the gentry. Margate, Hastings, Brighton and Weymouth were the most important, but many others, especially those with long promenades, were also popular. Sidmouth and Shanklin represent smaller examples. Many paintings of the period were of coves and bits of cliffs, often merging with marine work, and almost inevitably with considerable staffage, smugglers more often than fishermen. Many of the prints were quite different. These can be dubbed long-shore views, usually from a hill on one side of the resort looking along the promenade, and stressing the neat new terraces. The sweep of the coast and promenade would form the central line of the picture, acting to link foreground with middle distance. These prints may well represent the rather older tastes for the Classical of many of the resort visitors, while the artists' own preference was for the more modern Picturesque cove.

In many of the resorts whimsical Gothick architecture vied for attention with promenade Classical. The more modern resorts had many of these ornate cottages as fashions for resorts changed rapidly. 'Dawlish hath within a very few years come much into vogue', declared Swete in 1792.[58] Granville in the 1840s thought he detected an 8–10-year cycle in popularity of resorts, the local sequence being Weymouth – Sidmouth – Exmouth – Dawlish and Teignmouth – Torquay.[59] Prints of these places were sold locally, often produced by local printers.[60]

Estuaries

The estuarine scene so popular with watercolourists continued strongly with the rias of the south west particularly popular. One of the most favoured views, for example, was that of Sharpham woods on the Dart seen by boat. In general such estuaries remained popular only at high tide. Farington noted of the Plym estuary, known as the Laira, 'At high water the appearance must be fine but at low water much shore of a bad colour and naked effect, cannot be pleasing.'[61] Gilpin said of the Tamar, 'But they are beautiful at full sea only, at the ebb of the tide each lake becomes an oozy channel.'[62] Such preferences represent the continuance of the taste for lakes, begun in the previous period. Such a vogue would occasionally lead an artist to discard all topographic accuracy and provide what God had failed to do, as did Walmesley in his depiction of Okehampton Castle almost surrounded by an entirely imaginary lake (Figure 31).[63]

Industry

The slight popularity which industrial scenes had possessed in the previous period evaporated under the rules of Picturesque composition. For the first time there can be defined a small group of industries which forms the 'acceptable' face of commercial enterprise. The most significant industries within this group were those situated in the countryside and closely geared to agriculture. Agricultural scenes have themselves come under much scrutiny[64] and haymaking and harvest were by far the most popular, partly because they occurred at the time of year during which artists could be expected to be on tour. Even then, the workers were as often resting as working, and if the latter were usually well in the distance.

Swete singled out both the grist mills and the lime kilns of Devon for special praise, and there is plenty of visual evidence to show his was not

Figure 31 Walmesley, *Okehampton Castle, Devonshire*, aquatint, 1810, 19 × 26 cm
(Courtesy Devon Library Services). The ideal of castle overlooking lake, learnt in the Alps
and best found in North Wales, encouraged some artists to add totally fictitious lakes to
well-known castles. Elsewhere they added fictitious castles to real lakes.

an unusual taste. Both were dirty industries, the lime kilns especially so,
and in most cases they were shown working. In the case of lime kilns this
meant a filthy pall of smoke which few today would find attractive. They
were described as 'grotesque yet picturesque'.[65]

> To a lover of the Picturesque the Lime kilns and Grist mills of this
> county are objects of more than common attraction. I speak not of
> those kilns where the stone is calcined by means of furze for they are
> on heaths and brakes wild and naked, but where they are erected
> contiguous to the quarry. . . . As to the water mills the nature of the
> Scenery, the apparatus requisite and the effort produced by the mill as
> to convert the stream into a foamy waterfall and that generally where
> local circumstances are productive of the most striking contrast, a dark
> hollow formed by the buildings and overspreading trees, through the
> gloom of which the silvery waters rush.[66]

Klingender lists other major industrial attractions as Sunderland
Bridge, Barton Aqueduct, Marple Aqueduct, Chirk, Parys, Botallack,
Penrhyn Quarry, and pits at Cannock.[67] That these occurred, usually in
print form, there can be no doubt. However, the complete absence of any
of these subjects in the catalogues of the Royal Academy does strongly

suggest that their aesthetic importance could be greatly overestimated. Prints may represent a popular taste, as we have seen, but also on occasion may be produced for purposes other than the aesthetic pleasure to be derived from the scenes. Such would be equally true of photographs more recently. Industrialists and engineers may well commission prints of features of which they were proud, without convincing the artist of their beauty.

Quarries, which might be classed as industrial scenery, were sometimes favoured. Of Kenn quarry Swete said, 'Disuse has thrown around this Quarry a more Picturesque cast than perhaps any of the others possess,'[68] although there were certainly others quite frequently depicted, notably Cann quarry near Plympton. As one might expect, a degree of dereliction, with ivy, was preferred, and the drawing of rocks became a popular artistic exercise.

The other group of industrial scenes are the shipbuilding and marine scenes, though the distinction between the two may be of little consequence. Otherwise industry was firmly out of vogue. Because the stereotypes of counties were rapidly developing, Devon, not regarded as an industrial county, may not give clues to the whole country. For example, somewhat later in the century the depiction of Cornish tin mines became quite common, but the numerous Devon mines were scarcely ever shown, despite being frequently located in the very valleys which artists came to visit. Similarly there are few Devonian views of windmills, though these certainly existed, whereas in East Anglia windmills were a common motif, no doubt learnt from the Dutch. The Academy evidence, however, supports the Devon material, with the new factories very rarely appearing on its walls. The attitude to most industrial scenes at this time deteriorated from the neutrality previously evident. Industrial activity could form part of the background to a Picturesque view, as incidental extra rather than a required part of the composition. There were some exceptions, as we have seen, and the canals, in their heyday, were often highly regarded, as shown by Constable's boatbuilding scenes, and by Swete's suggestion that a canal at Axmouth would beautify the estuary.[69]

Towns

The urban scene was in transition. Classical architecture and terraces were still highly regarded, as in Bath, Tunbridge Wells and Cheltenham, as well as in London, where Hampstead was much the most favoured area. There were numerous prints of new public buildings in the provinces. Similarly there were still numerous artists depicting the larger and older provincial towns, such as Norwich, Exeter, Winchester and Oxford, but the Picturesque slums were only very slowly coming into

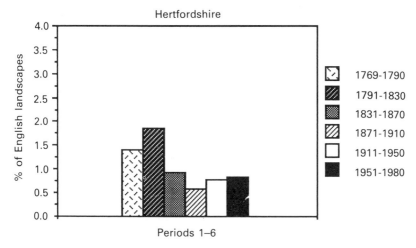

Figure 32 Histogram for Hertfordshire (Source: RA catalogues). The country houses have been Hertfordshire's major asset, and the county has been little regarded, considering its closeness to the metropolis.

favour. Just as the medieval country house was added to the Palladian in the portfolio of attractiveness, so artists began to find sketching material amongst good medieval and Tudor housing, often less for itself than for the staffage. Farington spent some of his time in Exeter among the half-timbered housing of the west quarter, but suggested this was not yet highly regarded.[70] Otherwise most urban scenes were of great Gothic buildings, or down by the river. The one genre which showed marked decline was the panorama. Such wide views could not be fitted into the constraints of the Picturesque rules.

Middlesex and Hertfordshire

If London's continued popularity was still involved largely with the Classical architecture and the river scene, this did not prevent London-based artists seeking more Picturesque views in the vicinity. Middlesex and Hertfordshire (Figure 32) show greater favour at this time than at any other and this is largely due to views of villages, including often the church, but also bridges and inns in what are now suburbs. Finchley, Enfield, Willesden and Harrow were all favourites, and there were numerous sites south of the river also, at Wimbledon and Morden for example. Apart from views on the Thames, these two counties largely show decreasing interest away from London. Country houses, such as Cassiobury and Osterley, were significant sites up to about 1830, and St Alban's Abbey at much the same time. Thereafter, the proximity of such places to the London studio failed to offset their lack of sufficiently

Romantic scenery. For a short while in the 1880s Bushey became the centre of a realist school under Hubert van Herkomer, but as late as 1889 Hertfordshire was regarded as 'in many respects an unexplored district as regards the tourist and the artist'.[71] Twentieth-century interest has been either in the inner suburbs of Middlesex, such as Camden and St John's Wood, not the 1930s estates, or further out there have been several views of Hertfordshire woods near the Buckinghamshire border. Rickmansworth and Watford have also had short bursts of popularity. Middlesex also shared, however, in the vogue for river scenes along the Thames discussed in Chapter 6.

Wales and the Lake District

The Picturesque tourist continued to visit the mountainous areas of the country and became more specifically interested in the mountains themselves. The North Wales visit became more diffuse in area, by 1800 moving away from a sole concentration on the valleys around Snowdon and the coastal castles, into Merionethshire, and especially Dolgelly, with Cader Idris almost as frequently painted as Snowdon itself.

In fact Mid Wales reaches the height of its very limited popularity at this time. Here is the classic case of an area which suffers from inaccessibility and perceptual shadow. Whatever the grandeur of the hills of Powis, they are lower and less spectacular than those of Snowdonia, and at least as difficult of access. The result has been a marked lack of artistic interest throughout the last two centuries, such that the area ranks

Figure 33 Graph for Wales (Source: RA catalogues). The two major peaks were both based in the north, but whereas the first was largely castles and lakes, the second was mainly rivers.

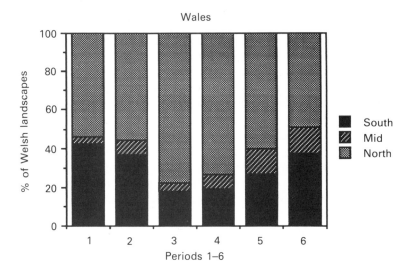

Figure 34 Distribution of Welsh landscapes (Source: RA catalogues). The lack of interest in Mid Wales is striking. The early importance of the south, especially Wye, only began to return with the interest in Pembrokeshire and the industrial valleys in recent years.

Figure 35 An engraving after C. Marshall, *View in the Vale of Llangollen*, from *The Gallery of Modern British Artists*, 1835 (Courtesy M.R. Pidgley). The river craze of the Romantic Period was at its height in North Wales, both here and at Bettws.

only 41st in pictures per square mile (Appendix 3). Mid Wales, with the Southern Uplands, the north Pennines and Bodmin Moor, represent major areas where the interest has been markedly less than might be predicted from their physical appearance. Any model of actual, rather than potential, attractiveness must take account of accessibility.

The same diffusion happened in the Lake District, where the long-favoured sites along the central axis from Windermere to Keswick were now joined by sites to the north and west, as far as Wastwater. Wordsworth's poetry must be seen as part of this fascination for the Lakes, not the cause of it, for the peak of popularity was already passed before his work was published. The same is true of the visits of Keats and Byron. In any case, as suggested previously the main attraction was the lakes, which resembled, or could be made to resemble, their greater counterparts in the Alps, especially Lake Geneva. Only in North Wales and Cumbria did the vogue for lakes not require surrogates. However, interest in Scotland was also moving north into the nearer Highlands, with Loch Lomond a firm favourite and the lochs of the Trossachs also beginning their rise to favour by the end of the Picturesque period, no doubt influenced by Scott. The history of this mountain taste has been studied elsewhere.[72]

If the lake was one icon of the period, the waterfall was another. Swete discoursed at length on five Devonian waterfalls, carefully distinguishing their aesthetic properties, but they did not match greater examples elsewhere. Experience is inevitably a major factor in our ideas of attractiveness whenever uniqueness or sheer size forms one of the criteria of judgement. Perhaps the best-known falls were the Aberglaslyn in North Wales and that of the Dargle in the Wicklow mountains, although Ireland had not yet become an important tour.

The Sublime

John Ward's picture of Gordale Scar was exhibited in 1812, and serves as a reminder that the concept of the Sublime was still very much alive. The most inoffensive bits of rockery were pressed into service to provide this need where nothing else existed. At the Valley of the Rocks, a little dry valley west of Lynton, Swete was 'imprest with dread' and declared that it 'had no thing of the picturesque about it, but compriz'd everything that was wild, grand and terrific.'[73] Most commonly perhaps sublimity continued to be found in storms at sea and the Eddystone continued to provide a marvellous lesson in awesomeness.

Despite the Sublime, and the survival of many ideas which have here been labelled Classical, the discovery of Picturesque qualities in a wide range of landscape subjects was the major achievement. The creation of mental maps of the Picturesque sites in various areas did not prevent simple mistakes. In Devon, Bickleigh Vale, on the Plym, was one well-known site. However, 40 miles north east is another Bickleigh, with a bridge over the Exe. The frequent mis-titling of pictures of the latter as Bickleigh Vale is surely evidence that artists were not always where they thought they were. The small, ivy-mantled bridge was the abiding image of the period and this motif continued, became stronger and transformed itself into the greatest icon of the mid-nineteenth century.

5

The Romantic Period 1830–1870

The year 1830 has been chosen to represent the division between the Picturesque and the Romantic periods. There is, however, no dramatic and immediate shift in the distribution or type of places preferred but rather a gradual development to a darker, more sombre, and markedly more umbrageous attitude to landscape. 'The presence of trees is, therefore, most essential to rural scenery.'[1] Many of the preferences of the previous forty years had by this time become somewhat stylized, and, arguably became even more so during this period. The Pre-Raphaelites, championed by Ruskin, realized this, but major change did not come about until after 1860. This period is, therefore, something of a hiatus, one during which landscape work became a dominant form, but one largely ignored by subsequent critics.

From 1850 onwards much evidence of taste is contained in the major journals written for artists containing articles about the popular sketching grounds. These include *The Art Journal*, *The Portfolio* and *The Magazine of Art*. Indeed these articles become a tediously repetitive part of many of these journals. Nevertheless they form a body of valuable corroborative evidence often detailing the reasons for visiting the particular sites. Ruskin's *Modern Painters* was published in 1851 with considerable influence, recently discussed by Peter Fuller,[2] and previously by Denis Cosgrove,[3] but Ruskin was not alone in espousing the new sciences of geology, meteorology and biology and claiming that artists must study the landscape scientifically. The interest in Professor Ansted's series of articles published in *The Art Journal* lies not in the aesthetic tags given to each geological type, but in the fact that an art magazine could publish the work of a geologist.[4]

This is not the place to discourse on the nature of Romanticism as a

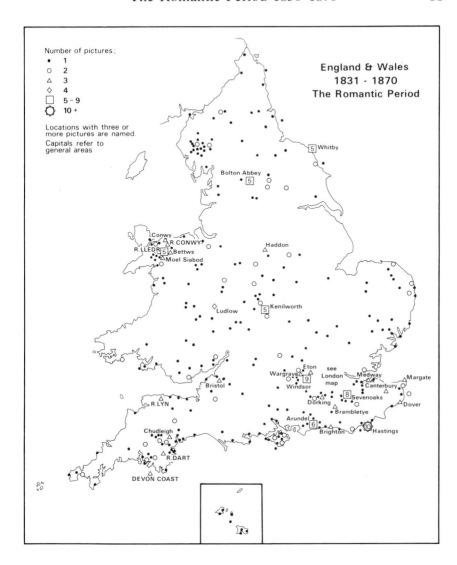

Figure 36 Map of landscapes depicted in Romantic Period, 1831–70, England and Wales (Source: RA catalogues).

movement in many of the arts. That has been well done by many, including Quennell.[5] Such writers nearly always date the Romantic period considerably earlier than here suggested. The reason for this apparent anomaly is not a different view of the Romantic idea, but simply that this work deals with the flowering of Romanticism, and other ideas, into dominant forms among all artists. The roots lie much earlier. Byron had been dead seven years before the period discussed here opens.[6]

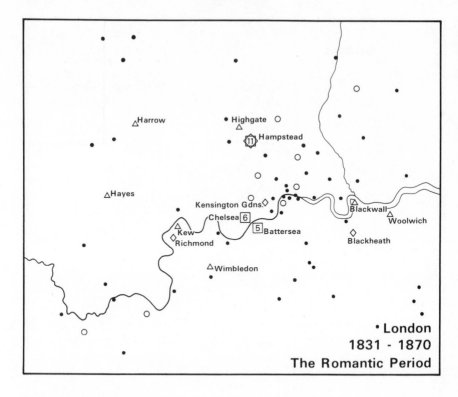

Figure 37 Map of landscapes depicted in Romantic Period, 1831–70, London area (Source: RA catalogues).

Travel

This was the time when travel became not only very much quicker, but also much cheaper. The advent of the railway and the steamship allowed artists to spend much less time travelling, whether at home or abroad. The steamship's importance in developing foreign travel is obvious, but its influence at home was also considerable, not only in the increased visits made to the Isle of Man and the Channel Islands, but also in the use made of coastal services. The normal way of visiting Lynton, for example, was by sea from Portishead.[7] Dartmouth too was commonly reached by sea from Portland.[8] A contemporary reviewer noted:

> Thanks to the facilities afforded by railways and 'excursion tickets' the glorious scenery of England is now made almost as accessible to dwellers in the metropolis as the parks of Richmond and Greenwich used to be half a century ago.[9]

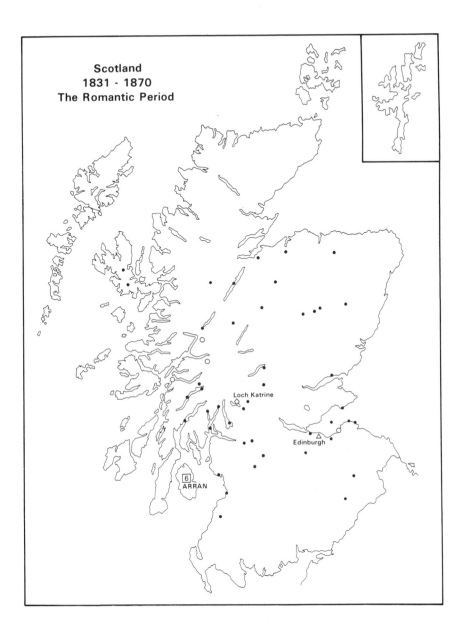

Inside the map:

Scotland
1831 - 1870
The Romantic Period

Loch Katrine

Edinburgh

ARRAN

Figure 38   Map of landscapes depicted in Romantic Period, 1831–70, Scotland (Source: RA catalogues).

The theory that improvements in transport were overwhelmingly important in discovering new landscapes is a tempting one. The rise to importance of Cornwall, for example, after the opening of the Royal Albert Bridge across the Tamar in 1859 is too obvious to be denied.[10] But this would be to forget that places at least as remote as Cornwall, such as North Wales and the Lake District, had seen peaks of popularity much earlier. Artists were quite capable of suffering the rigours of travel if the cause were good enough; evidently Cornwall wasn't.

If the railway did not of itself change the destinations of such inveterate travellers as landscape artists had long been, it certainly increased the numbers at the sites when they arrived. Complaints about tourists, which never of course included oneself, date from this time. Guidebooks flourished and Thackeray and Gustave Carus testify to the importance attached to these books, which usually divided the information into sections accessible from the railway lines. Thackeray remarked on the tourist in Antwerp always with Murray in his hand,[11] while Carus patronizingly commented on 'This species of glorifying nature which leads multitudes of idlers . . . up mountains and into valleys, in order to enable them to utter a few worthless commonplaces.'[12] The reason for Murray's ubiquity and popularity was its quality. Samuel Palmer recommended it strongly, at least *A Handbook for Travellers in Devon and Cornwall*: 'It was written by an artist and has a real savour of Devonshire perception, which will be found very rare.'[13]

Photography

The other great invention of the age which must concern us is that of photography, in 1839, but a discussion of its influence is delayed until Chapter 6, though not because its use in recording landscapes was deferred until after 1870. Indeed perhaps the most outstanding fact of the early days of photography was its immediate popularity, being used within a few years in some of the most remote corners of the world, as in Maxime du Camp's pictures of Egypt. The value of photography in showing people what the world was really like pre-dated even its use in displaying one's own physiognomy, though this was only due to the long exposure times. Its peculiar *verité* was very soon recognized. However, one of the greatest advantages of photography was its cheapness, especially in terms of time, which in turn led to the discovery of banal subject matter. Many commonplace aspects of landscape were not worth the efforts of a painter, but during the period here discussed, painters and others were learning from the photographers the fascination of the mundane, in fishing villages such as Newhaven and Whitby and elsewhere.[14] Only later did such subject matter become a dominant interest.

Foreign tours

Overseas touring was at its height. Italy was less important than previously in percentage terms,[15] but within Italy, Venice had now become the centre of interest, though a major group of English painters still existed in Rome, as Palmer testified, and there they met groups of artists from other countries.[16] Sorrento became the first site of what was to become one of the great genres, the Mediterranean coast view, and the Italian lakes were also much visited, not least by Ruskin. 'In our earliest thirst for travel Italy is the magnificent point to which our longings are most powerfully directed' suggested Henry Noel Humphreys, though others include Paris, for its theatres and gaieties, the Rhine for its legends and castellated crags, Switzerland for lakes and glaciers, and Spain for romance and the Alhambra.[17] *The Art Journal* gave 'Suggestions to Students of Art about to visit Italy'.[18] Alpinism has been studied by Dent[19] and by Robertson,[20] although the intense interest which they describe is not borne out by the numbers of pictures.

The development of steam-packet services tended to canalize interest along particular routes. The London–Antwerp route led to great interest in other Belgian towns, as well as to genre scenes and seascape views in Holland, most especially at Scheveningen. The final destination was often the Rhine tour, which enjoyed great popularity at mid-century, beautifully satirized by Thackeray in *The Kickleburys on the Rhine*, and by the antics of Brown, Jones and Robinson drawn by Richard Doyle.[21] The Newhaven–Dieppe route was also popular, providing a 'rest by the way for travellers to Paris'.[22] Both Paris and the Rhine led to comparisons being made with English landscapes, and the opening of the steamship services of the P & O was even more important. This led to tours of Greece, Turkey (which doubtless also benefited from being our ally in the Crimean war), Egypt and the Nile. Most of these trips, however, had the Holy Land as the main aim, as did Holman Hunt. Thackeray, in *Cornhill to Cairo*, was among the earlier visitors to Egypt and gives good descriptions of his perceptions of the Middle East, remarking 'I wonder that no painter has given us familiar scenes of the East.'[23] This situation was very soon to be rectified, with Edward Lear and David Roberts prominent in providing them.

Historical revival

The attractions of the Holy Land were undoubtedly influenced by the religious revival of the time. This revival does not seem far removed in sentiment from the fascination for historical subjects which dates from about 1850 and which had a profound effect on the subjects of art. The development of this historicism in painting, at least as evidenced by Royal

Academy titles, can be accurately dated to 1850. Tennyson's *Idylls of the King* were typical of a new interest in English folklore, in Medieval and Dark Age history, or more commonly myth. Pictures of any supposed Arthurian sites became common, few allowing mere evidence to get in the way of a good picture, and Sherwood Forest became a significant site for the first and last time. The great interest in Shakespeare seems closely related and led to the fascination for Stratford, as well as to many pictures purporting to depict Shakespearian scenes or using quotations from the plays as titles. This amounts to the discovery of Merrie Englande, most obvious in the sudden appearance of pictures of half-timbered buildings, narrow streets and even village scenes. A series of articles published in *The Art Journal* in 1851 on 'The domestic manners of the English during the Middle Ages' was unique at the time, but was soon to be typical.[24] Walter Scott's *The Lady of the Lake* was republished with illustrations by Birket Foster in 1853 and Daniel Maclise's famous picture of *The Play Scene – Hamlet* was dated 1853.

Foreign art

Major events were afoot in landscape art overseas. The influence of modern foreign art on English painting, however, was still slight, although the American school was highly praised. The German Romantic school, led by Friedrich, was also well regarded but there is little evidence of their preferred sites being visited by British artists, nor even of their subject matter being greatly popular. French painting, at the time when the Barbizon school was flourishing, later completely to alter attitudes to landscape, was widely ignored or derided.[25]

River scenes

River scenes were at their most popular in this period, conforming to a distinct type, as do so many of the genres of the period. The preference was for a medium-sized river, usually in its upland reaches where boulders and minor waterfalls were common. These are distinct from the Picturesque preference for incised valleys, or the Sublimity of high waterfalls also popular earlier. The valley sides are overhung with trees, high and steep, but not vertical. The trees seem particularly *de rigueur*. On Dartmoor, as the radial rivers reach the edge of the granite massif, they almost invariably cut deep gorges, entirely suitable for the Romantic genre. Only two of these, the Erme and Tavy, had gorge sections largely devoid of trees and they are the only two ignored by the Romantic artists. The stereotyped view almost invariably looked upstream, which allowed the fall of water to be seen, while providing a vista to link into the background. A downstream view would not provide the former, with the ground falling away from the viewer. Staffage was common, with the peasant in a red coat crossing a bridge becoming a great cliché. Optional extras in such views included a Romantic (i.e. dangerously unsafe) bridge and a watermill. The former was not the ivy-encrusted stone structure formerly preferred but a wooden plank bridge with handrail. Such bridges are so common a feature, frequently deployed by artists in highly unlikely positions, that one is tempted to think they may have been portable accessories. Benjamin Robert Haydon, near Plymouth, described the typical scene: 'The deep shadow of umbrageous trees, the green emerald masses of Foliage, the crystal ripple of the limpid springs, were fit to excite emotions deep and passionate.'[26]

Devon

Devon was the most popular county for some years and this popularity was centred on the Dartmoor rivers already mentioned, particularly the Dart itself and the Teign, and on the valleys of the East and West Lyn on Exmoor.[27] Samuel Palmer described the 'Rich glebes such as adorn the sides of Dartmoor'[28] and he 'idealized Devonshire just as he idealized Italy'.[29] As the graph (Figure 39) shows Devon's popularity had been high in the eighteenth century, when marine scenes and numerous country houses had provided material, but the Romantic river scenes and those on the coast at Torquay and elsewhere produced a distinct vogue, the decline from which Devon is still experiencing. Dartmoor, however, shared in the popularity of moorland scenes in the 1870s and after, but throughout the twentieth century interest has been firmly fixed on the coast and the fishing villages, especially Brixham.

Holy Street Mill, on the Teign two miles above Chagford, was one of the great sites, now frequently unknown even by locals, despite its continued accessibility. Page said of it, 'What a scene for Creswick. Close

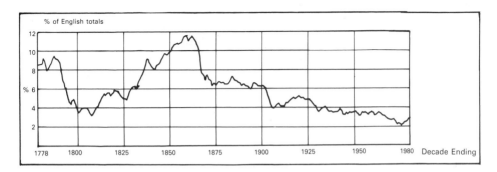

Figure 39 Graph for Devonshire (Source: RA catalogues). Devon's early popularity was largely marine, and of country houses, but the great vogue of the mid-nineteenth century was firmly based in the valleys around Dartmoor, and the River Lyn.

Figure 40 Birket Foster, *The Old Mill*, etching (Courtesy M.R. Pidgley). Possibly Holy Street Mill, Devon. The overshot mill was one of the clichés of Romantic landscape; invariably the only sign of the industry is the turning wheel.

Figure 41 David Murray, *The River Road*, etching, 1892, 53 × 35 cm (Author's collection). Not all favoured rivers were in the uplands. The pastoral reaches were also haunted by artists, especially later in the century.

at hand is the ancient mill, a building of picturesque dilapidation, rich, warm thatch and mellowed stone, that artists of high degree . . . have endeavoured times without number to transfer its beauties to canvas.'[30] Five miles downstream lies Fingle Bridge – 'almost as great a favourite with the artist as the better known one at Holy Street.'[31]

North Wales

This is also the time of the second, and greater, peak of interest in North Wales which was firmly based on the Conwy, the Lledr and other streams rather than on the mountains themselves. Bettws-y-Coed was the great centre, though Trefriw and Llanidloes on the same river were also popular and the Fairy Glen on the Aberglaslyn one of the required scenes. We can feel indebted to the artist in the *Art Journal* of 1887 (p. 273), for providing the frontispiece of this book and including other artists, an honest if not common practice.[32] Thus the two great vogues for Welsh scenery (Figure 33) must be seen as different in kind. The first was based on castles, lakes and mountain peaks, largely but by no means exclusively in the north. The mid-century peak was mainly of streams, rivers and waterfalls, primarily in Snowdonia, though the Usk was also important.[33]

Some small streams, like the Fairy Glen, continued to attract attention. One such was Chudleigh Brook, which according to Palmer was already becoming a veritable tourist trap.[34] Walter Crane, brought up in Torquay, was one whose family took regular trips there.[35] Today it is only well known by the rock-climbing fraternity. Another typical small Romantic Glen is Jesmond Dene, just east of Newcastle and convincing proof that convenience is a fundamental part of landscape attractiveness. Despite the railways a fairly ordinary little glen within 3 miles of Newcastle was still found more attractive than several spectacular valleys 50 miles away in the Cheviots.

Other upland rivers much favoured included those formerly idealized in Derbyshire (Dove and Derwent) and Yorkshire (Wharfedale and Wensleydale), but the same cannot be said of the Lake District. Though the area still produced many views, often from its more remote corners, the main vogue had clearly passed, although Lodore and Borrowdale cropped up on the Academy walls occasionally. This is not easy to explain, for Scottish lakes were popular, and so were Welsh rivers. Possibly the long trip to the Lakes was, with rail transport, just as easily extended to the Highlands. Any list of the popular rivers will inevitably exclude ones which were significant for local artists, however. Generally these umbrageous river scenes were the work of oil painters with the two best-known being Frederick Richard Lee and Thomas Creswick. Despite the comparatively long exposure times, which failed to render falling water as anything more than a blur, even the photographers happily depicted Romantic rivers.

In southern England some more pastoral rivers in the lowlands were also important, as much for watercolourists as oil painters. Holman Hunt found his scene for *The Hireling Shepherd* at Ewell, back to back with Millais working on Ophelia.[36] The middle stretches of the Thames, Medway, Mole, Wey and Arun were well frequented, by John Linnell, Vicat Cole and others not straying too far from the capital. Usually cattle or sheep, not pigs, browse by or in a river fringed with trees and rushes, almost invariably in high summer.[37]

This being the zenith of the river scene is an appropriate place to offer a short general review of the subject. During the eighteenth century small, usually rocky, streams had been much depicted, quite frequently with elements of the Sublime. The high waterfall was a lesser popular type, as were the great sweeping curves of the incised meanders as on the Wye and Dove. Wide estuaries were the watercolourists' preference where evanescent effects were more easily obtained, and they were usually seen at high tide, making them more akin to the lake views also highly popular but not easily found in England. As these types declined the highly standardized version here discussed became the chief view, and from then on rivers became continuously less popular. The preference for lowland, pastoral streams, usually of considerable size, which began in this period became much more pronounced with the Arun becoming one archetype, although the late-nineteenth-century boom of interest in highly populated views of rich, young people enjoying boating on the Thames was a particular fashion described by Jerome K. Jerome in *Three Men in a Boat*. River scenes continued to decline throughout the twentieth century, although there has been some self-conscious reworking of old sites. After 1850 prints still showed a few river scenes, but engravings were markedly few, although perhaps the engraving technique is not well suited to the type. Lithography and aquatinting seem to cope with trees so much better.

Coasts

The coast continued to increase its attraction, and the new preferred coastlines showed similar characteristics to the Romantic river scenes. The previously popular long-shore views, along continuous lines of cliffs, gave way to views with a shorter 'fetch'. The term is usually used to mean the distance waves have travelled across open ocean to reach a coast but it is convenient in this context to indicate a much shallower depth of field. Cliffs too were more indented, and rockier, frequently overhung with plants. Traditional resort views were still readily available in print form,

Figure 42   George Rowe, *Ilfracombe from Capstone Hill*, lithograph, 12 × 18 cm, *c.* 1828 (Courtesy Devon Library Services). The Romantic resort had less stress on sweeping promenades, and more concern with coves.

which suggests that the new taste had not penetrated very far down the social spectrum. Even these prints often depicted newer resorts, usually less equipped with long promenades. Torquay, Whitby, Scarborough and Ilfracombe were typical, though Bournemouth was also popular, more noted for its chines than its cliffs. Similarly, at the long-established Hastings, more views now concentrated on Fairlight Glen, as did Holman Hunt in *Our English Coasts*. At Ilfracombe one of the most popular views was of the chapel in the harbour, of which Ayton had earlier said 'The lighthouse is built in the form of a chapel, a whimsical fancy that has treated the genius of the place rather too cavalierly.'[38] Such whimsy was now highly fashionable. Most prints, however, showed the bathing coves and hotels.

Resorts were not the only views. Rocky, wild coasts began to become popular, not least in Cornwall, though there largely after the opening of the Tamar bridge in 1859. These are not coves full of boats and fishermen but moderately accessible bits of wild coast deliberately shown only as the haunts of nature. Marmaduke Langdale's view of Tintagel which won the Turner gold medal in 1866 is typical, fitting in not only with this genre but also with the historicism of popular legend.[39] These legends were becoming well documented, as in *Popular Romances of the West of England*.[40] Cornwall, which was to become the major focus of interest in the succeeding period, now became fashionable for the first time. The painter at Land's End could find, according to Tregellas,

Miles of grey and purple cliffs, cushioned with sea-pinks, and bordered
with golden furze and crimson heath, – stretches of yellow sands lining
the 'emerald crescent bays' – the silver sheen of the Atlantic – and a
changeful sky, everywhere await his pencil.

The same writer thought that the Lizard was flat and treeless, so 'appears
to promise little to the artist'.[41] The sea was regarded as a powerful
symbol of nature, energy and the futility of man, which inevitably made
wrecks a popular subject.

Particularly favoured parts of the coast now included Robin Hood's
Bay in Yorkshire, the southern coast of the Isle of Wight, and Sark. The
coast of Northumberland with its castles was also quite fashionable. In
general, however, long beaches were not highly regarded. *Murray's
Handbook to Devon and Cornwall* (1851) completely avoids mentioning
the great bays of Start, Woolacombe, Croyde and Braunton, despite
being meticulous in the description of all other parts of the county's
coasts.[42] Such scenes were not to enter into popular favour until the
twentieth century.

By 1850 traditional marine painting had largely ceased. A few artists
continued, often using ships in a symbolic way, as did Turner for *The
Fighting Téméraire*, or as Romantic objects in a highly charged landscape,
often with blazing sunsets or other means of emphasizing the effects of
nature. The interest in things geological, as well as meteorological, was
often demonstrated in coastal views, as also in the fantastic Sublime views
beloved by Francis Danby and John Martin. In 1839 the massive landslip
at Dowlands near Lyme Regis, visited by Queen Victoria, was described
by Carus as 'the wonderful labyrinth of ruins',[43] and was a favoured
subject for some years. Few other natural phenomena, in Britain at least,
so obviously spoke of the smallness of man, though the painting of the
Arctic wastes and Alpine crags was also popular.[44]

Appleton has suggested that the use of the theatrical term 'coulisses'
can be usefully deployed in many pictures, and stresses the purpose of
these side screens in providing niches in which refuge may be obtained.[45]
Certainly at this period his idea seems valid, with views along coasts with
a short fetch already mentioned. Carus notes the side screens at
Dawlish.[46] At Torquay (mid Victoria's Italy as John Betjeman called it),
Walter Crane noted the 'excursions on donkeys in the pleasant and
romantic places with which the neighbourhood abounded, such as
Anstey's Cove and Babbicombe'.[47] John Inchbold's view of Anstey's
Cove shows this taste particularly well, and also the use of a plateau
which Staley suggests was common in Pre-Raphaelite painting as was the
coulisse effect.[48] The value of the coulisse may be easily explained but the
plateau had been widely regarded as a boring landscape and it is difficult
to explain its popularity at this time, before the Heroic landscape, which
frequently exalted boredom, came into vogue.[49]

Towns

One of the most obvious characteristics of the Romantic was the flight from urban scenes. London was at its lowest point of popularity, and most of the towns that figure prominently on the map (Figure 37) do so because of their antiquarian, or more strictly, historicist interest. After about 1850 considerable interest was shown in the old half-timbered buildings such as those found in Ludlow, Dorking and Tewkesbury, especially in the small towns and villages of the south east. The love of vernacular architecture would be learnt mainly in the Weald, and from there Wealden forms of the cottage and farmhouse would be exported throughout the country. Some of the popular towns had obvious associational importance, the most significant being Stratford-upon-Avon, which was also blessed by appropriate architecture.

J. Penderel-Brodhurst gives a clear picture of the new taste in referring to Tewkesbury, set in 'pastoral scenery – so homely, and so legendary'. Having praised the 'half-timbering' and the 'irregular street architecture', he notes 'the ruggedness of the rooflines of these black and white houses', and the High Street is 'crooked, as most streets meet for the artist should be'.[50]

Cheshire

One county which depended for its peak of interest on this fashion for such architecture was Cheshire. Overall a most unpopular county, just

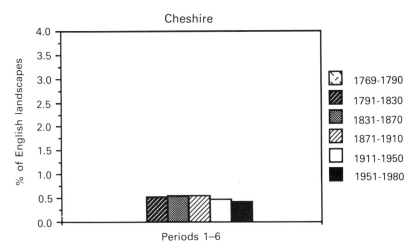

Figure 43   Histogram for Cheshire (Source: RA catalogues). Never a popular county, but the Dee was a favoured river for a time, and later the half-timbered buildings were much depicted.

reaching 1 per cent of the English landscapes in this period, it only ranks 38th in pictures per square mile (Appendix 3). There had been some interest in the country houses earlier, notably Tabley and Combermere, but it was the half-timbering of Chester itself, and of Little Moreton Hall, which created more interest. Since then the only clear genre has been for industrial scenes near Manchester in the last forty years.

Warwickshire

Warwickshire, too, owes its greatest visibility to the historicist interest of mid-century. Kenilworth and Warwick castles had long been popular, and there were some pictures of Leamington Spa, but around 1850 the county provides 2 per cent of the English landscapes at the Academy, though that still only ranks it as 25th by output per area (Appendix 3). It was the 'discovery' of Shakespeare which provided the impetus, Stratford itself luckily possessing the right kind of architecture as well as the birthplace. Transatlantic visitors, now such a traditional sight in the town, have a considerable history, for 'Shakespeare might be proud, indeed, of his county, that American paradise, which includes Warwick, Kenilworth, Leamington and Stratford upon Avon' was written in 1887.[51] Later, Warwickshire was unable to provide the dreary landscapes, or to meet the tastes of the twentieth century until the industrial areas of Birmingham became depicted in the 1960s.

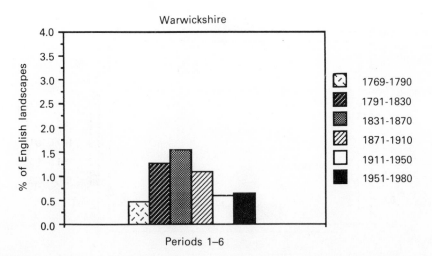

Figure 44   Histogram for Warwickshire (Source: RA catalogues). After 1850 the vogue for Shakespeare led to much interest around Stratford being added to the long-popular great castles.

Staffordshire

Staffordshire has had little to offer. Dovedale is half in the county but pictures thereof have been allocated to Derbyshire, the county with which artists have always associated it. Ranking only 38th by area (Appendix 3) the output has been not only small but very varied. Trentham and Alton Towers provided some country house views, Cannock some country town scenes in mid-century, but even the views of Stoke's bottle kilns have not made a substantial difference to Staffordshire's unfavourable image.

The general interest in country towns resulted in some having an outburst of civic pride, reflected in the output of prints of panoramas or of major public buildings, and often too of public parks, recently created and a considerable source of civic satisfaction. These were quite different from the Picturesque views exhibited at the Academy.

   Another such preference at mid-century which did not find its way very often into the Academy, but was clearly important in the print market, was the 'discovery' of the parish church. This is no doubt related to both the religious and historicist movements, and is seen in a flood of prints, usually lithographs, of the older medieval churches throughout the country. In Devon these were produced mainly by William Spreat in his series *Picturesque Churches of Devonshire*, but there are numerous other examples.

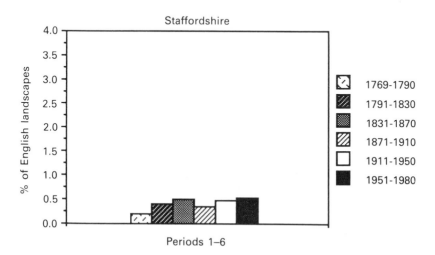

Figure 45 Histogram for Staffordshire (Source: RA catalogues). Until recent views of the Potteries and Black Country, interest had focused mainly on country houses and old townscapes.

Industry

Industrial scenes were rare, and became even more so after 1850. Industrial sites were being consciously avoided. For example many artists depicted the valleys which run off Dartmoor. Many of those valleys contained copper and other metal mines, but these were studiously ignored. They could not be accommodated within the Romantic ideal of those valleys, although the Cornish mines were sometimes depicted, if in a Romantic setting such as at Botallack. Perhaps the stereotyped image of Cornwall contained mines, that of Devon did not. Generally most of the 'Picturesque' industries remained popular, though lime kilns became much less frequent, at least when working. Shipbuilding also slipped in favour, perhaps with the development of iron and steel steamships in place of wooden sailing vessels.

The railways were very commonly depicted in the early days, but this flirtation only lasted until about 1850. The short-lived popularity of the railways as subject matter tends to confirm the importance of the

Figure 46 Birket Foster, *The Village Church*, wood engraving, from *Pictures of English Landscape*, 1863 (Courtesy M.R. Pidgley). The parish church came into vogue, though mainly in print form, as interest in the rural areas grew.

generally historicist interest after 1850 rather than a mere dislike of iron and steel. Even the South Devon Railway, depicted regularly by Oswald Angel and William Dawson, soon fell out of favour despite Klingender's idea that 'it seemed possible to combine the industrial with the idyllic, at least in the West Country.'[52] New bridges such as those at Sunderland and over the Tamar were also much depicted, but as with railways and churches this was more in prints and photographs than in paint. However, there were some foretastes of what was to become a major interest in the world of work. The paintings *Work* by Ford Madox Brown and *Industries of the Tyne* by William Bell Scott represent early attempts to create heroism in labour, which was later to become very much the mode.

Scotland

There had been a standardized tour of Scotland for many years, firmly rooted in the Lowlands and the Borders, but during mid-century this became a major focus of interest for English artists. Loch Katrine and the Trossachs, sites connected with Sir Walter Scott, provided one major centre, but Queen Victoria's interest in the late 1840s and the paintings of Landseer had much effect in spreading the taste for Highland scenery northward. Mendelssohn's tour, and the visit of Millais and Ruskin, may also have been significant. There were three main routes into the Highlands: that via Callander and the Trossachs, where beside the Falls of Leny Millais painted Ruskin on his rock, via Pitlochry to the Grampians, and via Loch Lomond and Inveraray. Many of the pictures displayed as much interest in the people, highly stylized and often stereotyped, and in the folk history, as in the landscape itself. Rob Roy and Flora MacDonald were much in evidence. Most of the Romantic interest lay in the valleys and the lochs, often with the typical river scenes of the period, rather than the barren mountains, which were to be the great vogue of the succeeding period. Glen Sannox and Glen Rosa on Arran were the two most favoured archetypes,[53] though interest in the islands further north was very limited, except where there was a special attraction as at Iona or Staffa. Landseer's role has been studied by Trevor Pringle, concentrating on the need to produce imperial imagery in an area still remembered as hostile.[54] At least one artist, F.R. Lee, who went to Scotland every year to paint and fish, deliberately chose North Wales one year because Landseer was in Scotland.[55]

Clearly the railways were influential in popularizing Scotland, as noted by Trevelyan: 'At the same time the new railway system of Britain opened out the Highlands of Scotland to pedestrians and tourists.'[56] However, artists had always succeeded previously in reaching unlikely places, so the railway was only an enabling factor.

Figure 47 Graph for Kent (Source: RA catalogues). No doubt aided by proximity to London, Kent has rarely been out of fashion. Views of castles, cathedrals, country houses and resorts were supplanted by coastal, rural and small town scenes.

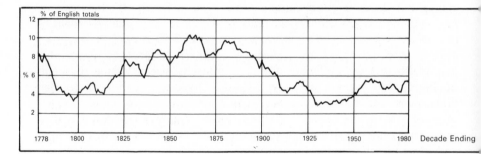

Figure 48 Graph for Surrey (Source: RA catalogues). As London expanded, Surrey became the source of rural sketches and later the home of the interest in the vernacular, and in heathland.

Concentration on the Romantic tours to the West Country, Scotland, Wales and even Ireland (where County Wicklow had been superseded by Kerry as the chief focus) could easily result in underestimating the importance of the lowlands. In fact for much of the period the most popular county was Kent (Figure 47) and Surrey (Figure 48) was also at its peak. No doubt a great deal of this interest was simply the result of the flight from London and the seeking of the nearest areas of rural, pastoral landscape. One movement was westward, up the Thames, long popular, and later to prove one of the archetypal areas of the late nineteenth century. Much more interest went south and east into the neighbouring parts of the North Downs, the Vale of Holmesdale and the nearer Weald, a process studied by Brandon.[57] Even the sandy areas of the Weald were beginning to prove popular; discussion of their importance is, however, deferred to the next chapter, as it was in the Heroic Period that the heathland scene flowered into a major genre.

Kent

Kent has provided more pictures at the Academy than any other shire county, and even by area ranks 5th (Appendix 3). As the graph (Figure 47) clearly shows, its greatest period was the mid-nineteenth century, providing 17 per cent of the English landscapes. Since then there has been considerable decline, probably the result of suburbanization and the growth of industry.

Early interest had been marine, at Dover and the Medway, antiquarian, at Canterbury and Rochester, coastal at the resorts, especially Margate and Dover, and country house portraits, with Knowle, Allington Castle and Charlton the most favoured. In the Romantic Period the major centres of Kentish interest remained much as they had been, though with much less stress on the great antiquarian buildings, such as Dover and Rochester castles and Canterbury cathedral. Interest in the resorts was comparatively muted also, although Broadstairs and Pegwell Bay, and Deal, joined the long-popular Dover, Folkestone and Margate. The Thames and Medway estuaries gave rise to many works, reminders that *Great Expectations* was written in this period. 'Dickens will, of course, be first in the mind of whoever looks on the mouth of the Medway.'[58] The pastoral valleys further upstream have already been mentioned, with Palmer's work at Shoreham typical in location if not in style. There was intense interest in churches, small manor houses and castles within the day-trip radius from London – the latter of course rapidly increasing.

As the suburbs spread so west Kent lost its attraction, and only in the twentieth century did the industrial shores of the Thames become interesting again. Nor could Kent offer the dreary moorlands favoured at the end of the nineteenth century – indeed it was the antithesis of these. However, more recently the smaller harbours, such as Sandwich and Deal, have come to the fore, together with revived interest in Picturesque subjects, and new interest in Romney Marsh, and the farm landscape, made famous by Rowland Hilder.

The Isle of Wight and many parts of Sussex were also much used, wherever trees, cliffs, rivers or sea could be combined with the works of man. In the case of Sussex interest dispersed from the coastal resorts, though they remained popular, into the surrounding villages and market towns. Arundel became a favourite, and the valley of the Arun was destined to become one of the main sources of inspiration fifty years

Figure 49 Helen Allingham, *Valewood Farm*, watercolour, from *Happy England as Painted by Helen Allingham*, 1909 (Courtesy M.R. Pidgley). Allingham was one of many artists popularizing the Wealden cottage scene towards the end of the century. The sentimental approach was also typical.

Figure 50 William Strang, *Lifting Potatoes*, etching, from *The Portfolio*, 1882 (Courtesy M.R. Pidgley). At last rural life began to be seen as burdensome, although it took time for the gracefulness of labour seen here to disappear.

later. The pastoral lowland stream was one of the few genres to reach across the major break in taste that began to build up in the 1860s, and of which the increasing fascination for the Highlands of Scotland was a forerunner. To the new fashion for Heroic landscapes we can now turn.

6

The Heroic Period 1870–1910

By far the most abrupt change of taste in landscape occurred in the years between 1860 and 1880, and this chapter takes 1870 to represent that change. Before 1860 there were few signs of the rising popularity of what Rodee has called the 'Dreary Landscape'.[1] Such landscapes form the most important element in the changes which took place in the last quarter of the nineteenth century. They include moorlands, heaths, fens, fells and marshes. Indeed to choose the term 'Dreary' to define the period is tempting, but there were other types also, and most of them seem to have in common that they were landscapes in which men, and more rarely women, could be seen in an heroic mould. By 1880 many of the great sites of the Picturesque and Romantic eras were almost deserted, at least by artists, though many remained popular as tourist locations; many still are.

Travel

Whatever the factors which brought about these great changes, improved transport facilities could not have been of much importance, for rail and steamship travel had been in existence for many years, and even by the end of the period the motor car was not likely to be available to many artists. The rail network reached its fullest extent, which may account in part for the deliberate seeking of remoteness, which became part of the Heroic ideal and a feature which has often been sought ever since. The bicycle also allowed greater flexibility within a short radius, at least with watercolours and other portable media.

Figure 51 Benjamin Williams Leader, *February Fill Dyke*, 1881, oil, 77 × 123 cm (Courtesy Manchester City Art Galleries). Perhaps the most famous of the 'dreary' landscapes so popular at the end of the century; rain, leafless trees, inhospitable cottage set in an endless landscape, such scenes were necessary to underpin the heroism of the new patrons' backgrounds.

Figure 52 F. J. Widgery, *Clapper Bridge, Dartmoor*, watercolour, 1896, 25 × 35 cm (Courtesy Royal Albert Memorial Museum, Exeter). The heathlands, moorlands and fens were usually depicted very colourfully, and with some object in the foreground. On Dartmoor old stone bridges vied with tors, archaeological monuments and ponies.

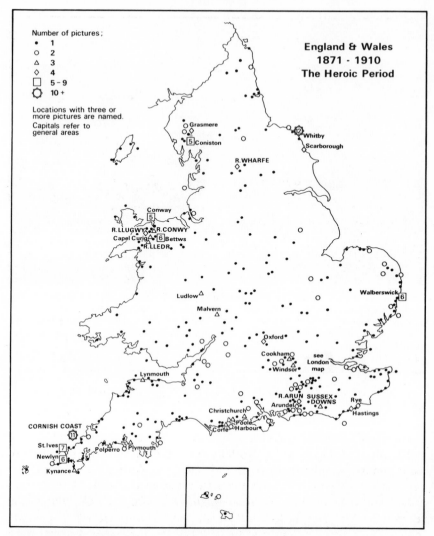

Figure 53 Map of landscapes depicted in Heroic Period, 1871–1910, England and Wales (Source: RA catalogues).

Art colonies

One major change was in the way artists visited landscapes. Most artists either lived in or at least depended on the London market. Previously they had gone on tours lasting two or three months in the late summer, though these became shorter when the railways arrived. The increased extent and more reliable rail network enabled them to live in remote areas and still visit the capital as much as they wished. Hence this was the

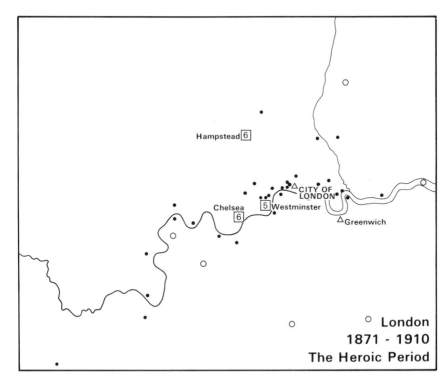

Figure 54   Map of landscapes depicted in Heroic Period, 1871–1910, London area (Source: RA catalogues).

great period of artists' colonies.[2] Many of these were abroad, and English artists often visited those in Brittany or in the Ile de France, but there were important centres in Britain too. Those at Newlyn and St Ives have been much studied, although the latter consisted largely of American artists before 1900. Others were at Whitby and Walberswick, both fishing centres, and at Bushey, where Hubert van Herkomer ran a painting school which was very much in the spirit of the times. Many artists were able, not to join colonies, but to live in their favoured location, as Albert Goodwin lived at Morte in North Devon.[3] Better communication enabled them to keep in close touch with the London market with only a few visits. The result of artists' staying all year in their favoured landscapes had much effect also on the times of year favoured by them, with winter becoming almost as common as summer on the Academy walls.

This is neither the first nor the last time when it is tempting to imagine there being both centripetal and centrifugal forces at work in British visual culture. The centripetal force is represented overwhelmingly by London, the only important artistic market and a great attraction in itself. It is represented in paint, print and photograph, setting itself up as the

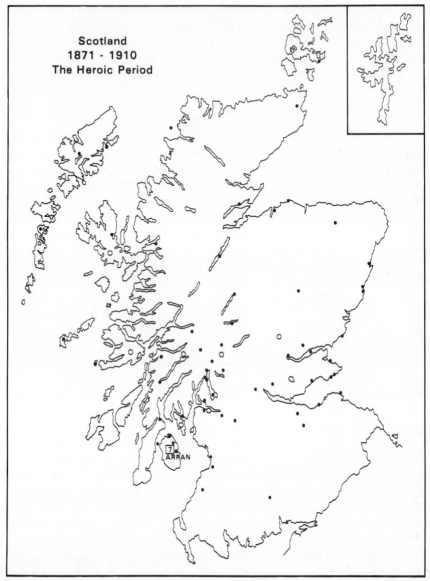

Figure 55   Map of landscapes depicted in Heroic Period, 1871–1910, Scotland (Source: RA catalogues).

seat of the avant-garde. However, when it ceases to be so, when metropolitan art is perceived as sterile, or tainted by academicism, the centrifugal forces operate and art becomes refreshed by ideas acquired by long stays in the provinces or abroad, most usually deriving from the simple, and innocent, activity of landscape painting.[4] The period under review here is the one when architecture and garden design were revivified by taking their exemplars from vernacular forms, and music also developed by taking seriously folk melody. In painting there was little left of a folk tradition, but painters learnt from the so-called primitive arts from overseas or, lacking the funds for foreign travel, looked carefully at the landscape of the ordinary countryman.

Foreign scenes

Foreign travel remained as popular as ever, but the preferred sites were much changed. Italy was by now second to France in popularity, and much Italian interest was Alpine. The Mediterranean coast scene, which had occurred from about 1850 onwards, was by now quite well established, especially in the Riviera di Levante and near Naples. This scene was to become the great cliché of the succeeding period. In France one of the major movements was to Brittany, where English artists joined the international colonies at Pont Aven and Concarneau, which had frequent links with the art colonies in Cornwall, not least in the person of Stanhope Forbes. The Forest of Fontainebleau which had been the heart of the Barbizon school, was also discovered by the English, and there may be a clear link with developments in England.[5] The French views of the forest had often shown it as a sombre backdrop to the rapidly developing heroic myth of the peasant. Perhaps Millet's *The Gleaners* and *The Angelus* can stand for this genre, and such work had great impact in Britain, which, however, lacked peasants. Although the farm labourer was sometimes accorded the status the French gave their peasantry,[6] the fisherman became the more common British equivalent, and one supported by biblical authority.

The love of the Alps continued to grow, becoming closely linked with winter sports. The Romantic interest also spread to Bavaria, especially to the little town of Rothenburg ob Tauber. The Rhine interest itself became less strong as artists sought ever more ornate examples of the half-timbered towns they had found at home. This love of Germany kept people travelling through the quaint towns of Holland, which provided much genre interest as well as architecture.

The fascination for Japan at this time is well known, but there was at least equal interest in the Maghreb and particularly Morocco. This and Egypt produced a major new genre. Former interest in the Islamic culture had been largely limited to the Levant and to Egypt, and to the great monuments there, the 'lions'. In Algeria and Morocco the major focus was the street life, the bazaars, medina, and the street Arabs, pictures full of colourful and picaresque urchins.[7] This fascination for the picturesque, or picaresque, and primitive was often gratified elsewhere, in Ireland quite commonly and in Orkney which was recommended for its inhabitants, 'of primitive habits and manners'.[8]

Patronage

By this time too there had been a major shift of patronage. The balance
of wealth between town and country had shifted dramatically, and was to
do so still faster in the agricultural depression. The rural aristocracy was
now less important in its patronage than the urban bourgeoisie, and there
was therefore less need to indulge the prejudices and points of view of the
landowning classes. Presumably these new urban patrons were content
with pictures of Heroic rural workers in a way which the older patron
could not have been. Possibly they saw in these images the heroes who
were, or should have been, their ancestors. Certainly this period seems to
set up that strange hierarchy of Heroic status among manual workers
which still seems to continue. Miners rank high in this table, possibly as
high as farm workers, but not so high as fishermen. Perhaps the zenith is
the lifeboat coxswain.

Tourism

Tourism had become a major industry, often viewed by the artistic elite
as an uncritical activity. In many cases the tourist was accused of liking
places either because of the guidebook's instructions or because of the
association of the place with the famous, though the fictional famous were
just as important. Fortescue remarked regarding Exmoor:

> The tourist reads *Lorna Doone*, buys a guidebook and hies him to the
> Doones' combe – if it be a fine day. He turns his back on the
> Badgworthy gorge and all its loveliness, and feasts his romantic vision
> on the grass grown foundations of what was very likely a pig's house. It
> is enough for him. These ruins are, as he is told, the Doones' houses:
> and Nature has no charms for him unless consecrated by the holy ink
> of the novelist.[9]

Photography

Photography had become a major method of depicting landscape; many
regarded it as an art form, though the battle on that issue was far from
over. Much of the time the photographers were content to depict the
same scenes as the painters, especially if they were concerned about
artistic status. There are many occasions, however, when photographers
helped to develop new genres. They were certainly in the forefront of the
fishing village interest with Hill and Adamson at Newhaven, and
photographs by Sutcliffe at Whitby often appeared in the *Art Journal*.[10]
Photographs had allowed most people the chance of immortality and
perhaps the rich found the character of the faces of the poor for the first

time in photographs, sometimes taken for strictly social reasons, as were the pictures of the Glasgow slums.[11] Certainly one of the features of the period was the banality of much painted subject matter. Wheeler has made a case that the ordinariness of many popular motifs was first found by photographers.[12] The work of P.H. Emerson remains one of the clearest examples of the new genre,[13] while the huge numbers of topographic scenes by Francis Frith, Bedford, etc. ensured that the British people knew their own country, and others, at least in images, to an extent vastly greater than heretofore.

Moorland

However, one major new genre owed little to the camera. The new interest in moorland was usually expressed in colour, thus most Devon guidebooks of the time used photographs to illustrate most of the county but preferred watercolours for the Dartmoor scenes.[14]

Moorland was the great discovery of the Heroic Period. This taste extended to heathland, and other comparatively flat, natural or semi-natural landscapes as well, and is quite distinct from the previous taste for mountains. The love of the mountains of Snowdonia or the Lake District was clearly *passé*, though the Scottish Highlands, which had been growing in favour since 1850, perhaps represent the half-way house between mountainous scenes dependent on sublimity, and these flatter, vaster places. They were found in Dartmoor and Exmoor, on the Pennines and northern Fells, in remoter parts of the Scottish Highlands, in the Fens and other marshes, including Broadland, and on the heaths, especially in Surrey and the New Forest. Peter Brandon has made out a case for the Wealden sands being the true home of the genre, with painters such as John Linnell being highly influential.[15]

The later Perthshire landscapes of Millais, such as *Chill October*, can stand as the classic examples of the genre, though for the low-lying areas Benjamin W. Leader's *February Fill Dyke* (Figure 51) can stand as exemplar, with Emerson's Broadland photographs, often including the Heroic rural labourer, equally impressive. The staffage gives the clue to the reason for the taste. Heroism has to be seen against backgrounds which emphasize the drudgery and the unpleasantness of the job in hand. Constable's carter in *The Haywain*, in full summer, is unlikely to attract the kind of sympathy demanded by such painters as Farquharson with his *Homeward He Plods his Weary Way*. That such sympathies were not confined to the visual arts is obvious from *Lorna Doone*, already referred to, and Hardy's novels. The lack of understanding of the realities of rural life may indicate that the former dates from the earliest days of the genre and is imbued with Romanticism, while Hardy was writing with closer knowledge and thirty years later. In art the need for the presence of staffage to point up the moral soon disappeared, and the landscape could itself stand for the reality of country life. All that was needed was the great sweep of heather, or reeds, plenty of atmosphere, usually wintry, wet or threatening, and some feature in the foreground. An archaeological monument would do very well, or a scruffy pony, or, on the Broads, a working boat.

Dartmoor and Exmoor

Dartmoor can serve to show how such areas were seen. The old descriptions of barren wasteland were replaced by adulation. Blaikie in 1885 described it as 'a pageantry of glowing moor and clear amber torrent, of quaint church towers, grey hamlets, desolate cleaves, fantastic tors . . . colour, light and shade, fleeting mist and sunshine. . . . The scene of desolation is complete and the stillness delightful.'[16] Desolation was still perceived, but was now a positive not a negative feature. At Cranmere Pool, Page found it 'difficult to exaggerate the sombre effect of this haunted spot. . . . In evening, purple, silence dun red and brilliant green.'[17] Such sentiments are a long way removed from Swete's comment in 1800, that the moor was 'of the most dreary nature, the Horizontal line on every quarter was formed by the Hills and Torrs of Dartmoor'.[18] However, Swete recognized that knowledge could lead to enjoyment, and remarked:

> the Author seems not to have had the most distant idea that from so desolate and barren a tract as Dartmoor, so much entertainment could have been reaped as has fallen to my lot to enjoy . . . the wearied eye recoils from the waste but the active mind yet urges it to roam along.[19]

Earlier still, Leland merely stated that 'Dartmoor is of very great compass, and is such a wild, moorish and forest ground as Exmoor is.'[20] As late as 1850 the Devonport Mechanics Institution was to 'offer money prizes for the best essays on the best methods of reclaiming the waste lands of Dartmoor'.[21]

Artists were working in the valleys on the fringe of the moor throughout the mid-nineteenth century. Sometimes local artists had their own favourites, although visitors tended to stick to the better-known gorges of the Teign and Dart. John Gendall of Exeter worked extensively on the Avon and William Widgery on the Lyd. Only in the later 1860s did pictures of the moor proper begin to appear, apart from isolated depictions of archaeological monuments, or tors. William Widgery was among the earliest, seeming to work his way up river, and was followed by his son, Frederick John. The wide expanses of purple heather seem to most present-day viewers highly clichéd, but at the time were quite new. In their case the staffage of hard-worked moor men was almost always missing, which may detract from the seriousness of the work, but that they can be credited with the popularizing of Dartmoor there can be little doubt.

On Exmoor the story was similar. In 1796 Swete described it 'a desert, all was wildness and barren nature'. It exhibited 'dreary uniformity'.[22] Exmoor was a 'filthy barren ground' according to Defoe, 'without feature,[23] and had 'not a trait of the mountain character' according to Marshall.[24] Although nothing like as popular as Dartmoor, the area attracted many artists, and the frequency of the title *The Doone Valley* is evidence that Blackmore's book was an important influence. The Scottish legitimation implied in the title of the article 'The highlands of West Somerset'[26] may well have been another influence. The fells of the Pennines shared in this vogue, and there were several pictures from the higher parts of the North Yorkshire Moors, as well as the Westmorland fells around Shap, and the central Pennines near Harrogate and Pateley Bridge. Most were in this genre.

Heaths

The essential ecological distinction between wet moorland and dry heathland largely eluded the artists, who depicted the southern heaths with some frequency. Peter Brandon has cogently argued that the heaths of Surrey especially around Hindhead were seminal, with the fashion spreading from there to other areas.[26] 'A richer and more luxuriant tract of country' said a book review of 1865, full of 'hills and dale, woods and pastures, perfumed heaths and breezy downs',[27] known by 1892 as 'John Linnell's Country'. [28] The other areas included the New Forest and the heaths of neighbouring Dorset. The preferred pictures were quite unlike those Picturesque scenes occasionally produced in the New Forest earlier, following Gilpin's account of his home patch.[29]

The New Forest had been compared to the Forest of Fontainebleau,[30] with a contrast between its 'stately woods' and its 'wide, wild, rugged heaths'. Indeed, the same writer continued, there are 'two areas of wild, unenclosed country preeminent for extent, unique beauty and romantic interest, Dartmoor and the New Forest'.[31] Tomson, writing about Studland, explained the purpose of staffage, praising 'the manly figures cast by the necessity of labour into many a posture that . . . appeals always . . . by its extraordinary rhythm and suggestiveness.' He too, as in so many other accounts, revealed the necessity for such places to be seen in comparison with the Highlands: 'Look to the left of you and you are in Scotland: for the moors of Scotland seem to be before you.'[32] Other favoured areas included the sandlings of East Suffolk, although they were 'rich neither in scenery nor associations, and all but unvisited by the tourist',[33] and several of the heaths in the London Basin.

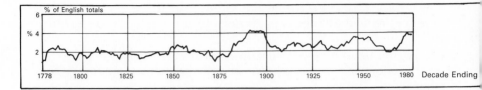

Figure 56   Graph for Norfolk (Source: RA catalogues). Despite the wealth of country houses, and the importance of the Norwich School of Painters, it was the popularity of Broadland and of old buildings which produced Norfolk's most important period. Popularity has been sustained with village and farm views.

Figure 57   E.M. Wimperis, *Marshlands*, watercolour, 1886, 36 × 54 cm (Courtesy Royal Albert Memorial Museum, Exeter). For the first time such places, notably in the Fens and East Anglia, came to be viewed positively. They supported the fashionable idea of the drudgery of rural labour.

Towards the end of the period, and for the first time, pictures of the Chalk Downs and the Cotswolds also began to appear on the Academy walls. These open, sweeping landscapes may have appealed for reasons akin to the moorland taste, but the fashion for downland continued much longer, which may be connected with the interest in formal structure shown by twentieth-century artists.

Marshes and fens

Although the vegetation was quite different the marshes of the Broads and Fens also shared in the taste for dreariness. P.H. Emerson's numerous photographs usually promote the reed cutter or farm labourer to Heroic status, as does E.M. Wimperis in his pictures of marshes. Once again horizontal formats, large expanses of similar vegetation, and uncomfortable conditions were *de rigueur*. Not surprisingly many of these works depicted autumn or winter, to emphasize the dreariness of the life. They were perceived as possessing an 'imprisoned strength and restlessness, chafing in a wilderness of hostile forces'.[34] Such scenes were no doubt assisted by the artists' residence in the area, and by the use of photography to overcome the problems of drawing in the cold and wet.[35]

Norfolk

More pictures of Norfolk were exhibited at this period than any other. The county only ranks 23rd in pictures per unit area (Appendix 3), and had produced a regular but small crop of interesting subjects. A few of these were scenes favoured by the Norwich school, Norwich itself and Yarmouth, but mostly they were of buildings such as Castle Acre, or country houses. Fenland and Broadland became depictable, Norfolk had much to offer. Of the two, Broadland was much the more popular, although King's Lynn became an attractive town. There was also much in the way of picturesque, medieval townscape and the numerous fishing villages of the coast. Later, in the twentieth century, Norfolk was to provide many rural scenes, but the major attraction was to remain the mudflats of the north coast, especially around Blakeney and Stiffkey, with their accompanying fishing boats.

Rivers

Such was the main Heroic scene, and the marked decline in the popularity of river scenery perhaps followed from the new requirements. Most moorland views included water, but more often a stagnant tarn than a babbling brook. Water had traditionally been used mainly as a prospect, but became a hazard in this period, yet another to be overcome by the rural people. It was frequently raining. The Scottish torrent in spate, complete with anglers, remained a common exception however, perhaps filling a rather different market. Depicting sport in a dreary landscape and in appalling weather conditions may have been a way of allowing the new bourgeois[36] patrons to share in the Heroic status of the labouring classes. Thus, in an article praising the Spey valley the writer could say, 'There are blackness and barrenness and yet no savage grandeur to make up for the want of pleasing features.'[37]

There was one major exception to these dreary views, however, which was also a river scene. This was the Thames boating scene which became a fad of the 1890s, although it continued well into the following century. It was quite the opposite of the dull and wintry landscapes generally so common. For once a book sums up the genre more easily than any one picture, for *Three Men in a Boat* was published in 1889 at the start of this fashion. The Thames between Oxford and London was by far the most important river, and Cookham, Windsor, Wargrave, Sonning, Pangbourne, Burnham Beeches[38] and Henley were all major sites. Most pictures were of the river in summer, many including young, fashionably dressed people in boats, with cattle or sheep by the bank. For once articles in the art literature seem to precede the fashion, and there were series in the *Art Journal* in 1883 and *The Portfolio* in 1884.[39] Some other rivers shared in this genre, though the boats were the added attraction of the Thames. The Arun was the most favoured of these, but the Sussex Ouse, Wey and Mole were important, and even the Great Ouse at Houghton and Hemingford Grey.[40]

Thames Valley: Buckinghamshire, Berkshire and Oxfordshire

Buckinghamshire reached its peak of popularity at this time, with Oxfordshire and Berkshire also being found attractive, although the latter, containing Windsor, had always been significant and Oxford itself would become a major twentieth-century favourite.

Berkshire has been the 7th most favoured county in pictures per square mile (Appendix 3). For many years this largely meant Windsor Castle, which accounted for about 80 per cent of the eighteenth-century pictures, though Donington Castle near Newbury was also favoured. With the rise of the pastoral river scene after 1850, the Thames increased in favour, and this taste, heightened by the late-nineteenth-century fad,

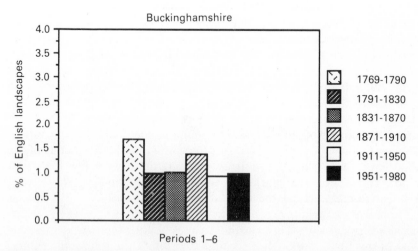

Figure 58 Histogram for Buckinghamshire (Source: RA catalogues). The popularity of the Thames meant that Marlow and Burnham Beeches became major sites. Later chalk downs also came into vogue.

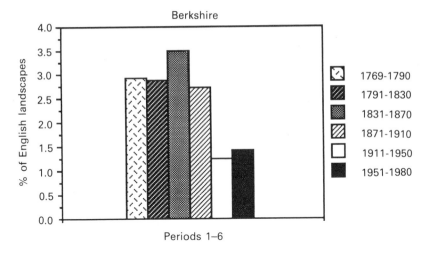

Figure 59 Histogram for Berkshire (Source: RA catalogues). To Windsor's popularity was added the views on the Thames around Sonning and Cookham.

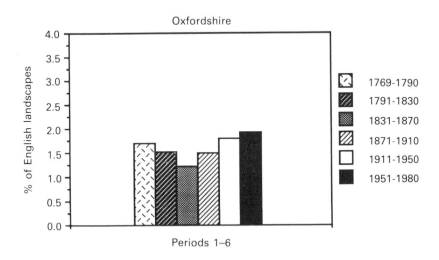

Figure 60 Histogram for Oxfordshire (Source: RA catalogues). Oxford has long been much depicted; later came Henley and other river scenes, and in the twentieth century many views in the Cotswolds.

has continued in being, especially centred on Cookham, the home of the Spencers. There have been many downland scenes as well, and during the 1920s Tidmarsh, the home of Strachey and Carrington, formed an archetype of the search for downland village scenery.

Buckinghamshire, ranked only 19th by area (Appendix 3), was much more dependent on the Thames, first at Eton and later at Marlow and Burnham Beeches. The downland was popular during the twentieth century, not least with Paul Nash, to whom Bevan in 1920 attributed so much of the taste for downland,[41] although much of the Chilterns was too wooded to attract the same favour as Dorset or the South Downs.

In Oxfordshire, ranked 10th (Appendix 3), the city and colleges of Oxford have always been the major interest, although Henley, Goring, Iffley, Shiplake and other villages became centres of the river scene. Only in the closing years of the nineteenth century did the Cotswold towns and villages, Burford, Chipping Norton and Banbury become attractive, thus giving the county a peak during the 1930s as the Cotswolds became the epitome of English vernacular architecture.

Coasts

The coast was much more favoured than the river. The fishing village became the second great stereotype of the period and shared with the moorland and similar views not the dreariness of the latter, but the heroism of the inhabitants. The fisherman, with considerable biblical authority, became the greatest folk hero of the age, and the fisherman's wife and family were granted almost as much status as the husband. The English were not alone here, for the Breton art colonies included painters from many nations, and the colonies at Worpswede and in Denmark also made great use of the stereotype.[42] Perhaps Scheveningen on the Dutch coast was the original model, though Concarneau and Pont Aven have become more famous. Right round the British coast artists stayed or settled in fishing villages, depicting the local population, the harshness and even drabness of their lives, and the fear of the sea which underlay it all. Wives looked out to sea waiting for the fleet to return, husbands mended nets or forged anchors, or brought home the pilchards. Newlyn[43] and St Ives were only the most important of the Cornish colonies, with Polperro,[44] Falmouth,[45] Looe, Penzance, Marazion and Fowey all much favoured. In Devon, Clovelly, which had appealed to painters since the 1850s, became swamped with visitors, while Appledore, Beer and Brixham all became popular.

At first cliffs and coves seemed a vital ingredient, as in the Gower and Pembrokeshire, at Whitby, Robin Hood's Bay and Runswick, at Crail and Pittenweem in Fife, Cullercoats[46] in Northumberland (visited by Winslow Homer), and many others. These were all some distance from

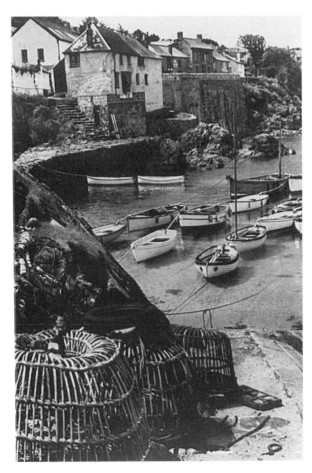

Figure 61 Donovan E.H. Box, *The Harbour at Coverack, in South Cornwall*, photograph, *c.* 1950 (Courtesy Country Life Publications). The origins of the popularity of what are today regarded as routinely attractive views lies in the Heroic Period, although staffage was then more important.

London and by the 1880s several low-lying centres, mainly in the south east, had also become important, of which the greatest colony was at Walberswick, at which the 'yearly increase in the number of artists' was noted in 1880.[47] Rye, Hastings, Christchurch and Bonchurch joined the East Anglian coast in importance, the latter including Blythburgh, Blakeney, Stiffkey and Aldeburgh as well as Walberswick. John Brett was typical of the attitude to fishing boats, though he also painted many views of sea and surf, often, like Henry Moore, looking straight out to sea, clearly representing sublimity through scale.

The Channel Islands

Although Cornwall's greatest heyday was to come in the twentieth rather than the nineteenth century, both the Channel Islands, treated here as if they were a single English county, reached their greatest favour in the 1880s with this kind of scene. There had been pictures of antiquarian

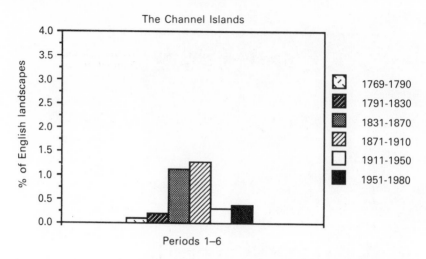

Figure 62 Histogram for the Channel Islands (Source: RA catalogues). In the early days Elizabeth Castle on Jersey was the most popular site, but the vogue subsequent to the steamer's arrival was largely coastal, notably on Sark.

sites, notably Elizabeth Castle, for many years, increasing rapidly after the first steamship service in 1823. Only towards the end of the century, however, did they attract in sufficient numbers for the Channel Islands to rank 3rd in depictions by area (Appendix 3). Jersey was 'an epitome of all that is beautiful in scenery' which the writer kindly defined as 'broad seascapes with rocks, granite cliffs, undulating woody streams, old harbours, old world farmhouses'.[48] The same writer notes the association with Victor Hugo, a very rare association with a foreign language writer. Sark[49] was as favoured as either of the two larger islands, while Alderney has never figured very large. The Isles of Scilly also failed to attract in large numbers.[50]

Isle of Man

The Isle of Man has followed a similar pattern, but at only about one-third of the level of the Channel Islands, only becoming 25th in output per area (Appendix 3). The attractions were similar, the 'romantic' coast scenery, especially the 'poetic savagery' of the south coast. 'Everything is epitomised, abridged, *petit*.' Port St Mary was the main attraction, as a fishing harbour, but the whole island seems to have attracted a less middle-class visitor than the Channel Islands, with a 'crushing, vulgar, scrutinising, touting crowd on the Douglas landing stage'.[51] Since the 1920s the Isle of Man has been all but invisible to English artists.

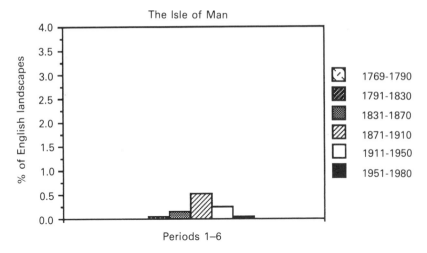

Figure 63 Histogram for the Isle of Man (Source: RA catalogues). Much less popular than the Channel Islands, but Port St Mary attracted some artists, as did so many fishing harbours.

Clovelly and the vulgarization process

Clovelly may be typical of the artistic history of these fishing settlements. Before 1800 it was merely inaccessible and rude; Maton describes the area as 'by no means remarkable for fertility nor is it novel or varied enough to be pleasing to the eye'.[52] By the time Daniell reached it in 1813 it was worthy of an illustration and the comment, 'Its singular inconveniences, informal chimneys and vertical street, have to the eye a very pretty effect.'[53] In the 1850s it was visited by writers, such as Wilkie Collins and Dickens, and artists such as Hook. The publication of *Westward Ho!* by Kingsley seems to have acted as the major spur. In 1879 W.W. Fenn wrote that it was, 'A mine of wealth for the artist . . . landscape or marine, picturesquely architectural, figure or animal painter. . . . Obviously the fishing boats . . . are among its principal attractions for the painter.'[54] The pictures concurred, and usually depicted the harbour though from many different angles. In 1896 the incumbent, Harrison, could write that Clovelly 'positively suffers from excess of attention and [has] become the victim of publicity', with visitors 'in battalions by sea and land'. The article continues in the most mysterious mode about Arthur and the Holy Grail, the native superiority of seafarers and 'the secret of the sea is whispered here.'[55] As popularity increased so the view became more stylized. All realism, which supported the Heroic ideal, was removed, until the standard view became that of the village street, complete with donkeys, panniers and roses. By the early twentieth century Clovelly was merely pretty. By 1954 even an artist

Figure 64 E.W. Tattersall, *Sunshine and Shadow at Clovelly*, photograph, *c*. 1950 (Courtesy Country Life Publications). This became the highly standardized view of Clovelly, as the product of a long process of vulgarization.

writing to an amateur audience felt obliged to apologize for liking the place: 'I know that the stern, strong, he-man type of artist dismisses Clovelly contemptuously as "pretty-pretty" but it was sheer wonderland to me.'[56] This process of vulgarization which seems to affect many genres of painting may be a natural consequence of artistic preference; it will be more closely examined in Chapter 9.

The heroic aspect of the fishing industry was clear in many accounts and had a distinctly religious flavour. One writer asked: 'Who has watched a herring fleet put off in the mellow sunlight has not felt painfully anxious as to whether all those boats . . . would come back again?' Later the same author thought that in his mind's ear he could 'hear the skipper murmuring grace' at the crew's meal.[57] Somewhat less sententiously another writer says,

> The sea . . . is a sentient thing. . . . There is something noble and hopeful in the sight of the labour of tilling the earth . . . yet, take it at its noblest and best, it lacks the fascination which the element of

danger adds to the calling of the toilers of the sea . . . [which] is an ever-present *memento mori*.[58]

Towns

The urban scene made a slow recovery from the disfavour into which it had recently fallen. Nevertheless, few major towns appear on the maps (Figures 53–55) and those which do, did not usually rely on urban scenes for their popularity, having pastoral interest as well, as at Oxford and Arundel. In London artists began to rediscover the interest in the Thames, with Whistler a major contributor, perhaps discovering through his fondness for atmosphere a way of rendering the river as acceptable pictorial material, despite its poor ecological state. Perhaps perceptions need to change sometimes to come to terms with altered environments, in this case the murk of London's river, and to endeavour to see the change as positive rather than negative. At this period, too, Chelsea, close by the river, became at least as favoured a district as Hampstead.

Outside London the emphasis on the medieval was very pronounced, with places such as Arundel, Oxford and Ludlow still in favour, but the great cathedrals and abbeys were no longer major subjects, and although castles were often depicted they were often those not previously of great account, notably Corfe, or those on the Northumberland coast, especially Bamburgh.

Northumberland

Indeed with the interest in the fishing village, especially at Cullercoats, as well as Bamburgh, Warkworth and Dunstanburgh, Northumberland was never so well favoured, though its rank of 35th by area (Appendix 3) suggests that the county was largely in perceptual shadow. The Cheviots have never been important. Newcastle and the Tyne have been depicted both for the architecture, and in the twentieth century for the shipyards. These had become a stereotype by the 1880s. 'The critics almost unanimously agreed that, because there was a great deal of smoke in the air, and dilapidation on the banks, and of mud in the water, it must be a picture of the Tyne.'[59] Jesmond Dene was discussed in Chapter 5 (p. 89) as an important Romantic glen. Occasional views of Hadrian's Wall have also appeared.

Cottages

In the countryside the landscape portrait of the country house and grounds had, by this time, virtually disappeared. However, the discovery of attractiveness in some villages was quite marked. The individual

Figure 65 N.H.J. Baird, *Old Houses, High Street, Exeter*, etching, 1880s, 20 × 12 cm (Courtesy Royal Albert Memorial Museum, Exeter). After the discovery of 'Merrie Englande' about 1850, such parts of many towns became features to be proud of.

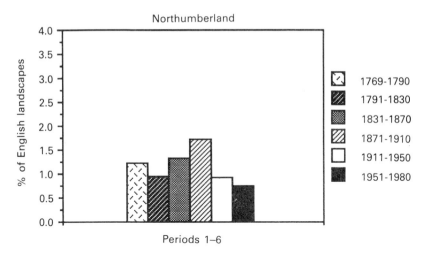

Figure 66 Histogram for Northumberland (Source: RA catalogues). The Romantic coastal castles were the most popular sites, but scenes of Cullercoats were also significant in the late nineteenth century. More recently industrial scenes on Tyneside have played their part.

cottage had been an occasional subject for many years, but the village as a whole had largely retained its reputation for rudeness, dirtiness and lack of civilization. Now, however, just those characteristics were beginning to be praised. The cottage and village were to become major stereotypes of art in the next period, but even these early views showed decided preference both in terms of area and building material. The preferred area was clearly in the Weald. Such villages as Amberley, Betchworth, Abinger, and Burpham possessed the tile-hung, often thatched houses which were regarded as the epitome of vernacular building, which preference was exported to other parts of the country. If half-timbering was not the local style, a certain lumpiness in appearance was to be preferred.

Surrey

The archetype of the English cottage was found in Surrey, as were the tastes for heaths and for downs. The peak of attractiveness lay before rather than after 1870 because of the early discovery of so many genres in the area. Of course, being so close to London, the county had never been unpopular, ranking 5th in total number of views and 4th measured by area (Appendix 3). The early views were often of the Thames, or of country houses, of which Albury was the most important, but there have always been many pictures of Croydon, Mitcham and other places long since swallowed by London. Surrey provided the nearest bit of 'real country'. The boom period started mainly with such pastoral scenes. Surrey 'holds within its narrow compass more than one busy and crowded, and withal picturesque town, and countless recesses that have all the solitude and many of the characteristics of a Highland valley.'[60] The favoured towns were Dorking and Guildford.

Slightly later, artists discovered the heaths, in 1879 still 'little known except to the painters who have now for some years frequented them'. Shere was the centre, a 'model village teeming with prosperous and flowery cottages' and so crowded with artists seeking views such as those by Helen Allingham that 'it promises to become in time a second Bettws-y-coed'.[61] Another writer even more mysteriously compares the heath with Capel Curig.[62] Having established itself for such different genres, and also some views on the North Downs, Surrey slowly became more clichéd and lost favour also as the suburbs spread southwards. The recent increase has largely been a result of artists' learning to see such suburbs in a more favourable light.

Nottinghamshire

Another county which reached the height of its very poor visibility in this period was Nottinghamshire, ranking only 36th in pictures per square mile (Appendix 3). The only two areas to be depicted with any regularity have been some views on the Trent, usually near Nottingham itself, and Sherwood Forest, the latter both as the home of Robin Hood and as a

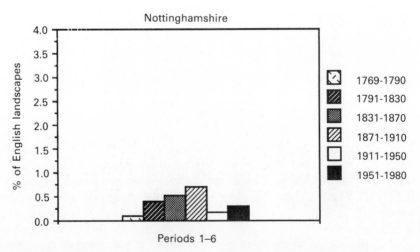

Figure 67   Histogram for Nottinghamshire (Source: RA catalogues). Apart from the country houses, only the discovery of Robin Hood and Sherwood gave the county any perceptual importance.

surrogate Barbizon. The lack of interest in the great country houses of The Dukeries, even in the eighteenth century, is perhaps surprising. This century the county has never provided more than 0.25 per cent of the English landscapes (Figure 67).

Scotland

Scotland, and especially the Highlands, was in many ways the standard of excellence by which others were judged. Southern heathland and Exmoor have been seen to be legitimated by Scottish references and they were not alone. Fortescue complained that Blackmore used the term 'glen' rather than the local 'combe' on Exmoor.[63] The Dart estuary, which had once been seen as a lake, and later as the English Rhine, was now claimed to be, 'more like some Scotch sea-loch'.[64] The string of articles in the art literature praising the Highlands was indicative of the popularity of the area.[65]

Arran remained the firm favourite, although the movement into the Western Highlands now extended at least as far as the Great Glen and sometimes beyond, especially to Mull and Skye, and even on occasion to the Western Isles. The Grampians ceased to be the main centre, and the Southern Uplands had now been almost abandoned, Scott's influence having run its course. The love of the fishing villages of Fife has been mentioned, and several locations on the Clyde were also seen in this light. After 1900 the popularity of Scotland fell dramatically, although remoter

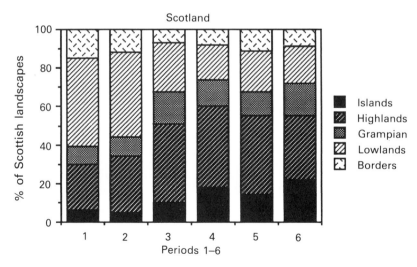

Figure 68   Scotland: distribution by region of the landscapes depicted (Source: RA catalogues). The main feature is the change from a southern- to a northern-dominated pattern in the Romantic Period.

Figure 69   Graph for Scotland (Source: RA catalogues). The great peak in the last quarter of the nineteenth century is obvious. The earlier, smaller vogue had been focused on the Tweed and the Lothian areas.

parts of the Highlands were regularly depicted. The interest in vernacular architecture did not seem to be satisfied north of the Border, and only Edinburgh itself remained a popular venue for English artists. To the present day the views of Scotland appearing at the Academy have remained of the type associated with a foreign country – the 'lions', stereotyped views of mountains and islands, the great and the good. English artists are still outsiders there.

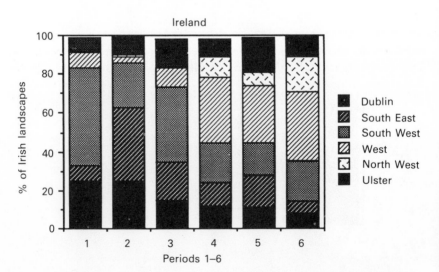

Figure 70   Histogram for Ireland (Source: RA catalogues). As the Scottish pattern was a northward movement, so the Irish was westward, from Wicklow, to Kerry, to Connemara, and to Donegal. However, the figures are never of the same order as those of Scotland.

Ireland

Some artists continued to visit Ireland, where the Romantic view of Kerry was giving way to more interest in Connemara and Donegal, which were perceived to have the quality of harshness which so much appealed. Nevertheless Ireland was never to recover the comparative popularity it had enjoyed in the early part of the century, when Dublin and Wicklow were the main sites. As in Scotland the same outsideness can be detected.

Industry

Industry had never been less popular. Despite some attempt to extend the notion of the Heroic worker into industrial settings, such as the work by Brown, it met with little popular acclaim, at least by those responsible for the Academy's selection. One writer asserted:

> As much as art has made of late – and justly – of the dignity of labour, it is not easy to find nobility in the grocer's shop, or in the pin-factory, or among the processes of the production of buttons.[66]

Even miners failed to achieve Heroic status until well into the twentieth century. Where pictures of industrial cities were found at this period they were only rarely of industrial subjects, those in Liverpool, for example, often being of the river. Even the rural industries, long since established as Picturesque, were little depicted. The days of the watermill and lime kiln were over.

This period, therefore, firmly established a quite new taste in landscape, which we have here labelled 'Heroic'. There was, however, an almost opposite fashion also at work, and we have traced the development of interest in the pretty river scene, the olde-worlde town, and the village. The latter taste was set to take over in the early years of the twentieth century the honest attempt at realism which the former represented.

7

The Vernacular Period 1910–1950

If the Heroic Period had started with considerable swiftness it ended with little more than a fading of its realistic strength to a much less powerful, but more sentimental, view in the early twentieth century. The rapid revolution in avant-garde art in France in the earliest years of the century had little impact on the subjects and places chosen by English landscape painters. However this influence did eventually lead to the decline of the landscape genre amongst the more progressive painters. The shift in subject matter that did take place was certainly under way before the First World War, and is hesitantly dated here to 1910.

Throughout the twentieth century the gap between the avant-garde and the mainstream artists has been very important. For many progressives membership of the Royal Academy represented 'the negative of ambition'.[1] Their work, which was already well on the way to abstraction before the First World War but moved back more towards the figurative after the war for a time, often avoided landscape as a subject, and where it was important the geometric, formal way of seeing it became popular very early. In fact many of the avant-garde artists missed the Vernacular tradition almost entirely. After 1900, therefore, rather than periods of taste which succeed one another, there are two main perceptions that accompany each other, often ill at ease with the other's existence. In sheer numbers what is here termed the vernacular outlook was dominant before the Second World War and the Formal outlook after it, but this is a generalization that should not be pressed too hard.

The second twentieth-century phenomenon is perhaps rather surprising: the speed of change of tastes slows down markedly. The enormously increased speed of transport by car and aircraft, and the vast increase in the numbers of the travelling public, may tend to obscure changing tastes

Figure 71 Map of landscapes depicted in Vernacular Period, 1911–50, England and Wales.
(Source: RA catalogues.)

among the 'visual elite'. Later in the century came major and successful demands for the conservation of landscapes, especially in the uplands, which have had a tendency to fossilize tastes. The separation of the elite of culture from the elite of power has meant that those who have the power to conserve places and direct tastes have not themselves been at the forefront of changing ideas. Change, therefore, has occurred more at the pace of the slowest member of the convoy than that of the leaders. The tastes fossilized by conservation law have not been those of the artistic fraternity even at the time of the designation. Thus moorland, for

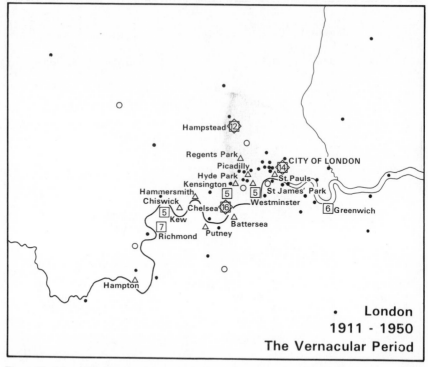

Figure 72   Map of landscapes depicted in Vernacular Period, 1911–50, London area
(Source: RA catalogues).

example, had long since ceased to be a major concern for forward-
thinking artists when National Park legislation enshrined moorland's
attractiveness in the years after the Second World War. This slow change
is partly due no doubt to the nature of the data, for the Royal Academy
became more and more the home of safe, middle-brow art. The more
advanced artists tended to exhibit in the New English Art Club. At
St Ives in the 1930s the rows between the old guard, led by Borlase Smart
and Julius Olsson, and the new abstractionists, led by Barbara Hepworth
and Ben Nicholson, used language which today seems to place far too
great importance on such a trivial affair.[2]

The term 'Vernacular' is used for the period to indicate the two main
features of the landscapes of the early twentieth century. One was the
continuance of the themes of the Heroic without the realism which
accompanied it, until the result was a sentimental and Romantic view of
the workers and their workplaces. The other was a reaction against
metropolitan and international standards and a search for the local and
special. This shows itself as a preference for objects which were perceived
as demonstrating the local character of an area, not of major significance.
Views of grand country houses by known Palladian architects gave way to

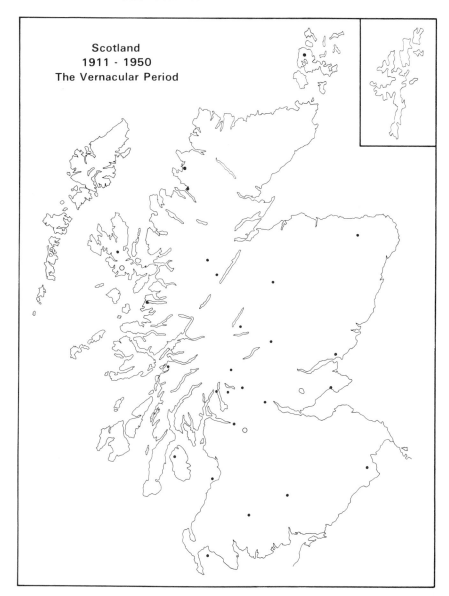

Figure 73   Map of landscapes depicted in Vernacular Period, 1911–50, Scotland (Source: RA catalogues).

views of old thatched farmhouses. Well-known 'lions' in the towns were replaced by views of bits of villages, and major metropolitan vistas were less popular than suburban housing.

Figure 74 J.A. Brimble, *A Somerset Lane at Bratton, near Minehead*, photograph, *c*. 1950 (Courtesy Country Life Publications). The ideal rural, vernacular scene. A bit of village, with rounded forms to the cottage, and thatch. Sheep, rather than cattle, hedges in bloom and a noticeable absence of people.

Transport

The major transport development during the period was clearly that of the motor car, which immediately made large parts of Britain accessible in a way they had never been before. The ability to go more or less anywhere with great ease, even taking oil-painting equipment, meant that remoteness was a feature only now to be found on islands or in the furthest-flung parts of Scotland. Those places, including Skye, the Outer Hebrides and parts of the north-west Highlands, certainly enjoyed popularity in this period, with John Dickson Innes's views of North Wales or Arenig perhaps typical. However, the other effect of the motor car was to discover the universal attraction of British farms, villages and rural countryside all over the country. Oddly the car seems to have discouraged artists from driving very far to find their subject matter. The key to this apparent paradox probably lies in that other feature of motor transport – the ability to stop wherever one wants. Consequently solitude was as easily found within a few miles of the artist's home as anywhere else. Artists too more and more commonly lived in villages, and the addresses of exhibitors at the Royal Academy can be used to confirm this. The rural farmsteads, villages and cottages once only rarely depicted outside the south east were sought all over the rural parts of England. Sussex, the main example of a county having its peak in this period, was much aided by its convenience by car from London.

Conservation

During the same period, and partly for the same reasons, the outdoor movement became very powerful, and this is well documented.[3] Hikers pervaded the countryside, and the tension between farmers, often the owners of the preferred landscape, and hikers, grew accordingly. At the same time farming had become an Heroic activity, and its preoccupations became the stuff of much writing and broadcasting.[4] The publication of *England and the Octopus* and *Britain and the Beast* demonstrated a very clear elitist, though frequently left-wing, antipathy to the working classes, now able to get into and thought to be ruining the countryside.[5] If the outdoor movement in the south was largely middle-class, this was certainly not true in the north, with the mass trespass on Kinder Scout in 1928 and many other areas of the Pennines being opened up to walkers. The publication of books, very often by Odham's Press and profusely illustrated with monochrome photographs, not only reflected the enormous interest in British heritage but also encouraged it and largely defined the beauty to be seen. To a large extent it was those features which during and after the Second World War became protected by a whole series of Acts of Parliament and have to an extent been fossilized into the map of 'Picturesque Britain', which formed the fashion of the time.[6]

The ability to reproduce photographs in books brought to a much enlarged audience the ideas of what constituted attractive scenery. In addition, the widespread use of the camera as a normal adjunct of the typical tourist was, therefore, coupled with the view from the road, which in turn led to a distinctive way of composing pictures of attractive scenery.[7]

Foreign travel

With the obvious exception of the interruption to foreign travel during the First World War, artists travelled abroad more frequently than ever before. France was by now the first choice of most, with several areas of interest. The Mediterranean coast scene became absolutely dominant and is discussed here because the influence of this genre was so pervasive that it became sought everywhere, in Britain and overseas. Such scenes had been depicted since 1860, but they were now mainly from the French Riviera, although Sorrento, Capri and the Riviera di Levante also provided many. Cezanne and Van Gogh were considerable influences on the Riviera's popularity, but the interest in Cezanne's preferred inland scenery along the Calavon and at Mont St Victoire was largely limited to more advanced artists and did not attract the majority until after 1945.[8] Paris was the undisputed artistic capital with views of Montmartre perhaps the most common cliché, though there was still much interest in the fishing ports of Brittany and the Channel coast.[9]

Interest in Italy was centred on the Alpine lakes and the towns of Tuscany, with Florence overtaking Venice in popularity and many small hill towns such as San Gimignano highly favoured. Spain began to share in the Mediterranean coast scene along the Costa Brava as well as the well-established interest in the older towns. Germany's popularity, which had been considerable along the Rhine and in Swabia, naturally disappeared during the First World War and showed no sign of serious recovery during the inter-war period, though whether this was due to political considerations is uncertain. Certainly the emergence of Fascism in Italy and Spain does not seem to have deterred artistic visitors. The Low Countries also lost all their popularity, perhaps because they had come to be seen as *en route* to Germany. Many more artists visited and depicted America but the influence of the formal American views of industrial landscape, such as those by Charles Sheeler, was delayed till after the Second World War.

Figure 75 R.P. Bevan. *A Devonshire Valley No.1*, 1910, oil, 51 × 61 cm (Courtesy Royal Albert Memorial Museum, Exeter). A very early example of landscape seen as geometric pattern, by an artist with much continental experience.

Impressionism and Cubism

A further prime cause of changed tastes in this period was a major shift of painting style. We have seen how the development of a new medium, such as photography, effectively produced a new way of seeing and therefore a whole new range of seeable subjects. The same is true with style and technique. Before the First World War Impressionism was taken up avidly by mainstream painters, some fifty years after its appearance in France. The avant-garde were more concerned with Cubism and Post-Impressionism, which is one of the main causes for their earlier adoption of a formalistic view of landscape. Impressionist subjects included the rippling surface of water and orchards in blossom, both views which particularly suited a style which laid the paint on in flecks and small brushstrokes. These subjects rapidly became popular in England, and places where orchards were plentiful, such as the Vale of Evesham, became regularly depicted, not only in paint but by other means as well.[10] Orchards had not been a major subject previously, and even water had not usually been depicted with the rippled surface which now became normal. The presence in England of Walter Sickert and Lucien Pissarro during the inter-war years was no doubt significant in promoting this general style.

Another major change followed the development of abstract art, especially Cubism. Before 1900 there were occasional panoramas over rural landscape, but these did not concentrate their attention on the landscape as a pattern, the linear patterns of the hedgerows and the colour patterns of the crops. Among the first painters to produce such work was Robert Bevan (Figure 75) who, after spending time with Gauguin in Pont Aven, moved on to Paris where Picasso and Braque were developing Cubism.[11] Returning to England he took up residence in the Blackdown Hills and created pictures which show much evidence of Gauguin's influence as well as that of the Cubists. Does the modern love of hedgerows, and of the landscape as pattern, descend from Cubism? This is an intriguing idea, though one that more properly belongs to the succeeding chapter, because although such scenes occur in about 1910 they do not become widespread till later, and then largely with the progressive artists.

Film and postcard

The invention of film created a new medium, which has not been analysed here, though some have considered its importance as a former of taste.[12] Although few film-makers may have originated new fashions in landscape, they certainly formed a most powerful mediating factor between artist and public, transferring the artists' perceptions to a public quickly and effectively. Surely none of the moody, romantic paintings of Dartmoor so common at this time could have had the impact of the Basil Rathbone version of *The Hound of the Baskervilles*, with the Grimpen Mire stretching from the very door of the Victorian mansion. If in earlier times the print had been the main pictorial souvenir for the visitor, and later the photograph, in this period the rise of the landscape view as a picture postcard again mediated between elite and public. The subject matter of landscape postcards is a vast store of potential information to assist the study of the perception of particular places over time.

War

The greatest events of the period were, of course, the two wars, and the influence of the first on artists' perceptions of Germany has already been noted. Within the United Kingdom, the result of war was greatly to increase the proportion of landscapes of British as opposed to foreign places. The appointment of Official War Artists, in both wars, did not directly lead to much landscape work, as they were obviously depicting human effort, though some of Paul Nash's views of Flanders are highly memorable. There is, however, a discernible trend towards patriotic landscapes – depicting the scenes for which people thought they were fighting, although they no doubt depict officers' views rather than the places which the private soldiers thought worth fighting for. In the First World War such views were actually promoted by the government, as witness the downland view of Figure 76. There was also considerable artistic interest in the battle areas, not only by the Official War Artists. In the first war the coastal towns of Picardy were popular, probably due to paintings done on leave from the Front. Only in the second war was there much to be painted at home, while still imagining oneself in the front line, and John Piper's paintings of wartime destruction are typical of many subjects in almost every local collection in the country. The danger of such pictures is the tendency to make attractive even subjects which the artists thought ugly and were depicting only as records. Such is the result of putting frames around pictures, as is demonstrated by the problems of many socially concerned photographers. Even wartime photographs of destruction can now be seen as nostalgic. So while some artists depicted the battle, or the country to be fought for, the official historian of the Royal Academy could note that in 1916 'others seemed to be specially designed to keep at bay the horrors of the time'.[13] There were also considerable restrictions on free movement during the wars, in 1915 'no sketching, photography, or note taking [was] allowed on any part of the coast' of Woolacombe Sands.[14]

Figure 76 First World War parliamentary recruiting poster, *Your Country's Call* (Courtesy Trustees of the Imperial War Museum, London). The Scottish soldier invites us to protect the newly popular downland with its bucolic villages.

The fishing village

The most outstanding feature of the new period was the geographical spread of the fishing village scene, which had come to such prominence in the Heroic Period. Newlyn was the favourite of previous artists who had concentrated their interest on the fishermen and their families at least as much as on the landscape. The newer scenes were much less interested in the people but more concerned with the fishing tackle, the boats, nets and gear, always now seen as pretty and charming rather than as the equipment of a dangerous and harsh existence. This prettiness, coupled with sentimentality, is sufficiently ubiquitous to provide a tempting title for the period, but the overwhelming interest in rural villages and ordinary buildings suggested that 'Vernacular' was equally truthful and less condemnatory. The fishing villages concerned now extended all round the coasts of Britain. The Cornish villages, Newlyn, St Ives, Polperro, Mullion, Mevagissey, remained among the most important. In Devon, Brixham came to the fore, with Beer, Appledore and Clovelly also important. A century previously Ayton had suggested that Appledore 'contains two parallel rows of small, neat, compact dwelling houses which afford no very interesting matter for description.'[15] In this period the 'typical' view of Clovelly discussed in the previous chapter became the norm. Other fishing villages had no cliffs or coves, once regarded as essential components. Once the boat itself became established as the focus these could as easily be seen against a background of mudflats and marshes as against cliffs, and many villages of East Anglia joined Walberswick in fashion, together with several in Sussex, e.g. Bosham, Itchenor and, above all, Rye.

The coast

The dominance of the coast in the perceived map of Britain, which had emerged during the Heroic Period, was reinforced during this vernacular period. While the fishing cove type, with its original home in Cornwall, remained, the interest now spread to the south-eastern coasts, with much less in the way of rough seas and cliffs. Indeed Rye became the archetype – a village rapidly becoming gentrified, with small boats and mudflats. The books of C.H. Benson beautifully depict the strange cross between Bloomsbury and Newlyn which existed there and in many other harbour areas, e.g. Brixham, Bembridge and several in Sussex, especially Shoreham.[16] The focus of interest was now marine, with boats and their tackle at the centre. The fisherman was no longer seen as an Heroic figure who needed to be set against the violence of nature, rather he had become picturesque staffage, as countrymen had been seen a century before. Several considerable artists were involved, such as Oskar

Kokoschka at Polperro, but only rarely was the interest extended to big ships or commercial ports.[17] One author attempted to demonstrate that perfect beauty lies in a logarithmic spiral, showing this by examining three paintings and a Brixham trawler,[18] thus summing up the fascination for all things nautical by reference to accepted canons of beauty. The relationship between these views of fishing harbours and the Mediterranean coastal view is a close one. Both rely extensively on colour, as well as finding a point of view which stresses the informal arrangement of houses in these villages.

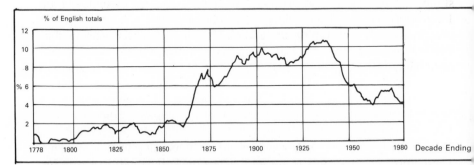

Figure 77   Graph for Cornwall (Source: RA catalogues). Despite a very late start in popularity, Cornwall became the main centre of the fishing village genre, first popular in the 1880s but the mainstay of landscape art between the two wars.

Figure 78   Steel engraving after Clarkson Stanfield, *St Michael's Mount, Cornwall*, from *Stanfield's Coast Scenery*, 1836 (Courtesy M.R. Pidgley). Early views of Cornwall were nearly always of the 'lions'.

Cornwall

Cornwall reached its greatest popularity during this period, having been in vogue since 1860. Ranking 8th by area (Appendix 3), for some years Cornwall was the most favoured county outside London. It has always been seen as coastal. Before the vogue most scenes were of St Michael's Mount or similar 'lions', with Mount Edgcumbe a major country house. Between 1860, when artists began to arrive in large numbers, and the 1880s when the Newlyn school got under way, the main views were of stormy headlands, usually without any signs of man's existence. From 1880 to 1950 Cornwall provided the archetype of the fishing cove and village, gradually becoming more clichéd. The substantial decline since 1940 reflects this, and many of the more recent views have been inland, including those of the clay-pit landscape near St Austell, or of abandoned tin mines.

Bays

Long, sweeping, usually sandy bays began to be popular for the first time. These provided a coastal genre less widespread than, but quite distinct from, the fishing harbours, and were usually depicted as empty beaches, providing a long-shore view, with the beach itself creating a curving line down the centre of the picture, by no means dissimilar to the use of cliffs in the early resort views. Such places had long been unpopular, but now the great bays of North Devon, for example, were depicted frequently by Albert Goodwin, who lived there, and by David Bomberg among many others. Theirs was a very different perception from that of Richard Ayton, who described Woolacombe in 1813 as 'another dreary flat three miles in extent called Woollocombe Sands'.[19] In the mid-nineteenth century *Murray's Handbook* made extensive reference to the coasts of the county, but completely ignored Slapton Sands in South Devon and Saunton, Croyde and Woolacombe in the north. Such a simple structure to a landscape did not appeal to the Picturesque or Romantic minds.

These coastal genres also saw a geographical extension, not only 'infill' on those coasts already popular, but also an extension to ever more remote places. Some artists sought out remote parts of the coast to make their own, the best known being Graham Sutherland with his paintings of the coasts of Pembrokeshire. There he showed marked interest in the details of landscape, giving them a symbolic significance which he used to highlight his statement about the place. Some islands, especially Skye, shared in this interest in the remote coast and there were many pictures of remote bays in the Highlands.

General review of coastal scenes

The coast has never been unpopular for artists, but has shown a distinct rise in popularity over time. In the Classical and Picturesque periods, apart from the popularity of marine scenes, the interest was usually in major promenade-type seaside resorts, Brighton being an exemplar. There followed a move through the nineteenth century to more and more Romantic coastal resort settings, with rockier small coves, and views with a shorter fetch. Ilfracombe was typical of these later resorts. Views overlooking such places, and long-shore views, were popular and doubtless had important souvenir elements. In addition there was interest in rias and estuaries, usually in watercolour from the Picturesque Period on. Later the fishing village, with Newlyn the exemplar, replaced the resort during the Heroic Period, and indeed the fisherman became the essential hero of the time. To this genre must be added the pure seascapes, wide pictures of waves with only the merest hint of land or boat, such as those done by Henry Moore, which fit the ideals of an Heroic landscape and the sublimity of the sea very well. Only in the twentieth century did long sandy beaches become popular together with an extension of the fishing village genre to low-lying coastal villages, usually with interesting vernacular architecture, plus mudflats with boats. This is the Rye type. In the recent past a further genre has been added, the interest in really violent coastal scenes, often in Scotland or Ireland, though Hartland forms a good local study. These are the places now regarded as natural sketching grounds, with the formality and geometric qualities of the rock formations being of particular interest. Even in 1918 Hartland Quay was 'a place to see to shudder at'.[20] *Murray's Handbook* thought it exhibited all 'the dreariness which characterises the Carbon-iferous formation'.[21]

Rural landscapes

The views of inland rural England did not change a great deal during the period in either subject matter or location, although there was considerable extension to produce a much denser pattern. Moorlands, marshes, fells and heaths remained very popular subjects but were now seen in a much less harsh and heroic light. Certainly they were no longer dreary. Muted colour had always been at the heart of such views, but atmosphere was now added, with swirling mists becoming a cliché, and bright colours, especially the purple heather and yellow gorse. The inclusion of people was less common, though an animal, or more often an archaeological monument, often formed a repoussoir or even the chief subject. The heaths perhaps provided this sunnier scene more easily than the moors. Hardy was seen by many as a progenitor of such an attitude to

Figure 79 Alan Cotton, *Hartland Quay*, oil, 1970, 152 × 112 cm (Courtesy Royal Albert Memorial Museum, Exeter). The black, hard coast south of Hartland Point, previously ignored, has become the most favoured bit of Devon's coast in recent years.

landscape,[22] although this surely implies considerable misreading of the general tenor of his work.

The river as the central feature of landscape work very largely disappeared during this period; that most traditional way of leading the eye from foreground to background, of looking up a river, was by now *passé*. However, valleys were far from *passé*, and those in the chalk country or the Cotswolds were very much part of the new popularity of those areas. In particular the Sussex valleys and those on the eastern slopes of the Cotswolds were the subject of many pastoral pictures, although the stream itself was usually of much less significance than the cattle or sheep (never pigs), the hedgerows and the villages. Estuaries, however, made something of a comeback, and atmospheric views in watercolour, with a light mist on the water, a few boats and distant fields were a distinct genre. The Medway, the south-western rias and the long indentations of the Essex and Suffolk coasts were the main attractions.

Downland

Until 1900 the only parts of the chalk downland to be frequently depicted were those near to London – the North and South Downs – and these were outcrops too narrow to give the feeling of the rolling plain which was the new taste. In 1813 Ayton had referred to those in Dorset as 'those open downs offering only the contrast of a dry desert with a wet one'.[23] Even after 1900 the large expanse of Salisbury Plain itself took many years to become highly regarded, though that may have something

Figure 80   A postcard postmarked 1905, inscribed *Devil's Dyke near Brighton – view of South Downs looking East, showing the pretty Sussex village of Poynings*. Both tastes, for downland and for Sussex villages, were comparatively new.

to do with its inaccessibility due to its military use. W.H. Hudson's very popular *A Shepherd's Life*, published in 1910, began by noticing the lack of appreciation for Wiltshire, apart from Salisbury Cathedral and Stonehenge, and suggested that 'these downs may be neglected, since, if downs are wanted, there is the higher, nobler Sussex range within an hour of London.'[24] Perceptual shadow in the middle of southern England! Hudson blames Gilpin for some of the downs' unpopularity but admits that Gilpin 'certainly expresses a feeling common to those who are unaccustomed to the emptiness and silence of these great spaces'.[25] In 1795 Maton was delighted to get into Devon's valleys, 'unlike the wide downs and frequent wastes, silent with desolation' he had left behind in Dorset.[26] As late as 1888 the lack of knowledge of the downs is well indicated by an article on 'The Wiltshire Avon' which not only includes pictures of Stratford-upon-Avon but also mistakes the Dorset Stour for Constable's river.'[27] That such a mistake could not only be written but escape editorial scrutiny in a major art periodical says much about the lack of interest in both Constable and Wiltshire.

Wiltshire

Consequently Wiltshire has only ranked 27th in the list of English counties when its area is taken into account (Appendix 3). It has had two peaks of popularity. The first, in the Picturesque Period, was accounted for by very specific sites, notably Fonthill, Salisbury Cathedral, Stonehenge and Stourhead. Thereafter only a few pictures of Picturesque

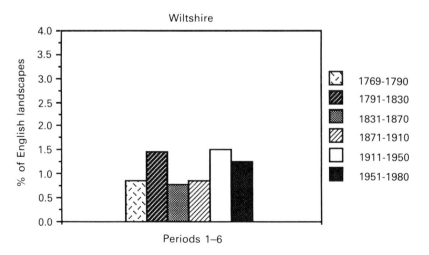

Figure 81 Histogram for Wiltshire (Source: RA catalogues). Apart from its 'lions' (Stonehenge and Salisbury Cathedral) the county was largely overlooked, even when hillier downs were in vogue.

townscape, such as Malmesbury, and pastoral river scenes occur until the interest in downland villages developed after about 1920. Avebury has been a favourite for some, including Paul Nash, but the villages along the Wylye and other chalk valleys have accounted for most.

Dorset

Dorset's early popularity was almost all concerned with the country houses, and with pictures of Weymouth and, later, Lyme. Since Hardy, and there are sufficient picture titles including his fictitious place-names to be sure of his influence, Dorset has become much more popular. At first this interest was largely coastal:

> Only of late years has the strip of Dorsetshire coast between Weymouth on the west and St Alban's Head on the east . . . become generally popular with the brethren of the brush. . . . No foliage breaks the rolling outline of the Downs . . . it is the coast which forms the attraction of this locality for the artist. (1879)[28]

Within a few years this had changed dramatically. The coast remained popular, and Swanage took part in this, but it was the Purbeck range and Corfe Castle which became the centre of interest. Poole Harbour also provided a popular location for boat scenes, and several small towns were depicted for their vernacular buildings. Consequently Dorset has raised itself into 14th place when ranked by area (Appendix 3).

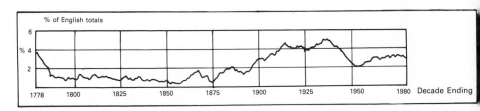

Figure 82   Graph for Dorset (Source: RA catalogues). The late-nineteenth-century surge of interest may well stem from Hardy's influence, but was coastal as well as downland.

Gloucestershire

The Cotswolds shared in this interest, with Bibury and Burford only the most favoured of many Cotswold villages. Ashbee's centre at Chipping Camden is right in period, and the fascination here was the double one of rolling landscape and the supreme example of genuine vernacular architecture. The 'simplicity and beauty which constitute the chief interest of Cotswold building'[29] which drew Ashbee there became the chief example of the glory of the vernacular to a generation of British architects, and all readers of Batsford books.[30] That Gloucestershire

Figure 83 G.F. Allen, *A Little-known View of Arlington Row, Bibury, Gloucestershire*, photograph, *c*. 1950 (Courtesy Country Life Publications). The Cotswolds very rapidly took over from the Weald as the model for vernacular architecture.

should see its zenith of popularity at this time (see Figure 83) is not surprising. Apart from views in the Wye valley, only Bristol had been shown any consistent favour before the late nineteenth century, both around the gorge and in the terraces of Clifton. The Bristol school of artists had done much to make the city well known in artistic circles, and Tewkesbury and Gloucester had provided Picturesque townscape, but it was through the late discovery of the Cotswolds that the county found most of the new icons of the twentieth century – vernacular cottages, villages, farmsteads, patterned fields – all within its boundaries. As these have become slightly *passé* the county has declined, although there is some recent interest in the Forest of Dean, never before much used.

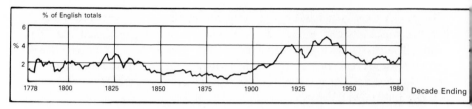

Figure 84 Graph for Gloucestershire (Source: RA catalogues). Early views were usually of Bristol or the Wye. The inter-war vogue was almost entirely based in the Costwolds, which shared in downland favour.

Sussex

Sussex, however, was the county which most closely matched all the requirements of the new fashions, enabling it to rank 3rd in total number of pictures and 6th by area (Appendix 3). Its resorts, such as Brighton, had been depicted since the eighteenth century, though Hastings has shown greater flexibility in providing material for all coastal tastes. There were major country houses to be depicted, not least Turner's Petworth. The Arun had been a model of the pastoral river since at least 1850, but the village was Sussex's greatest asset. Coastal boating scenes flourished at Rye, Shoreham, Pevensey, Itchenor and Bosham. Rottingdean was a well-favoured spot as well as the better-known resorts – except for Worthing, and especially Bognor, which never seem to have attracted aesthetic interest. The great change of attitude began well after W.W. Fenn, the most prescient of the many writers of sketching ground articles, wrote in 1883:

> The downs are not, and never have been held in the estimation they deserve . . . it is the fashion to say of the South Downs that they are 'not paintable' and to stigmatise them as a treeless waste bordered by a shipless sea . . . they have gentleness, softness and other endearing attributes.[31]

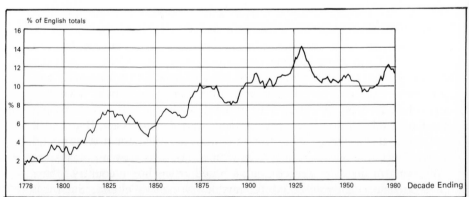

Figure 85 Graph for Sussex (Source: RA catalogues). The most favoured county in the twentieth century, with the South Downs and villages being added to the established coastal scenes, and the little harbours such as Rye.

The South Downs provided sweeping curves, and hill forts; the Vale of Sussex was scattered with dozens of villages which possessed the tile-hung, thatched, cottages surrounding the cricket on the green which became the stereotypes of the English village, and from whence, together with Surrey and Kent, the idea of vernacular architecture's pleasures spread throughout the country.

The attitude to rural life became one of faintly patronizing bucolic nostalgia. The harshness of Hardy's knowledge of the rural life was replaced by the sanitized and flowery view of Eden Philpotts.[32] Cornfields, harvesting, ploughing, haymaking, cattle, orchards and rutty lanes had become sufficiently remote from the daily life of the artist, and his patron, to be seen without people and as a bucolic dream. This was the time to be drinking cider under a haycart with Rosie. East Anglia at last came into its own. The region which had produced Gainsborough, Constable, Cotman and Crome at last began to be discovered by the metropolitan artists. Constable was recognized as providing the right imagery a century before it was needed,[33] and was discussed for the first time in the *Art Journal* in 1903.[34] John Nash painted the same country, from his base at Wormingford, and as the map (Figure 71) indicates he was far from alone. Many of these views made their debt to Constable clear, and we see the beginnings of appreciation for what is now the only Area of Outstanding Natural Beauty to bear the name of an artist.

The way in which certain places are seen because of their association with the great will be discussed in Chapter 9. Foreign places were often visited because of their association with great painters, but in this country the writer's landscape was always more popular – even with painters.

The Village

At last the English cottage, village and farmstead became attractive features of the landscape. Throughout the country, but especially in the Cotswolds, the south east, East Anglia and Essex, the village 'bit', the cottage and the farm became standard scenes. The village scene was typically of a few cottages, almost always irregularly arranged, with glimpses of the church and bridge and occasionally the pub. Several of the classic models have already been mentioned – Bibury and Burford in the Cotswolds, Amberley, Burpham and Steyning in Sussex, Betchworth in Surrey, Bardfield in Essex, Appletreewick and Burnsall in Wharfedale. Of course building materials varied with location, but by no means any village would do. Often metropolitan based artists had a country retreat to which their friends would be invited for the weekend. Such was Carrington's Tidmarsh near Pangbourne, or Applehayes, near Clayhidon in Devon, where Robert Bevan met his friends including Charles Ginner and Spencer Gore.[35]

The choice of villages was by no means random. In Devon three distinct types emerged. One was the fishing village, such as Appledore, Beer or Dittisham, where the boats usually formed an obvious focus. The other villages were either the granite-walled, thatch-roofed villages on or around Dartmoor, with Widecombe, Buckland-in-the-Moor, and Lustleigh as the chief exemplars, or those built of cob with thatched roofs, mainly in east Devon, with Otterton, Newton St Cyres and Broadhembury being particular favourites. Soft cob and hard granite seem at first to have little in common, but they both produce a lumpy and rounded form which seems to be the preference. Certainly the villages of the South Hams or North Devon, generally built of slaty stone with very hard outlines and sharp corners, were nothing like as popular. At Studland, 'The main charm of these little buildings is that they fit absolutely into their peaceful and entirely natural surroundings.' The same writer continues that 'from the new houses the wise man will naturally turn his eyes.'[36] Uniformity, such as found in the many estate villages, was not highly regarded. As late as 1877 Hine had complained that in Devon, 'As a rule [our towns and villages] are extremely unpicturesque and are far less attractive in this respect than those of Warwickshire, Berkshire, Cheshire or Somerset.'[37] Less than sixty years later Mais could write, 'In nearly all Devon villages the prevailing colour of cottages is a spotless white which gives them an air of gaiety.'[38]

The farm

The farmstead was a more obvious genre, often viewed to show as much of the buildings as possible. Although the odd tractor might be allowed, the yard should be untidy and varied, preferably of a mixed or animal-rearing farm. Efficiency was not attractive. They were often seen in winter, with bare elms forming a background, especially when depicted by the Essex group of artists such as John Aldridge and Edward Bawden, or by Hilder in Kent. Bateman's views of Cotswolds farms were very similar, and Piper's views at Betchworth in the 1920s[39] clearly come in the same category. Trees were often depicted bare of leaves, and it was not till after the fields had been newly ploughed that Bawden thought, 'the water-colour season in central Essex is drawing to a close.'[40]

The cottage

The cottage has a much longer history as a genre. During the early nineteenth century they were frequently called hovels, but were not uncommonly depicted, though care must be taken to distinguish between the *cottage ornée* and the labourer's home. Prout's views of tumbledown, picturesque shacks, apart from the high quality of the soft ground

Figure 86 Tristram Hillier, *Beach with an Old Breakwater*, oil, 51 × 76 cm (Courtesy Royal Albert Memorial Museum, Exeter). Some parts of the coast offered geometric possibilities which more advanced artists appreciated long before they became the norm.

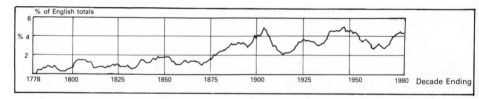

Figure 87   Graph for Suffolk (Source: RA catalogues). Despite Constable, Suffolk did not become the quintessential rural county until this century. Many views depict his landscapes, however, and also the small coastal towns.

etchings, were not untypical, unroofed yet apparently housing a large family of suspiciously well-fed and rubicund children. For the rest of the century the cottage occurred occasionally, though usually as background rather than main subject. Those of Helen Allingham at the turn of the century are much prettier (Figure 49). Interest focused almost equally on the riotous garden, which formed such an inspiration for Gertrude Jekyll and other garden designers at the time, the cottage itself, warm, neat and be-rosed, and the inhabitants, almost invariably young, female and winsome. The new purchasers of art were not landlords to the rural poor, indeed they were often *nouveaux riches* demonstrating their nostalgia for the homes they would like to have come from. Today Lowry performs the same role for the new patrons as Allingham did for hers. It was a powerful image – so powerful and long-lasting that today large numbers of splendidly decrepit cottages, sometimes whole villages, are being remade by their new wealthy owners in the image which Allingham created.

Suffolk

The demand for scenes of farms, villages and cottages inevitably led to the favour in which Suffolk was held. Ranking 20th by area (Appendix 3), the county had previously been popular, except with a few idiosyncratic characters such as Gainsborough and Constable, only for its country houses. Then came the boom at the end of the century in marsh scenes and the villages along the coast, Walberswick and Blythburgh being the most important. They represent the peak just after 1900. These coastal sites were not abandoned, but after 1920 the scatter of interest throughout the county, and especially in West Suffolk near Bury St Edmunds, has been largely the result of farm and village scenes.

Cambridgeshire and Huntingdonshire

Huntingdonshire has the distinction of having fewer pictures than any other county, per square mile (Appendix 3), and only one centre and vogue of interest. Ten of the total of twenty-nine pictures were exhibited

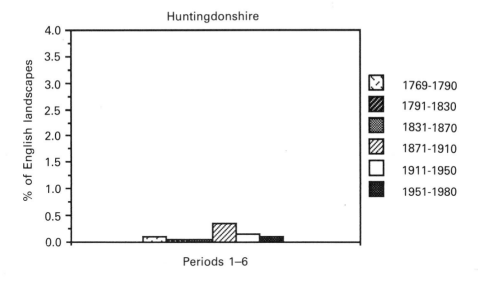

Figure 88 Histogram for Huntingdonshire (Source: RA catalogues). A most unfavoured county, with only the River Ouse being at all commonly depicted.

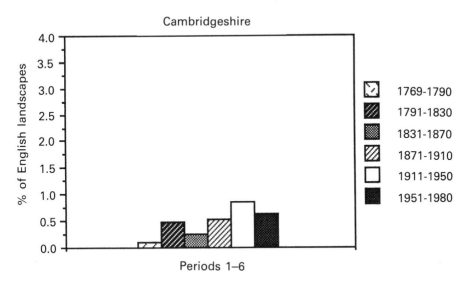

Figure 89 Histogram for Cambridgeshire (Source: RA catalogues). Ely cathedral and the Cambridge colleges have been important, and the Fens became so late in the nineteenth century.

between 1900 and 1924, and most of them represented the Great Ouse near Houghton – a rather late vogue for a pastoral river.

That Cambridgeshire has fared better, with 178 pictures exhibited and ranking 32nd by area (Appendix 3), is mainly due to the presence of the Cambridge colleges, popular in the twentieth century, and Ely cathedral, one of the most favoured, during the early nineteenth. To them have been added several views in the Fenland, mainly dreary landscapes of the last quarter of the nineteenth century.

Industry

At last industry began to recover, or in some cases acquire, its attractiveness. Boats had been in vogue for many years, but steam had lessened the attraction of ships. Now ships and ports began to be rediscovered. William Wyllie was a major figure, but so were many of the war artists, such as Nevinson working in Southampton, and Wadsworth at Plymouth and Liverpool, interested in the geometric possibilities of shipping and cranes. Liverpool, Glasgow and London Docks were particularly favoured. This geometric interest was important in several types of industrial scenery, and was more formal than vernacular in character, though well under way by the 1930s. That period of industrial stagnation and depression awoke artists not only to the plight but also the artistic possibilities of the North. J.B. Priestley's famous *English Journey* was followed by the photographers Bill Brandt and Humphrey Spender, and the setting up of Mass Observation in Bolton. Paul Nash depicted the northern canals in murals, again usually as patterns of colour. This new way of looking at industry clearly had its roots in the United States.[41] There artists such as Charles Sheeler depicted some industries, grain silos being a favourite, in a very clean way, applying great washes of pure colour, often with the black grid of lines from cranes or other large machines. However, most of the favoured industries in Britain, unlike America, were obsolescent and some derelict. If there were very distinctive visual forms attached, so much the better. Thus the pithead winding gear of mines, notably in the unique landscape of the South Wales valleys, was popular, as were the bottle kilns of the Stoke potteries, where Arnold Bennett's work may also have had associational importance. The shipyards, ports and canals were also long-established industries in decline. The new industries growing up, along the Great West Road for example, were not seen at the Academy.

London

London itself did return to favour, however, although the preferences had changed markedly from its previous vogue before 1850. There were

Figure 90   M. Drummond, *The Park Bench*, oil, 61 × 41 cm (Courtesy Royal Albert Memorial Museum, Exeter). The Camden Town Group were among many who began to depict suburban scenes, usually with a genre element, in the early twentieth century. The more sedate inner London suburbs were most favoured, never those under construction.

still plenty of pictures of Hampstead but Chelsea was clearly more important. What is more the Hampstead pictures were by now quite likely to be similar to those in many of the Victorian/Edwardian suburbs, such as St John's Wood. Here members of the Camden Town Group and Spencer were only the first to depict quite ordinary houses and their gardens. The houses were usually terraced villas with bay windows and several storeys, not the simple terrace of the Public Health Act housing, nor the suburban semi-detached houses which were being built at such great speed throughout London, and indeed everywhere else. Nevertheless the novelty of such work was very marked, often with considerable interest in the small front gardens, usually using an Impressionist technique. Chelsea was the centre of an artistic quarter, with many views including the Thames, which was popular from Hampton to Woolwich.[42]

A few larger towns were significant other than those popular for industrial reasons, or for individual buildings – such as Lincoln and Durham cathedrals. Among these were Oxford and Cambridge, where there were many pictures of the colleges, much more frequent than before. The artists of this period may have become part of intellectual society to an extent that they had not previously achieved. This seems to be in tune with a period when artistic theory and history was very much at the centre of scholarly thought, and the quite numerous pictures of Bloomsbury may not be unconnected.

Scotland

North of the Border there is more difficulty in understanding the output. Certainly Edinburgh had become the most important centre, sharing in the revival of urban scenes, and Glasgow was also often seen, though usually along the Clyde and with ships. The Galloway region attracted a few artists but in the Highlands there was a distinct dispersal, probably a result of motor travel. The great centres such as Arran and Glencoe were now replaced with a scatter of depictions of the western highlands. There were very few of the Grampians or Buchan. North of the Great Glen a few artists submitted scenes of desolation and remoteness but the Highland fad was certainly over.

Ireland

Ireland was more favoured than previously. The fashion for Irish scenes had developed with distinct regions being favoured at various times – except for Dublin which produced a few pictures throughout. Wicklow, with a concentration on the Dargle, was followed in the mid-nineteenth century by Kerry, where Killarney was the focal point. One article in 1850 was written 'to induce many persons to visit them [Killarney Lakes] who have been accustomed to make annual tours to the Continent'.[43] The suggested tour was the upper lake, Torc and Muckross Abbey, Mongerton, Dunloe, the Three Lakes, Weir Bridge and Innisfallen. The Dublin Exhibition in 1864 may have been instrumental in attracting more visitors to the country, not only to Kerry but to the 'wilds of Connemara' and the *terra incognita* of Donegal'.[44] Most articles and pictures stressed both the romantic sunsets and the picturesque and faintly amusing rites of the peasantry.[45] Later County Donegal and Connemara came to prominence, as they did with many Irish artists such as Yeats as a Celtic fringe consciousness developed. English artistic visits fell off after the troubles of the 1920s and there were more pictures of Northern Ireland, notably along the Antrim coast, especially Cushendun and Cushendall, although the Giants' Causeway had long been a 'lion'. Recently the depiction of Ireland has decreased, as much in the south as the north, but the outline given here is that of English artists. As with Scotland there can be no assumption that Irish views of Irish landscape are similar.

8

The Formal Period 1950–1980

For the avant-garde a formal attitude to landscape had started long ago, probably from 1904, when Cubism was developed by Picasso and Braque in Paris, but the middle ground of artists, to which most of the exhibitors at the Academy belonged, were almost fifty years in adopting it. A formal, geometric way of perceiving landscape has much in common with abstract art, which throughout the inter-war period, and for some years after the Second World War, was the position maintained by the more progressive artists. Indeed the use of abstraction was effectively the definition of progressiveness. The argument between realism and abstraction frequently became heated, as happened in St Ives with the clash between the two societies.[1] Only after the second war did abstraction invade the large central area of artistic endeavour at the professional level. Landscape was not regarded by many artists as suitable subject matter for this cerebral new activity but people like Robert Bevan and the Camden Town Group, though much earlier, found themselves unable to avoid landscape.[2] For the purposes of this kind of study, of course, the degree of verisimilitude between depiction and reality is quite unimportant. If a locatable place or landscape subject was the inspiration for a picture the fact that it might be quite unrecognizable is beside the point.

Aesthetic theory

In many ways, Modernism was not merely abstraction but a return to an accepted canon of aesthetics. It was thus closer in its tone of voice to the Classical rather than the Romantic. The language deployed had a cold and calculated air, with pure form a prominent concept. That many

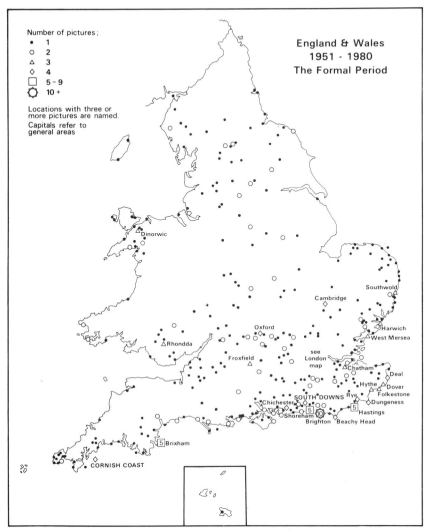

Figure 91 Map of landscapes depicted in Formal Period, 1951–80, England and Wales (Source: RA catalogues).

should rediscover an interest in the structured and ordered world of Classicism is not surprising and this is seen in the revisiting of many Classical sites, in Bath, at Stourhead and in London. The fascination for the geometry of nature, and interest in painterly structure, developed with and after Cezanne, whose great hero was Poussin. The preference for form over content resulted in the reduction of many scenes, landscape or otherwise, to their most simple components. In the study of art, whether historical or theoretical, this led to the subject matter of the work being largely ignored. Effectively all pictures were regarded as

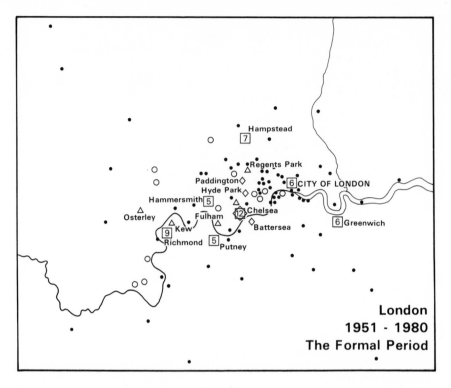

Figure 92 Map of landscapes depicted in Formal Period, 1951–80, London area (Source: RA catalogues).

being a pleasing, or otherwise, arrangement of shapes, lines, textures, and colours on a flat surface. The importance of the meaning of the objects or people depicted was largely lost. In some cases a *reductio ad absurdum* led to blank sheets or canvases. Inevitably this led to a preference for the simplest landscape forms.

Photographic work, which had difficulty in being completely abstract, was also infected by the Modernist principle. This demanded the special attributes of the photographic medium being exploited, and a set of photographic principles developed in the United States which often took its inspiration from landscape but imposed on it the clarity and form which derived from the peculiar qualities of the medium itself – including the preference for the banal and ordinary. These were made most obvious by the f64 Group and the subject was often posed as much to display the medium as the qualities of the landscape. The landscape work of Edward Weston and Paul Strand was most influential on British photographers such as Bill Brandt. and resulted in a preference for surface texture and formal qualities of light and shade.[3] At this period photography was more influential in its approach to landscape than any

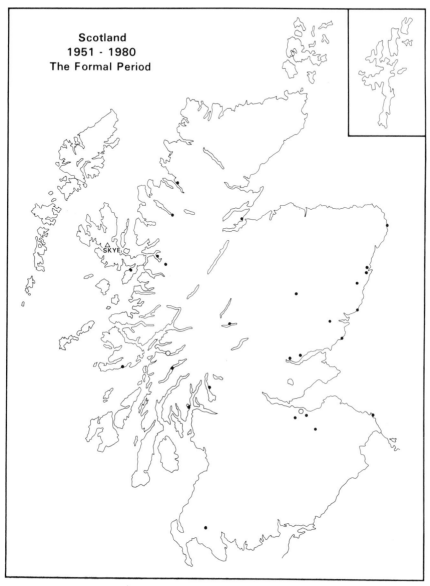

Figure 93 Map of landscapes depicted in Formal Period, 1951–80, Scotland (Source: RA catalogues).

other medium, 'It is nearly always the professional photographer, whatever his preoccupation, who reveals landscape.'[4] The use of the camera by the tourist then changed the way visitors saw places.[5]

Mediating influences

If photography provided some of the new 'ways of seeing', film and later television also became a major source of imagery. In the 1930s, through the series of books depicting Britain, and the beginning of journals such as the *National Geographic* and *The Geographical Magazine*, people had become much more aware of the appearance of the world, usually a static and monochrome world. The change since then has been of enormous dimensions so that the sheer number of images of landscapes seen by people, usually in movement and in colour, is out of all proportion with previous generations. Much of this influence has derived from the United States, in both television and film. John Gold has demonstrated the way in which films of imaginary futuristic townscapes were instrumental in bringing those townscapes into being.[6] There is little doubt that more and more places were being altered or maintained to fit a preconceived picture of how they should look.

Artists abroad

Abroad, artists dispersed the existing stereotype of the Mediterranean coastal village scene throughout the whole Mediterranean basin, and outside it to the Algarve, and to the islands, most importantly the Balearics in the 1950s and, after they had been so successful as to attract a major holiday industry there, to the Greek islands, finding ever more remote places as the tourists caught them up. The obvious way in which this pattern developed, with hoteliers following the paintbrush, has not yet led to tourist boards deliberately promoting art exhibitions to 'seed' the vogue for their area of responsibility. Overseas the major preference for formal scenes is not as obvious, though the Mediterranean fishing villages often became studies in the juxtaposition of bright colour fields.

The English interest in the rural vernacular spread to the continent, and especially to rural France, with the archetypes being found in the Dordogne and Vaucluse, and to rural Tuscany. After the war the popularity previously accorded to Italy returned very quickly. By 1950 Italy was again a major destination. Germany had not recovered in popularity since the First World War and did not begin to figure again at the Academy until the 1960s; and it was a further decade before pictures of Japan, quite highly regarded in the 1930s, began to return.

Many more views of the United States and Canada began to be seen, including the stereotypes of American landscape now so familiar.[7] In general, however, the visits of the artists abroad do not seem to have led to such obvious legitimating of British landscapes as previously occurred. Indeed sometimes the reverse seems to be true.

Travel

Car-ownership expanded dramatically so that all parts of the UK mainland were accessible with great ease. In addition air travel has become a normal method of reaching more remote areas and, in particular, islands, almost all of which are much more accessible. The impact in the Mediterranean has already been noted but at home, too, this led to the opening up of all the offshore islands. Oddly the final result of all this accessibility has been, as hinted in the previous chapter and confirmed in the present period, to find remoteness near at home. Certainly many more artists were now enabled to live permanently in the country all year round, and the consequence has been a much more rounded view of the country in all weather conditions and times of the year. At last the snowy winter scene, beloved by the Dutch back in the sixteenth century, has become part of the English vision of their world.

Aerial views

The view of the landscape from the air may have influenced some American Abstract Expressionists, as hinted by those who favour the notion of the Abstract Sublime.[8] There has been little obvious impact on the view of Britain, at least in terms of figurative aerial views. Peter Lanyon's fascination for gliding was an obvious exception. However, aerial photography has become a commonplace with oblique aerial views of the property adorning many house walls. This is obviously a modern version of the Landscape Portraiture of the eighteenth century, but has not, in general, been accorded similar artistic status.

The replacement of the black-and-white photographic books of British landscape with new colour aerial photographs in a new generation of books such as *Britain from the Air*[9] may have come too late to have greatly influenced the choice of landscapes as recorded in this book up to 1980. That it is likely to do so in the future can be seen by analysing the types of scenery favoured in these books. Higson suggests that the masterful aerial shot has important meaning in the context of film and television, and this may well transfer to the other arts.[10] Such aerial views inevitably see pattern and geometry, as much in the towns as in the countryside, and reflect a quite different view of Britain from that portrayed by John Dixon-Scott and others in the Odham's books of the 1930s.[11]

Tourism and advertising

Stereotyping of landscapes has been greatly encouraged by the development of the holiday industry, with its inevitable brochures, and to the

Figure 94   Hamford Water, Essex, from *The Aerofilms Book of Britain from the Air*
(Courtesy Hunting Aerofilms). The new fashion for aerial photographic books, in colour, is
creating new landscape preferences, based usually on pattern.

increase of advertising generally which uses landscape, British and
foreign, to create an ambience seen as appropriate to the product. The
influence of such advertisements as Summer County, Marlborough
County, Ginsters Cornish Pasties, John Smith's Bitter, Timotei shampoo
or Bounty bars on tropical beaches is incalculable, but undoubtedly very
important in deciding which features of a place are meaningful.[12] There
can be little doubt, for example, that the meaning of a palm tree has
changed dramatically from 1864 when it was a religious symbol of the east
and Judaea.[13] Generally advertising tends to reinforce existing myths
(prejudged impressions about meaning which may sometimes be true).
The view of Yorkshire produced by a combination of beer advertisements,
James Herriot and *Last of the Summer Wine* could scarcely be more
different from the Yorkshire of mid-nineteenth-century pictures of Bolton
Woods and Whitby harbour.

Judith Williamson's analysis of the referent system of nature, as a selling point in advertising, has been shown to be strongly developing since 1930.[14] This may be one cause of a totally different way of looking at landscape rapidly developing at present. As Modernism has run its course, so since 1980, which is the last year of our analysis of Royal Academy titles, a new ecological view of landscape seems to be gaining ground, as discussed in Chapter 9. The rapid decline in London's popularity in the 1960s may have heralded this. It is likely that the Formalist view of landscape described in this chapter has died, interestingly maintaining the approximately 30/40-year cycle which the period dates in this book would appear to suggest, though several of the breakpoints in the periodicity have been evolutions rather than revolutions.

Residence

Artists still tended to live in one place and depict it regularly. One obvious example is the work of Kyffin Williams in North Wales, but there are many others such as Sheila Fell at Aspatria and R.O. Dunlop at Rye, as well as the well-known group at Great Bardfield in Essex. Luckily at the Academy such artists do not seriously distort the general pattern as there are many artists who only submit occasional work.

Industry

The landscape of industry and of associated towns has at last become of real significance, although a glance at the maps (Figures 91–3) will demonstrate that industry still ranks a poor third after coastal and rural views. In general industrial landscapes have never been of front-rank importance, unless we include a group of occupations, such as agriculture, fishing and milling, which have traditionally been accepted as attractive but are not usually thought to be industrial processes. Of course, the failure to think of these as proper industries may be a result of their attraction. In the Classical period there were pictures of industry, though their quantitative importance has been exaggerated, and if one were to restrict the term only to factory and mining enterprises, would be quite insignificant. Such attraction almost disappeared in the Picturesque, except for mills and limekilns, and even the Romantic period only showed some interest in railways and that for a short time. Klingender's statement, that

> The iron industry had not yet lost its picturesque character. Still surrounded by romantic scenery, the great ironworks, with their smouldering lime kilns and coke ovens, blazing furnaces and noisy forges, had a special attraction for eighteenth century admirers of the sublime[15]

Figure 95   Will. F. Taylor, *Colne, Lancashire*, photography, *c.* 1939, from *Our Nation's Heritage*, edited by J.B. Priestley, London, Dent, 1939 (Courtesy J.M. Dent & Sons). Just as the hard realistic views of fishermen in the 1880s became the romantic cliché of the inter-war period, so photographs of the industrial areas, intended, as this was, to convey a social message, have become the romantic clichés of the present.

must not be taken as a suggestion that such pictures abounded.

The late nineteenth century's interest in the Heroic worker was normally limited to the primary trades – farm workers, fishermen and a few miners. Where such work did occur the interest was almost entirely directed at the workers themselves, and not on the built forms of the industrial landscape.

The revival of industrial interest may have come from American work, and concentrated on scenes with outstanding forms and unusual shapes – cranes, kilns, scaffolding and mine winding gear.[16] Certain other industrial features became popular. In Cornwall the disused engine-houses, especially the spectacular view at Botallack, became so attractive that they now form a logo for the county. Like so many favoured industrial sites they are disused. Ever since the historicist attitude first became obvious about 1850 industries have had to await the patina of age before becoming aesthetically pleasing. If not actually derelict, the industry must be seen as an interesting survival. Lancashire mills, now quite well favoured, were made so largely by L.S. Lowry, and they were in decline even then. The Welsh mines have become attractive since the war, so much so that the Rhondda appears in Figure 91 as a site of significance, and the same could be said of the bottle kilns of Stoke on Trent. Very recently there have been several pictures of gasworks but this interest post-dates the arrival of natural gas which has made them redundant. One exception to the rule is that of waste heaps, most dramatically the white hills and pits with green pools of the kaolin pits near St Austell in Cornwall. Others include the slate quarries of North Wales, as at Dinorwic.[17]

By 1928 Vaughan Cornish was expressing the opinion which has been the norm in England since 1850 in saying, 'The forges of the Black Country impart volcanic splendour to the night, but modern manufacture contributes little by day to the Scenery whose natural beauty it impairs.'[18] In this sense, little has changed. Few industrial forms of the present attract artists. Unlike the railways in their day, motorways and airports have been ignored. A few forms, such as Fylingdales early-warning station, or Goonhilly, do seem to find their way into Academy exhibitions, perhaps because, as W.G. Hoskins remarked of the latter, the forms do not relate to the earth.[19] The industrial north has become a visual stereotype, created partly by Priestley's *English Journey*, and reinforced by the photographs of Brandt and Spender. These highly Romantic scenes have now found their way into advertising.

Docks were attractive from the time of the First World War until the container revolution and the coming of the Link Span Terminal and Roll-on Roll-off ferries. Despite the increasing preference for industrial landscape, a result largely of the desire for easily assimilated forms, this has remained firmly historicist. Post-war industry has been almost universally ignored; there are virtually no nuclear power stations, trading estates or hi-tech buildings on the walls of the Academy except in the architects' room. Despite the listing of some Art Deco factories on the Great West Road, these have not yet found their way into popular preference. The general picture is clear. If artists start to depict certain industrial forms, that form of industry is doomed.

Lancashire

Lancashire has been viewed more favourably since 1930 than before. However, only 405 pictures relating to the county have been exhibited since 1769, so the county ranks only 33rd by area, and bottom if ranked by the output per 1,000 population (Appendix 3). Of these 405, about one-third represented Furness which district has here been included as part of Cumbria. The docks at Liverpool have provided a steady trickle of pictures throughout the two centuries, and Manchester too has been occasionally depicted for its industrial scenes. Towards the end of the nineteenth century there were some fell views from Rossendale and Ribblesdale, but the contention that between Preston and Blackburn there 'lies a tract of country which possesses all the charms of our English landscape' was not widely accepted.[20]

Figure 96   P. Nash, *The Sluice Gate*, 1920, lithograph, 36 × 41 cm (Courtesy Royal Albert Memorial Museum, Exeter). The formal opportunities presented by industrial landscapes were exploited by major artists long before they became the commonplace of art.

The more recent increase in favour has been largely in pictures of industrial towns, with Lowry's among them. Salford, St Helens, Bolton and Wigan have joined Liverpool and Manchester, usually with views of striking industrial scenes. There is some evidence of very recent interest along the coast, especially by photographers, but this post-dates the Academy evidence.

The coast

The coast has remained by far the most important class of landscape scene. The concentration of pictures all along the coast from the Wash to Cornwall is the most obvious feature of the map (Figure 91). Two types of coast are added to the portfolio of attractive varieties. One of these is the long sweeping sandy bay, often in semi-abstract style. These have been noted in the inter-war period, but now became much more popular with their formal quality of the central line of shore, with clean sea and cliffs clearly stressed. The other type is the remote line of cliffs, often jagged and frequently seen from above. The coast between Hartland and Bude, often shown in a 'sublime' state with the sea crashing against the

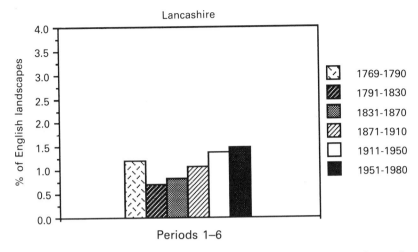

Lancashire

Figure 97 Histogram for Lancashire (Source: RA catalogues). Never a much-favoured county, apart from Furness, the industrial and port views of the twentieth century have exploited the formal elements of the landscape.

black cliffs, has become much frequented by local artists.

Modern photographers have become very keen on views of people at the seaside, usually the working class about their traditional holiday. Paul Theroux's interest in the 'shallies' is typical of this preference, showing an amused, detached, quizzical and rather patronizing, if slightly envious, look at seaside behaviour. In fact, one characteristic of many pictures is that beaches are inhabited.[21]

At the other extreme are the pictures of remote coastal areas, including for example Cape Wrath, Anglesey and the Lleyn peninsula, while the boat yard, mudflat and old sail loft retained most of the popularity they had enjoyed throughout the century, though the treatment became more formal. The favour in which both Dungeness and Beachy Head have been held is easy to explain. The one is flat, remote, and can be rendered very simply, as Nash depicted Dymchurch previously. Beachy Head, as the greatest of the chalk cliffs, with the Downs just behind, equally gives a flavour of simple forces opposing each other.

The third type, the harbour scene, remains, partly as a survival from the 1930s, partly as an Anglicized version of the Mediterranean coastal view, and perhaps also because of the advantage of the shapes of boats and shore. During this period many of the fishing villages became more important for their yachts and pleasure craft. Places such as Cowes and Burnham on Crouch had not previously been much favoured, but any prejudice against mere pleasure craft had by now been dissipated. The Heroic figures which had first attracted were certainly not now a requirement; possibly they no longer existed. The owners of the yachts were also, no doubt, potential purchasers of art, so perhaps these pictures resemble those of Bath in the eighteenth century – artists clustering round the watering holes of the potential customer. Certainly the small former port of Topsham, near Exeter, is one of the major subjects of local artists, though scarcely depicted before 1930, and is also a district in which many artists and patrons live.

Such small towns, once fishing ports, form the staple base of most coastal work. While Rye itself has become overworked, similar sites have been found on every coast. Even the shores of the Solway Firth and Morecambe Bay, long unpopular, are now commonplace, notably at Bawdsey, with Oliver Hall's work.

Lincolnshire

Such coastal views have been largely responsible for Lincolnshire having something else to offer other than the cathedral, which accounts for about one-quarter of the 238 views exhibited. For its size the county is most unpopular, ranking 43rd (Appendix 3). Boston occasionally adorned the Academy walls as Picturesque townscape, usually with the church as part of the scene, and Crowland Abbey had also once been a site, as had several country houses, notably Brocklesby. Since about 1920 such views have been joined by views of Grimsby and other coastal locations, often mainly mudflats, though even Skegness has been occasionally seen. The

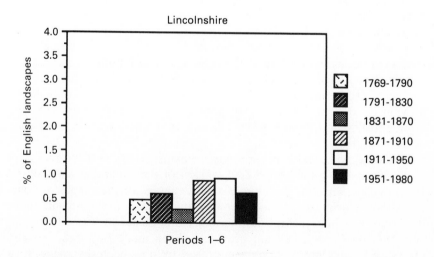

Figure 98 Histogram for Lincolnshire (Source: RA catalogues). Apart from its cathedral, only the mudflats of the coast have regularly been used artistically.

villages and farms of the county do not seem to have shared in the revival of interest in such features elsewhere

London

Towns have seen a revival. London, in particular, rose to a peak of importance such that in the 1960s it accounted for 20 per cent of the total landscapes of England (Figure 99) and one could add in another 4 per cent for Middlesex (Figure 100). During the 1970s, however, London saw a spectacular collapse of its popularity, reduced to 12 per cent by 1980. Although all the traditionally important riverside views, in Richmond, Putney, Chelsea and Greenwich remained much painted during the boom, there is plenty of evidence of the main centre of interest moving into the West End. Here there were many pictures of the Classical squares and terraces, and of the public parks, usually depicted with many people, reminiscent of the beach scenes but also of the pattern of London pictures in the eighteenth century. There are many cases in this Formal Period of the return to the scenes beloved by Classical artists, which may show the relationship between Modernism and Classicism.

The suburban views of the Vernacular Period also survived and developed into areas such as Camden and Paddington, but never into the suburban estates of the 1930s further out into Middlesex. Nor are there pictures of the small Victorian and later terraces consequent on the Public Health Acts. Nor again do we find artists operating in the Abercrombie New Towns, however important architects and planners may have found them. Roofscapes were one of the shortest lived of genres, being a

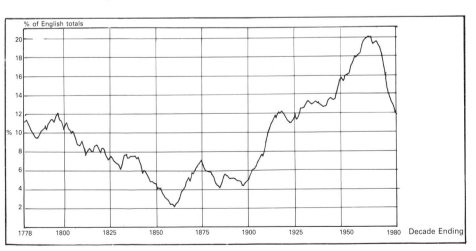

Figure 99 Graph for central London (Source: RA catalogues). The marked avoidance of London in the mid-nineteenth century has been followed by its dominance during much of the twentieth, with much less emphasis on 'lions' than had been the case. The rapid decline in the 1970s may well be a result of environmentalist attitudes.

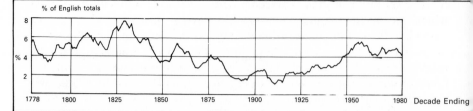

Figure 100   Graph for Middlesex (Source: RA catalogues). From being the most convenient piece of countryside for metropolitan artists, Middlesex suffered with industrialization and suburbanization. Only as those landscapes have become more acceptable has it begun to recover.

favoured view of the 1950s but scarcely seen before or since, though the evidence of titles may not be relied upon with certainty in this case.[22]

A survey of 309 pictures exhibited between 1950 and 1980 can be broken down as follows:

Individual buildings	32,	of which St Paul's Cathedral 10, and Hampton Court 4.
Parks	26,	of which Hyde Park 9, Regent's Park and Holland Park each 4.
The river	41,	of which the docks 7, Tower Bridge 6.
Districts	120,	of which Chelsea 22, Hampstead and Highgate 13, Putney and Hammersmith each 9, Kensington 7, Chiswick 6, Camden, Strand-on-the-Green, Paddington, St John's Wood, Twickenham, Fulham, Brixton and Peckham each 4.
Streets	40,	of which 20 are West End.

Such a crude breakdown can only raise questions, but a detailed study of London's art would be able to date preferences with much more detail.

Middlesex

Although Middlesex had its most popular period in the 1820s it is discussed here, alongside London, the expansion of which has done so much to depress Middlesex's attractiveness in the eyes of painters. Most of the considerable favour it once enjoyed was of four types – its major buildings, such as Osterley or Hampton, the small villages which were to become suburbs, the views of Hampstead Heath, a gentrified area since 1800, and views along the Thames. In the 1880s it was thought 'not a beautiful county . . . its unbuilt-upon acres are cultivated to every hedge and headland. . . . It needs these atmospheric effects [evening mist] to give the magic touch which differentiates the barren and desolate from the suggestively pictorial.' The same writer, however, hints at the process which has been already discussed, in saying that the 'canal is just emerging from the matter-of-fact stage of its existence'.[23] Suburban industrial Middlesex as a whole has, since 1945, emerged from the matter-of-fact stage and become acceptable pictorial material, with the inner suburbs, bits of canal or railway line, and older and more decrepit industrial areas in the fore.

The northern towns, many of which occur on the map (Figure 91) for the first time, were, unlike much of London, seen for their back streets. Though no single town has become the stereotype, several were important, such as Leeds, Huddersfield, Halifax and Ilkley. Rain on a stone flag pavement alongside a terrace row has become a cliché especially of the photographers. Here the Heroic worker has lived again, usually the mill workers of Yorkshire, or the steelmakers and shipbuilders of the north east, or miners anywhere the pits are threatened with closure. Landscape and genre become hopelessly confused. Inglis has asserted that townscape is always politically knowing, and the political implications of these pictures are all too clear. The romanticizing of the industrial past, seen not only in art but in the new heritage museums of the north, is remarkably akin to the promotion of the fisherman a century ago.[24]

The great interest throughout the country, noted in the previous chapter, in depicting the bomb damage during the war is in marked contrast to the almost complete ignoring of the reconstruction which followed it. Both the rebuilding itself and the finished products have been studiously avoided by artists.

Rural scenery

In the countryside no new landscapes were discovered, but some rather neglected ones became much more significant. If trees had been essential to the Romantic painter, perhaps their absence is the most notable feature of the Modernist. The chalk downs were ideally suited to be shown in an almost linear form. Rarely seen as soft and bosomy, they were now hard, flowing outlines capped by symbolic forts or clumps. West Penwith was also ideal – a virtually treeless peninsula where the forces of nature and the structure of the land were at their most obvious. Not that the natural forces were to be seen through cloud or mist – the modern sky is usually clear and mist is clearly out of fashion. All such places, where the bones of the land are near the surface, were now in favour.[25]

Some areas could also offer a network of hedges or stone walls which could add a surface pattern of great interest. This was certainly true of

Figure 101 R. Slater, *On Bodmin Moor*, watercolour, 18 × 34 cm, 1980s (Courtesy Royal Albert Memorial Museum, Exeter). Bodmin Moor is smaller and lower than Dartmoor, and further from London. Consequently such pictures as this are comparatively rare.

Penwith and of the Cotswolds, but the Peak District and Yorkshire Dales were the archetypes of this patterned view. No doubt such scenes were favoured by the growth of the rambling movement in the 1930s, the subsequent designation of both Peak and Dales as National Parks, and their continued popularity on television programmes and advertising. The hedge patterns might be less popular than stone walls but throughout lowland England the view across the fields from the downs was much favoured. The archetype is to look down on a wide panorama, often across a valley, with the subject being the pattern of walls or hedges on the far side. The village or farmstead at the bottom often forms a refuge.

The farmyard scene had begun to be popular before the war, and its popularity was much enhanced by the work of the Great Bardfield group in the 1950s and by Rowland Hilder's work, largely in Kent. This genre has spread throughout the country during recent decades, with Suffolk becoming the epitome of the English farming scene. The farms depicted have changed somewhat, in order to keep just behind modern farming practice. There is nothing new in this. A century ago a critic could write, 'so many pictures . . . seem to proceed upon the assumption that steam-plough and reaping machine do not exist, that the landscape contains nothing but what it did a hundred years ago'.[26] Today the time gap is nearer thirty years. Intensive pig or poultry units have not been depicted, nor have smallholdings until very recently. Similarly there has been a distinct decline in some areas recently; as there are so few views of the modern East Anglian large-scale enterprises, there can be little doubt that this decline is due to the removal by the farmers of the favoured features – notably the hedgerows, and the farmyard with a varied assortment of implements and animals. The photographs taken by Ravilious in mid-Devon, traditionally the least attractive part of the county, show this very well,[27] and the same interest is confirmed by the multitude of Country Life museums springing up all over the country. That East Anglia, the epitome of the modern taste for farm scenes, should have been so much in the forefront of recent agricultural developments has led to vociferous opposition. Just as the public began to enjoy a new genre, the reality was taken from them.

Essex

Essex ranks 15th in the proportion of pictures per square mile (Appendix 3) and its proximity to London has guaranteed it some consistency of attraction. In the earlier years some country houses, notably Audley End, were favoured, but most of the views were of Epping Forest or of places close to London, largely rural scenes then, with many marines and associated scenes along the Thames estuary. Interest slackened in the late nineteenth century, despite there being areas which might have provided

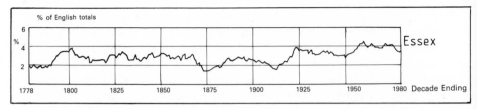

Figure 102   Graph for Essex (Source: RA catalogues). Proximity to London, and Epping Forest, have resulted in some steady popularity, but only recently have the mudflats of the coast, and the farmsteads, become acceptable pictorially.

dreary landscape. One writer 'marvelled at the ugliness of the landscape.'[28] In the twentieth century Essex has been well placed to provide both the boats-and-mudflats genre, at West Mersea, Burnham on Crouch, Harwich, Walton-on-Naze, as well as the long-popular Southend, and the vernacular interest in villages, farms and rural life, in the north-west area and in Constable Country.

A sizeable proportion of these modern views of farms and rural scenery are winter views. The leafless elms of the hedgerows became a feature which distinctly helped the pattern-making ideas of the time. Just as new farming robbed artists of a landscape only recently loved, so did Dutch elm disease.

The Formalist artist is interested in structure. Ewart Johns has pointed to the great interest shown by Italian Renaissance artists in how the landscape is made and the converse English interest in its appearance. Since he wrote this has become less true. The cold curves of the chalk downs have become one of the most popular geological formations. The bare-and-windswept taste is often accompanied by a particular fascination for archaeological and similar features to highlight the age and timelessness of the view. Nash's love of Wittenham clumps is well known, but places such as Avebury, Chanctonbury Ring, even remote Callanish, have become much depicted, not now in the swirling mists of Romance but sharply defined and cleanly cut.

One distinct feature of the time has been the reworking of motifs and landscape features from the past, and especially from the eighteenth century. The Classical and Picturesque are back in vogue. Sometimes this is quite conscious, as John Piper has retraced the Picturesque in Wales,[29] but more often it shows itself in an attraction to the Classical country house, and to the garden or park. Bath is back in fashion, and so is Stourhead. The same historicist idea may be behind the many self-conscious pictures and tours 'in the steps of the master', the master usually being Constable or Turner.[30] The normal curve of popularity for a landscape feature means that, once discovered, a new attraction remains in the portfolio of taste to be reworked, but this is the first obvious case in the statistics of a revival of former interests into a major feature.

The importance of Oxford and Cambridge is obvious on the map (Figure 91), and the greater links between art and scholarship were noted in the 1920s. These links have continued and strengthened. Indeed, since the Second World War, art courses in higher education have blossomed at least numerically. Consequently many artists are employed, full- or part-time, as teachers at these institutions, which are frequently quoted as addresses in the catalogues of the Royal Academy. This has tended to concentrate professional artists in certain cities, with obvious effects on the popularity of those places. Other artistic centres, such as Edinburgh, Glyndebourne, and Aldeburgh have also benefited.

Outside Edinburgh, however, interest in Scotland has been at a very low level, although north of the Highland boundary fault there is now revived interest in the east rather than the west. While Aberdeen and Buchan cannot be said to be a new vogue, the western Highlands do seem rather *passé*.

Yorkshire

One major county about which little has been said specifically is Yorkshire. Its graph (Figure 103) shows that taking the county as a whole there has been little variation in its favour. In total number of pictures exhibited it ranks 5th, but only 28th when its great size is taken into account (Appendix 3). This comparative continuity masks, however, major shifts in the locations used; Yorkshire is after all large enough to have most landscapes within it, and a detailed study of its image would be particularly interesting. Early interest was focused on the castles (especially Pontefract, Coningsburgh and Bolton), abbeys (Kirkstall, Fountains, Rievaulx) and country houses (Castle Howard, Allerton Park), but even before the Romantic period, interest shifted to the river valleys, especially Wharfedale, and to the coast, first at Scarborough and

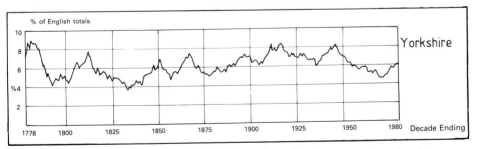

Figure 103   Graph for Yorkshire. (Source: RA catalogues). The county's size and variety has enabled it to provide most artistic requirements, but the centres of attention have changed from the abbeys and houses to the valleys, especially Wharfedale, to the coasts, and now back to the dales and industrial areas.

later at Whitby. As the coastal interest became dominant so there was a dispersal of interest to the smaller coves, Staithes, Runswick and Robin Hood's Bay becoming more important. There were many pictures of the Pennine fells as well, notably around Pen y Ghent and Ingleborough. At that time such scenery still needed legitimating: 'The dales have a scenery of their own, quite distinct from, though with various relations to that of Derbyshire, of the Lakes, of the Highlands and North Devon.'[31]

Since 1950, of a sample of 80 pictures, only 11 were of the coastal belt, with 27 of the Dales, fells and moors, Wharfedale now being second to Wensleydale. There were 14 of the industrial West Riding, with Leeds, Bradford, Sheffield and Huddersfield all quite attractive, and also Hull. Canals and mills were common, steelworks and power stations rather less so.

Durham

There have been 299 pictures of County Durham exhibited, and of these almost half have been views of the cathedral, a view from across the river which has remained a staunch favourite throughout the two centuries. The remaining pictures have been distributed in a way one has now come to expect. A fairly broad scatter in the eighteenth century was replaced by views on the Tees at High Force and Barnard Castle in the mid-nineteenth century. The more recent work which has caused some increase in the county's perception has come as much from the industrial east as from the west, and places such as Easington and Hartlepool have

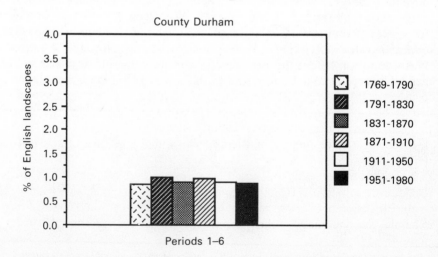

Figure 104 Histogram for County Durham (Source: RA catalogues). The great view of the cathedral has dominated the county's figures, although views on the upper Tees and later in the coalfield have also occurred.

provided one of the archetypes of the modern industrial Heroic scene, usually with cloth-capped miners prominent as staffage.

Use of this kind of methodology

Before proceeding to consider the possible causes of the patterns disclosed over the last six chapters, some discussion of the advantages and disadvantages of this approach is appropriate. The approach is, perhaps, noteworthy for the very large samples of pictures involved, 75,000 for the Royal Academy study backed up by the computer analysis of 6,500 Devonshire pictures. Such large numbers allow the data to speak for themselves.

There are numerous studies, not only by art historians, which examine the work of one artist or a small group. Such work must take very great account of the conditions of production, the patronage, and the environment of ideas in which the artists found themselves. Many artists did not set out to portray a particular place, but to answer questions that lay within the realm of art and aesthetics.

The aim of the techniques used in this book is somewhat different, and perhaps more limited. They attempt to produce a starting-point so that the system by which perceptions, of places and landscape icons, permeate a society, can be eventually revealed. In order to achieve this several other kinds of study will be needed. One such would be to examine a particular icon's history, to see how one image or type of image permeates the entire culture. Daniels has done this for Constable's *Haywain*.[32] Such studies could be extended to the examination of a complete genre – such as the fishing harbour – and as in all such work, the appearance of the image on a chocolate box or tea tray is of great evidential value.

A second approach would be to elaborate the maps in this book, which inevitably represent a London-based view. There are numerous more local art exhibitions which could be used to trace in detail the pictorial history of their areas – Kent, Sussex, Yorkshire and East Anglia suggest themselves as worthy of close attention.

Places also have images of themselves, and the history of the self-perception of particular towns and other areas can be studied by an examination of the guidebooks and advertising which attempt to sell the locale, especially if it is one which has depended on its image for tourism or the attraction of new industries. Preliminary investigations suggest, for example, that the image of the Channel Islands has changed from 'British home-from-home' to 'a taste of the continent' to 'Britain's South Sea islands'.

The story of man's use of the land could thus be complemented by the story of man's perceptions of it.

9

Processes and possibilities

After six chapters which have tried to lay out the evidence of changing artistic preferences, this final chapter can begin to speculate on what might cause these very rapid changes, though several of the more obvious influences have been touched upon already. After speculating on the processes which might be underlying the changes noted, the book concludes by looking to the future. There is certainly some evidence to show that artists are at present going through another period of rapid change, which is altering attitudes quite fundamentally.

Throughout it is important to remember that this book has only studied the landscape perceptions of a very small group – the professional landscape painters and other artists of England and Wales in so far as they relate to landscape subjects and locales found within the British Isles. Their influence has been assumed by many to be very great, although exactly how the influence of artists and other taste-formers is passed on to the general public is a question which requires a major research effort. Bliss, referring to Edward Bawden's work around Great Bardfield, said, 'He and John Aldridge with their landscape paintings made that countryside familiar to visitors to the Academy.'[1] Donald Meinig made the same assumption when discussing the way in which photographs and paintings make actual landscapes become symbolic place.[2]

Artists are inevitably outsiders. Even when they depict their own home areas they do so with a detached observation which has its own rules, as have the observational constructs used by architects, planners, etc., again even when looking at their own homes. As Griffiths has shown, insiders and outsiders have quite different attitudes to conservation, and the problem of conservation is near the heart of the future possibilities for this method of analysis.[3] Things may be conserved for many reasons, among them recreational purposes, such as many parts of our moorlands. Historical examples are preserved for research and educational purposes, such as the gardens at Westbury on Severn or many archaeological sites. Other sites are conserved because they contain a diversity of flora and fauna not found elsewhere, or as scientific exemplars in other disciplines, though as yet there are no Sites of Special Artistic Interest. But many places and buildings, as well as objects, are preserved because they are thought to be attractive. Such thinking most obviously underlies Areas of Outstanding Natural Beauty and conservation areas in towns. If attractiveness is such an ephemeral feature as much of this book suggests then serious doubt must be cast on the wisdom of conserving objects merely because the current generation find them attractive while assuming that succeeding generations will agree.

Locals and visitors

Though all artists are outsiders in the sense used by Griffiths and Relph,[39] there are still differences between local artists and visitors. Lowenthal noted that landscape itself was an outsider's concept: 'attachments which ignore scenery are most common to residents, for whom physical features are lineaments of socially charged landscapes.'[4] There is no evidence of local artists giving much greater emphasis to people rather than places, but locals do often visit different places from visitors and are usually the first to discover new places. The first artistic visitors to Clovelly were either Devon men or systematic tourists. Similarly, of the two gorges on the Teign, the visiting artists usually depicted the lower gorge at or near Fingle Bridge, but the locals penetrated further upstream to see the Gidleigh gorge. The role of the local expert may be very great. When Joseph Farington visited Devon in 1809 he acted on the recommendation to visit John Swete at Oxton House, having already discussed his tour with Bishop Fisher at Salisbury.[5] Swete gave him a list of the places worth visiting, and this seems to have been a service he often performed. To what extent Swete had his counterparts in other counties, and the extent of their role in drawing the Picturesque map of their territories are matters worthy of serious research. Their role probably ended with the arrival of the guidebook.

An additive pattern

The existence of 'short term caprices in tastes and fashions' has been noted by other writers, though usually in a way somewhat dismissive of their importance.[6] In terms of locale these certainly occur and the changing fashions for different seaside resorts has been noted. There are

a few places once of very great attraction which now seldom appear in
the lexicon of places to see. In Devon three can be noted. Berry Pomeroy
castle was one of the great sites not only of the county but the whole
country, a ruined, ivy-clad fortified manor set on a hill and fulfilling all
the requirements of a Picturesque *memento mori*. It is still conserved by
English Heritage, but is certainly not in the same league as it once was.
The case of Chudleigh Rocks is yet more impressive in its disappearance.
Of the twenty-three pictures of it in the Devonshire sample of pictures,
the last was in 1862. Even four years later Samuel Palmer recommended
it:

> Worth seeing, if you don't stop short as the tourists do, on the wrong
> side of the chasm gaping at the opposite cliff – while the real spectacle
> is what they are standing upon. I found it all strewed with Pic Nic
> bottles and broken plates.[7]

Today, still quite accessible, the place is abandoned to a few rock
climbers and locals walking the dog. The third case is Holy Street Mill, on
the River Teign above Chagford, perhaps the greatest site for mid-
nineteenth-century painters working the valleys running off Dartmoor,
and now almost unknown even within the county.

These three sites are, however, exceptional. While locales show a
greater tendency to short-term caprices, preferred subjects are very
persistent. A new preference, for village scenes, farmsteads, wooded
valleys, tends to arise with considerable speed and reach its peak of
importance very quickly, but the subsequent decline does not remove it
from the catalogue of the aesthetically acceptable. No doubt the genre
becomes overworked, and loses favour, but it remains available to be
reworked.

Thus the pattern, at least of subject types and largely of attractive
locales also, is an additive one. New ideas are continually being added to
the list, old ones decline but do not disappear. This may suggest that art
is an extractive industry which must one day exhaust its supply. However,
new classes of landscape objects are continually being made, to increase
the supply. Nevertheless, in looking at the aesthetic preferences of any
period it is vital to note what is absent – what scenes are not depicted.

Access: political constraints

Among the first major group of factors which affect the patterns of
perception with which this book has been concerned are those which
affect the ability to reach certain places – broadly, accessibility.

The most obvious of these factors is that certain places are simply not
visitable at certain times. The most outstanding cases are only seen
abroad – English artists, for example, did not depict many German scenes

between 1940 and 1944! Such restrictions on travel, as also the tendency of the Austrians to be suspicious of sketchers, sometimes arresting them for espionage,[8] were rarely applicable at home. However, in the First World War Goodwin noted that 'no sketching, photography or note-taking [was] allowed on any part of the coast'[9] for security reasons, and such restrictions must have had occasional effect.

Visits to Scotland and Ireland may well have been curtailed for political and military reasons, the former in the eighteenth century and the latter more recently. The political content of some of the pictures of the Scottish Highlands during the later nineteenth century has been discussed by Pringle.[10] During recent wars artists have been concerned to depict the destruction, as much at home as overseas, and also to produce archetypal views of Englishness, such as those noted during the Second World War.

Access: propinquity

Political constraints apart, the problems can be divided into those of geographical propinquity and the results of new methods of transport. There is a clear preference for the landscapes of those counties nearest to the national artistic capital of London, most notably in Middlesex (before it became suburbanized), Surrey, Kent and, later, Sussex, but also along the Thames into Essex and Berkshire. Their importance is greatly enhanced, of course, when they happen to possess landscape features popular at the time. Holman Hunt and Millais searched the environs of Ewell for a suitable site for a 'cornfield' painting.[11] Later the Surrey heaths were the birthplace of that new interest, and the Weald as a whole became a laboratory for discovering new ideas in the nineteenth century.[12]

Propinquity was also a factor in the provinces. Bickleigh Vale, the gorge of the River Plym, for example, was much the most favoured of the Dartmoor valleys in the Picturesque period, undoubtedly because of its proximity to Plymouth. Another local spot, however, was too out of the way to be noticed till long after the taste for its type of scenery had begun. This was the Yealm estuary, largely ignored until 1900. Page in 1893 noted, 'One would expect these waters to be haunted by artists, but such is not the case. . . . It does seem strange that a spot within such easy reach of Plymouth should be so little known.'[13] In Northumberland the popularity of Jesmond Dene must be attributable to its closeness to Newcastle. Artists did, however, travel great distances to find landscapes not available nearer home, even when transport conditions were next to impossible. The early popularity of Cumbria and North Wales demonstrate clearly that the grander the scenery the further the journey.

A sliding scale

Perhaps the discovery that artists travel as little as possible in seeking their preferred landscapes may seem facile, but if the same were true of the population at large, the implications for landscape planning would be considerable. Landscape attractiveness must be seen as a sliding scale, with more and more unusual features being necessary to achieve popularity further from centres of population. In conservation terms this would mean applying more stringent criteria further away from the cities. The numerous techniques which attempt to supply an objective assessment of landscape quality usually ignore propinquity to centres of population. Such systems may highlight attractive landscapes which could be more heavily used but they will not actually attract unless action is taken to improve accessibility. Similarly the importance of rather unexciting landscapes near to the town may well be overlooked. The importance of such places has been highlighted by Common Ground,[14] though their work concentrates on the importance of places to residents. Visitors too are usually based somewhere, hence the insignificant little River Sid, close by the resort of Sidmouth, has always been more popular than the much grander rivers of north-west Devon, such as the Wolf, Thrushel and even the Torridge.

Diffusion

Another result of propinquity is the process of diffusion. This occurs with reference to both locations and subjects. Where most artists were visitors rather than residents there is a clear movement away from certain centres. Again this is most obvious abroad. The earlier visitors to Egypt were content to depict the 'lions' – the Sphinx, Pyramids, etc. Only later did they begin to look further afield, and at ordinary life. The same is true of Tuscany where there was a clear move from Florence to a group of favoured Tuscan towns, and finally to the rural areas. This certainly happens also at home. The earlier visitors to North Wales stuck closely to the road from Llangollen to Carnarvon and Bangor. Only later did they penetrate into Merionethshire. Equally it took artists some time to reach Wastwater and Eskdale in the Lakes. In the Highlands the tastes first developed in the Trossachs and Arran and then spread further north towards the Great Glen.

In terms of landscape subjects diffusion has been much discussed in earlier chapters. The discovery of the Mediterranean coast scene on the Bay of Naples and its subsequent spread to the French Riviera, Spain, Majorca and now the Greek Islands, is obvious. The diffusion of the heathland scene, and the views of villages and cottages from the Weald to the rest of England, has already been noted. For many years the idea of

the Vernacular meant the local architecture of south-east England. The
Essex or Kentish farmstead has now spread throughout the country, and
the Cornish fishing village is just as likely to be found in County Antrim,
Fife or Yorkshire.

Remoteness

In the twentieth century there have been some occasions when the rule of
propinquity has been reversed. Some artists have sought remoteness
apparently for its own sake. This no doubt follows the rule that when a
thing becomes difficult to attain it becomes more valuable. In the remoter
parts of the Scottish Highlands – or even more in the western or northern
isles, and in parts of Ireland, the landscapes depicted do not apparently
differ from those traversed to reach them. This positive value to
remoteness only seems to operate in landscapes which are perceived as
'natural', even if they rarely are. It is found in the innermost recesses of
Dartmoor where the most central point, Cranmere Pool, has retained a
certain cachet despite now being only a few hundred yards from the
military road. It is not found in remote farmed landscapes; where these
are depicted the difference between them and more accessible, usually
richer and more agriculturally advanced areas, is stressed.

Propinquity was seen as a disadvantage by one nineteenth-century
writer. W.J. Loftie noted that 'People go to Gloucester or to Tewkesbury
to look at patterns of domestic architecture, while Guildford is too near
to be visible.'[15] The figures for the popularity of Guildford do not,
however, support his statement, although there have certainly been cases
where places have remained 'invisible' despite their accessibility.

Transport

Changes in the transport network are the cause of changing tastes most
likely to come readily to mind. During the two centuries under discussion
the network has changed dramatically, continually increasing the
accessibility of most places.

The turnpike seems to be the first great change which affected the
travelling artist, for although the canals were used to carry passengers
they do not seem to have much affected the localities or subjects
depicted. The turnpike road did not create the possibility of touring for
the mass of the population, but many artists managed to afford it. The
result was that travel to the remoter corners of the kingdom was made
much easier – but by no means all remote corners were visited. As is
usual throughout the history of transport development, the new system
acted only as a permissive factor. Certain destinations were made easier,
but artists did not depict things simply because they could get there.

Figure 105 T. Rowlandson, *Honiton, Devonshire*, pen, ink and watercolour, 30 × 43 cm (Courtesty Royal Albert Memorial Museum, Exeter). One of the coaching stops much favoured for quick sketches.

However, the turnpike stopping-places, usually inns, provided distinct nodes of activity. In Devon a string of such places developed from Honiton, to Exeter, Chudleigh, South Brent and Ivybridge, and finally Plymouth. Rowlandson's little glimpse of Honiton (Figure 105), and the dozens of pictures of the bridge at Ivybridge attest to this. The great boom in Picturesque travelling permitted by the turnpike certainly makes Esther Moir's description of the period as 'The Discovery of Britain' quite understandable.[16]

The arrival of the railways clearly had similar effects. There are too many cases of the arrival of the railway being followed by increased output of pictures for the evidence to be ignored, and the popularity of the new system is clearly attested by the numbers of depictions of the railway itself. Perhaps Cornwall is the most obvious case, with the opening of the Tamar Bridge being followed by increased popularity, but the actual figures of pictures of Cornwall (Table 3) during that decade suggest that even there the case is not completely proven. The railway did not teach new tastes, though during the famous poster campaigns of the 1920s and 1930s it may have been influential in mediating them. The railway's greatest achievement was to provide transport for the bulk of the population, and hence promote popular tourism, together with its concomitant anti-tourist sentiment. Blaikie was only expressing the normal, if elitist, view when he thought that much tourism and changed attitudes to nature were induced by the railways and commended eighteenth-century travellers whose judgement was not 'enslaved by popular guides'.[17]

As tourism developed so the railway sometimes had a negative influence on artists' perceptions. As the masses arrived the artists left. Lynton represents an example of a place where the arrival of the railway heralded a decline in artistic interest.

The development of the steamship permitted the popularity of many foreign places, and was undoubtedly instrumental in assisting ideas

Table 3 Cornwall: number of exhibits 1849–69

Year	No.	Year	No.	Year	No.
1849	2	1856	5	1863	4
1850	6	1857	0	1864	9
1851	4	1858	1	1865	6
1852	1	1859	1	1866	9
1853	4	1860	2	1867	6
1854	0	1861	8	1868	2
1855	1	1862	6	1869	3

Source: Royal Academy catalogues

gleaned from Greece, North Africa, etc. to penetrate into Britain. Both the Channel Islands and the Isle of Man also had to await regular steamship sailings for their popularity, and the paddle steamer made Arran by far the most favoured part of Scotland for many years. In addition coastal steamers were important, especially in the Bristol Channel, the south coast and North Wales. Walter Crane as late as 1881 took ship from Ryde to Torquay, not as an outing but as the easiest form of transport.[18]

Evidence for the importance of the bicycle is difficult to acquire, but cameras and watercolours were easily carried. At much the same period as the bicycle mania came the rise to importance of the country cottage and village, especially close to London in the Weald, and a connection between the two may be worthy of investigation.

The motor car was probably instrumental in encouraging the highly dispersed pattern noticeable in the maps from the 1930s onwards. As remoteness became ever more difficult to find, so the car enabled the artist to discover the newly acceptable pictorial material such as farms, fields and villages in his own back yard. The picturesque bits of previously unexplored counties were tracked down and became the object of concern to prevent their being spoiled, as Goodey has shown in Northamptonshire.[19]

The growth of air travel had considerable impact abroad, especially in encouraging visits to the Mediterranean islands. At home most islands had long been easily reached so the impact was much less.

Aircraft, motor cars and even bicycles have not been themselves the subject of art, at least pictures of them were not frequently to be seen on the Academy's walls. Railways and steamships were, however, acceptable pictorial material in their earliest years – up to about 1855 – and have become so again recently. Recent pictures, however, have, like so many industrial pictures, been of obsolescent versions – steam trains not diesels, ocean liners not container ships. Even the road scene, quite common from the 1930s onwards, has always concentrated on small country roads, not on arterial highways. They are frequently used to produce a deflected vista, previously achieved with the upriver view. Canals, popular before industry became unacceptable, have succeeded in continuing to provide artistic fodder, presumably because they were obsolete.

Associational attraction

Many locations attract because of their associations, or perceived associations, with the famous. Writers seem to be the most attractive heroes in this respect, even to artists who might have been expected to pay more attention to their fellow painters. There are two distinct types of association. In some cases the attraction is to the home or sometimes grave of the hero, which therefore takes on the characteristics of a shrine, with the landscape itself being secondary. Such cases include the pictures of Shakespeare's Stratford, Scott's Dryburgh, and Balmoral, or, at a local level, the several pictures of Reynolds's home at Plympton. Many pictures of country houses, even where not specifically commissioned by the owners, were very conscious of the ownership of the property, and the articles advising artists on sketching grounds often include as much family history as other material.

In other cases the visit is to the landscape described by, depicted by or associated with the hero or heroine, and Haworth, Tweeddale, Hardy's Dorset, Landseer's Highlands, Blackmore's Doone Country and Kingsley's Clovelly are obvious examples. The attraction is easily measured because so many titles make specific reference to it, often by quotation. A few painters have been causal factors in this way, the most important being Constable, although such recognition was, in his case, long delayed. Certainly the work of Richard Wilson was in many artists' minds when visiting North Wales, with the title *Wilson's Lake* sometimes being used.

Much more often, artists, like all visitors, made decisions based on the reports of trustworthy friends. Because Farington first visited Devon on the advice of Lysons scarcely makes Lysons an associative influence on Devonshire.[20] The recommendation may not be a personal one. Palmer first determined to see Devon after seeing a 'a bad print' of Watermouth Castle in a shop window in Great Russell Street in London.[21]

As part of the discovery of Merrie England after 1850 a good many associational attractions were to mythical or legendary characters. Glastonbury and Tintagel were seen as Arthurian sites, the Fens were seen as Hereward's, and Nottinghamshire saw its greatest period of popularity as the home of Robin Hood. Shakespeare too was first lionized at this time, very much as part of the discovery of English heritage.

Art theory

Landscape art not only derives locations from other artists, but also feeds from art at least as much as from landscape. There seems little doubt that an appreciation of seventeenth-century Dutch painting influenced both the development of panorama painting generally and the subjects depicted by the Norwich school and many others in the early nineteenth century. Earlier the work of Claude much influenced both subjects and ways of presenting them, perhaps even a whole way of seeing. In his Devon notebooks John Swete was reminded of Rosa at Watcombe, of Gilpin at Mount Edgcumbe, of de Loutherbourg at Beer, of Claude at Axmouth and of William Payne in many places. Similarly the work of the Barbizon school almost certainly influenced the later love of heathland in Surrey and elsewhere.

190

Oil paintings

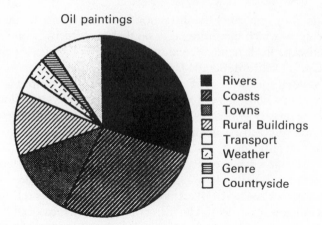

(a) Oil painting. Not well adapted for buildings, but ideal for leafy streams.

Watercolours

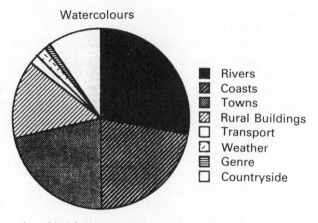

(b) Watercolour. Ideal for atmospherics, not only on the coast but on the moorlands.

Engravings

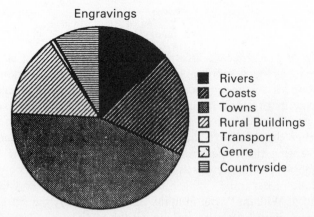

(c) Engraving. A linear medium well adapted for representing buildings.

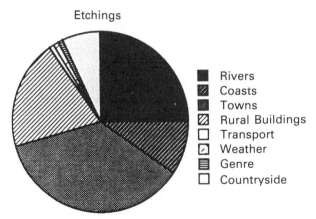

(d) Etching. The preferred print medium for river scenes in the mid-nineteenth century.

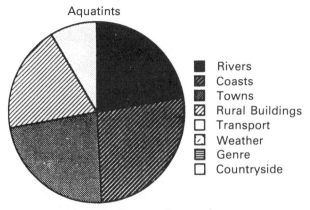

(e) Aquatint. Similar to watercolours, with much use for coastal scenes.

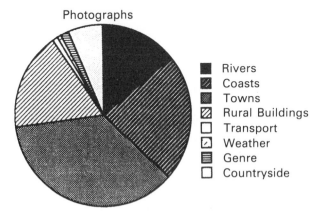

(f) Photograph. Over half are buildings, though the pattern influenced, of course, by the fashions prevalent since photography's invention.

Figure 106 Subject types for different media (Source: analysis of a sample of 6,000 landscape depictions of Devonshire).

Technique

If one artist's style can call into being an entire way of viewing landscape, as Claude's did, a technique can do the same. The Impressionist way of handling paint sought subjects which were enhanced by it. One was the surface of water, first on the Seine but later in the many estuary and river scenes of the early twentieth century. The Suffolk coast was largely seen in these terms, as was the Thames after Whistler. Even more obvious was the discovery of the orchard. The orchard was so overlooked as a subject that in a county as famous for its orchards as Devon not one depiction has been found of an orchard in blossom prior to 1890. Thereafter, it became a popular subject, both there and elsewhere, especially around Evesham. Artists needed Impressionism to see orchards. Perhaps, too, Cubism is necessary in order to see landscape as pattern, to admire the chequer-board of colour and line which is the subject of so much modern landscape art. Did Picasso teach us, by a tortuous skein, to appreciate the English hedgerow?

Medium

The medium itself is of critical importance. We see through the medium of depiction. Figure 106 shows the balance of different subjects for various media, and the differences are quite clear. The engraver's use of line makes it the natural medium for depicting buildings, whereas the aquatint is very close to the watercolour in its use. Even within subject areas there are important differences. The estuary view is very much the watercolourist's scene, whereas the Romantic upstream view of a river in a wooded gorge is usually in oil. The watermill, however, was in 1855 thought 'not a very attractive subject for an oil picture'.[22] Trees usually are in oil, mists in watercolour. The moor and marsh scene was also usually a watercolourist's view, the portability of the medium being an advantage. Smiles points out the significance of this:

> It is evident that the topographic print, by its very nature, was precluded from treating seascape or coastline with any success unless such scenes were made interesting by ships or architecture. Water colour on the other hand, was perfectly suited to render the evanescent effects of atmosphere, surf, sea and rock that the mid-century tourist had come to admire.[23]

The photograph appears to be biased towards buildings, as are most of the print media, though the photograph inevitably favours towards twentieth-century tastes.

John Jakle has stressed the importance of the relationship between the tourist, the landscape and the camera.[24] The colour photograph is now such an important part of the tourist experience that the extent to which what we perceive favourably is determined by the characteristics of a good colour photograph may not frequently be apprehended. Bernaldez *et al.* have suggested that Madrid students are still able to view landscape without the demands of photographic composition being interposed, but that the landscapes they then appreciate are significantly different from those preferred in photograph form.[25] Behind what makes a good photograph lie not only the demands of the medium itself, apparently favouring buildings, but also the impact of the whole of art history. To what extent are tourists constrained in what they see by the camera in their hands? Will the replacement of that camera by a portable video significantly affect what is sought? The demonstration here that artists' perceptions are significantly affected by the medium they use raises questions of considerable importance, as yet scarcely examined.

Patronage

The influence of patronage on the subjects depicted by artists is in some cases obvious – notably in the country house scenes – the landscape portraits of the late eighteenth century. The extent to which artists have always been constrained by the wishes of the purchasing public is a vexed one, although John Barrell, Dennis Cosgrove and others have strongly urged its importance.[26] The rise of the industrial bourgeoisie to the position of patron may well have permitted the 'realistic' portrayal of farm workers and fishermen towards the end of the nineteenth century, but discouraged the similar portrayal of industrial workers. In this century the market-place may have resulted in the distinct split between avant-garde and mainstream art. The former was producing art for a self-conscious artistic elite, the latter for an expanding middle class often with working-class origins. The popularity of obsolescent industrial scenes may be due to purchasers' wishing to maintain contact with roots that they have effectively left. Even where sales are not in question the role of the audience is important. The tourist takes many pictures with an audience in mind – whether it is the family or a wider circle. Although this book has been concerned with the tastes of artists, there can be little doubt that the tastes were wider than that, or the artists would have starved. That does not, of course, mean that the tastes were universal.

Trickle-down effect

If one question raised but unanswered in this book is the relationship between medium and perception, another is certainly the means and speed of the dissemination of perceptions through society. There are distinct intervals of time which elapse between the avant-garde discovering a new landscape feature and its widespread adoption by the middle-ranking artists under discussion here. The love of the geometric patterned landscape was evident with Robert Bevan as early as 1910, but did not become a major theme till after 1950. The moorland stretches of Dartmoor reached favour with our mainstream artists about 1870, but the area was designated a National Park in 1951 following major campaigns throughout the 1930s. Even then it was a middle-class taste, and according to Burgess remains so.[27] Many writers in the art literature assumed that the popularity of landscape painting was 'evidence of the way the love of landscape is penetrating the community'. The same writer thought that,

> the undying verse of Scott, Byron, Wordsworth and others never at their best could appeal to the multitude as will a faithful transcript of them by brush and colour . . . the painters have taught us much of what we ought to look for.[28]

One writer put it much more simply: 'Where artists lead the way the crowd soon follows.'[29] Heathcote thought, 'There could be no doubt that landscape paintings . . . helped to create attitudes.'[30] Just how, and how fast, this trickle-down process acts remains to be discovered. How does the taste emerge from the group who actually see art to those who don't? Which media act as mediators in this respect? What roles are played by film, television, postcards? Here is indeed a large research agenda. The answers, however, will be of considerable importance. Very considerable time and money is currently spent persuading people to view certain places favourably, usually to boost the tourist industry. If the 'natural' process by which this happens can be uncovered, much more efficient manipulation of the tourist market could be achieved.

Centrifugal and centripetal forces

Among the processes which appear to be at work in creating the pattern, though insufficiently precise to be dignified as causes or laws, is the existence of both centripetal and centrifugal forces, sometimes with one in the ascendant, sometimes the other. The centre, at a national level, is almost always London though Edinburgh and Dublin may act in a secondary role. The small artistic centres act as a counterweight to London. The essential similarity which united Constable's Dedham Vale, the numerous late-nineteenth-century art colonies such as those at Newlyn and Walberswick, Herkomer's school at Bushey, the tours to the Lakes, Scotland or Wales, even the haunts of the recent Ruralist Brotherhood, has been that they were not London. They did not possess the metropolitan, academic, art market nor its political flavour. Rural landscape perhaps always acts as an anti-metropolitan force. As Inglis has reminded us, however much the appearance of the landscape has been moulded by power politics, it is usually seen as fundamentally innocent. Gainsborough wanted, 'to walk off to some sweet villages where I can paint Landskips' and escape the market-place of Bath.[31] Joseph Wright similarly found himself 'continually stealing off and getting to landscapes'.[32]

Perceptual shadow

The notion of perceptual shadow has already been introduced. Just as some places lie in the rain shadow of mountains, so some places are less favourably regarded than their landscape might lead one to expect because they are overshadowed by greater attractiveness or grandeur. Bodmin Moor is a particularly good example. A fine piece of moorland, it is both lower and less extensive than Dartmoor as well as being further from London. Consequently few artists have depicted it, and it is designated only an Area of Outstanding Natural Beauty, and not a National Park. The Welsh borders and the central Welsh mountains seem other obvious cases, as have been the Southern Uplands of Scotland after the associational impact of Scott faded.

Some other places seem to be usually visited *en route* to others. The most obvious case is abroad for the Low Countries were visited *en route* to Germany and the Rhine. When that area lost its attraction for political reasons after 1914, the popularity of the Low Countries also collapsed. Llangollen's popularity was largely due to its being on the route to North Wales, and at a more local level the turnpike stops might be considered of the same kind. Undoubtedly Okehampton Castle's enormous popularity was helped by its position on the main road to Cornwall.

Legitimation

The process of legitimation has also been encountered. Although clearly visible in the pictures, perhaps the guidebooks are an even better explanation of the process. Swete thought the estuary of the Dart was like a lake[33] and this epithet was stressed throughout the early nineteenth century as late as 1844, when Carus thought it appeared 'as if it were a lake'.[34] Later the description 'The English Rhine' was so commonplace as to be later described as 'absurd and unjust'.[35] One idiosyncratic writer thought its only rival was the Meuse between Namur and Dinant.[36] Rather later it was 'more like some Scotch sea-loch'.[37] As tastes changed so did the legitimating epithet. At Mount Edgcumbe, Carus thought that 'In fine weather and with a bright sun, one might think oneself on the Gulf of Naples', though Torbay was the more common surrogate for Naples Bay.[38] On Bodmin Moor, he suggested, 'one might almost think oneself over the steppes of Siberia.'[39] Lynmouth tower was built in

Figure 107   W.H. Prior, *The Dart Estuary*, from *Pictures of the Great Western Railway,
VIII – The Mouth of the Dart, Devonshire* (Courtesy M.R. Pidgley). The places with which
the Dart has been compared have changed frequently with changing fashions.

imitation of those on the Rhine, although more usually the place was seen
as the English Switzerland.[40] This 'seeing in terms of established
concepts'[41] has been more studied in relation to European legitimation of
overseas landscapes. Vallis also notes that 'To the first English settlers
[Australia] was readily seen in terms of the Romantic tradition then
sweeping Europe.'[42] Legitimation is also given away by the use of
language, as when the Teign estuary is called a 'loch',[43] or the common
use of the Scottish 'glen'.

These phrases, intended to make new places acceptable by comparison,
sometimes become rather absurd. 'The hills [of Derbyshire] mimic Alpine
scenery to perfection' says one writer, claiming 'Monsal Dale the very
Tempe of Derbyshire'.[44] Perhaps the finest is the likening of the cement
works and gasworks of the Medway estuary to the ruins of Palmyra.[45]
That these legitimations were as influential on artists as writers is very
clear from the pictures. Paintings of the Dart estuary show a sequence
from those closing off the sea and at high tide (lake), to those showing
the castle overlooking the water (Rhine), to tidal pictures with no signs of
towns (loch).

Vulgarization

The way in which Clovelly, originally the subject of fine paintings and
writing, changed into a location which artists apologized for visiting has

already been discussed. The work by Hook and other painters in the mid-nineteenth century was of a varied kind, but by the early twentieth century the pictures became merely copies of themselves, and the view itself became standardized. By 1934 even S.P.B. Mais, usually quite able to be sentimental, had to defend the place by wondering, 'whether over-praise or over-photography can really spoil beauty'.[46] This vulgarization of locations, and of subjects, may begin in the manner suggested by Yeend King, writing in 1885:

> I am not sure that there are not spirits so perfectly unable . . . to bear the weight of their own responsibility, that when looking for subjects, they only recognize them by their drift of empty colour-tubes and old paint rags. Then they know there must be something in the vicinity, for somebody had been there before. In this way a number of beautiful haunts, charming though they are in themselves, year by year afford the material for the same stereotyped views: and one knows from the Academy catalogue exactly what the composition of the picture must be, and almost puts up a prayer that no one should be allowed to paint the 'Fairy Glen' or the 'Church Pool' for a matter of forty year at least.[47]

As the vulgarization process produced stereotyped images, these became accepted as the stock-in-trade of particular areas. The lack of pictures of Devonshire mining has been noted. Cornwall was accepted for its mining landscape which was frequently depicted. In Devon the mines remained invisible; they failed to fit the image which the artists carried in their heads.

Exceptional and typical

A final pattern to emerge from the statistics is the search for the exceptional and for the typical. The extraordinary is almost always popular, be it Snowdon, St Paul's or Windsor Castle. Often, however, the artist would greatly exaggerate the exceptional feature, especially if the effect of the Sublime were intended. Kingsley complained that 'the lying painters paint [the Ehrenbreitstein] just three times as high as it is.'[48] At the other extreme, when a particular feature is sought, such as farm, or village or cottage, its very typicality is its most admired feature. Meinig has postulated the existence of a few archetypal landscapes in America.[49] In the case of the discovery of the English village, very few villages have been found sufficiently typical to serve the need, and those that have represent a distinct settlement form.

A glimpse of the future

The tone of this book has varied from the tediously factual to the outrageously speculative. To try to identify the most recent movements in artistic perception, and suggest where these are leading, may be a logical conclusion, but it will also aspire to heights of speculation and even intuition not so far attempted.

Certainly, however, some of the graphs suggest major changes are afoot. The collapse of interest in London during the 1970s has been accompanied or succeeded by distinct upturns in several remoter areas – Wales, Cumbria, Yorkshire, Devon, Norfolk and Suffolk. It is far too early to be sure that these are significant trends, rather than short-term caprices, but they do fit some of the trends which can be discerned by looking at recent exhibitions of landscape work, and by talking to artists and students about their interests.

The most obvious feature is that there is a lot of it about; the death of Modernism is being accompanied by a remarkable resurgence of interest in landscape work. As happens so often when the academic, metropolitan notion of art loses confidence in itself, artists turn to landscape as naturally as composers look to folk and popular traditions. While landscape depiction has increased markedly, it has been joined by the new phenomenon of 'land art' – although 'landscape involvement' might better indicate the purpose. Many artists, usually trained as sculptors rather than painters, spend time in the landscape, making objects usually from local materials which are intended to highlight the properties they find there. The work of Andy Goldsworthy, David Nash, Richard Long, and the exhibitions of work in National Parks, the work at Grizedale and the Forest of Dean, can all stand witness to this. From using timber, sculptors proceeded to manipulating growing trees, and now to planting them. This close involvement with nature is one thread in the most recent movement, and one that is closely connected with the eco-movement.

A second thread is that of community involvement. Relph's[50] categories of insideness include 'empathetic insideness' which is very close to the objectives of caring for very local places, as promoted by Common Ground. There is a very wide gulf between the attitudes of the trained artist and those of a local community, similar to the outsideness problem experienced by any professional but exacerbated by ideas of exclusivity and creativity which artists find it difficult to shake off. Often interpretations of landscape or place by artists reveal more about their own heads than about the landscape. However, there is much determination in some quarters to break down this barrier and concentrate on the local, the particular and the human meanings of landscape objects.

These two threads of community involvement and eco-consciousness have resulted in a distinct preference for the untidy, for the vernacular in the sense used by J.B. Jackson,[51] rather than the vernacular preferences of the Bloomsbury artists between the wars. The latter have now become official 'good taste', supported by conservation legislation and promoted by the National Parks and the National Trust. Many artists are now

Figure 108 Robert Clement, *Dartmoor*, 1985, watercolour, 25 × 18 cm (Author's collection). The most recent preference is for an untidy landscape, replete with shacks and barbed wire.

concentrating on landscape objects which might be perceived by most conservationists as unacceptable – suburban housing, allotments with old sheds, decrepit farmsteads with barbed wire in rolls and corrugated iron roofs, rank and weedy spaces left over after planning or farm rearrangement, pylons and gasworks.

In some cases the artists have continued the tradition of painting the obsolescent. The suburban houses are those of the 1930s, not the 1980s, the farmsteads are those which by any modern standards would be uneconomic, and the gasworks have also outlived their usefulness. Nevertheless they also evince an attitude which is opposed to the landscapes of good taste. The raucous seaside resort, such as Blackpool or Morecambe, is preferred to those perceived as genteel; Tintagel is preferred to Boscastle, the remote, rural communities of north-west Devon are preferred to the rich farmland and gentrified villages of the south east of the county.

We seem then to be entering a new period of artistic perception, clearly one where centrifugal forces are dominant, for which the term 'scruffy' might be apt, though the 'Environmentalist Period' might be a more dignified term. This is far from firmly established, and contains within it some unexpected elements. Just as the Post-modernist movement in architecture has made a serious reappraisal of Classical ideas and motifs, so artists have also begun to revisit Picturesque and Classical houses, gardens and towns, reacquainting themselves with the tradition of their discipline.

As the ideas of this new movement spread through society we are given a splendid opportunity to demonstrate the trickle-down effect and measure the time-lag involved. When will be the first occasion when a rusty corrugated-iron barn is conserved for posterity?

Appendix 1

Sources of the statistics, graphs, histograms and maps

All the quantitative material derives directly from the catalogues of the Royal Academy Summer Exhibitions from 1769 to 1980. The catalogues give the following information:

1   Artist's name.
2   Title of exhibit.
3   Medium – usually inferred from all the works in a single room being in a similar medium.
4   Rank of artist (if ARA or RA).
5   Number of exhibit.
6   Address of artist, from the Index. This is frequently a club, college or gallery rather than a home address.
7   Other works by the same artist, from the Index.

The exhibitions have varied in size dramatically. The first in 1769 had 136 exhibits, but this rose rapidly to over 1,000, and to a peak of 2,245 in 1914. Average 1,317 exhibits per annum, a total of 279,244 works.

The first stage is to discard the works which were not pictures. Sculpture is easily distinguished, but the architecture less easily so. Pictures by architects depicting their own works were discarded, but those depicting other buildings were included.

The remaining 80 per cent are pictures. The titles are then used to distinguish which are landscapes. This is not a certain method, although the inclusion of a place-name was taken as an indication that the place was important so such pictures were generally included. In total 76,569 pictures were regarded as landscapes. (For a sample study see Peter Howard, 'Changing Taste in Landscape Art', unpublished PhD thesis,

University of Exeter, 1983, pp. 57–60.)

Of the landscapes 30 per cent proved to be unlocatable other than to country.

The locatable landscapes are then available to be mapped, and graphed. They are grouped into areas based on the historic counties of England.

The histograms

Where the proportion of pictures of a county or area did not rise above 4 per cent of the total for England at any time, simple histograms are used. For each of the six periods distinguished in the book the number of pictures of the county is expressed as a percentage of the total number of locatable landscapes of England.

The graphs

Where the proportion of pictures of a county or area rose above 4 per cent of the total for England, and in some other cases where the graph shape was of particular interest, graphs are used. The plotted figures represent the number of landscapes of the county over the past ten years expressed as a proportion of the total number of locatable landscapes of England over the same period. Thus the first figure plots the proportion for 1769 to 1778, the second 1770 to 1779, the last 1971 to 1980. This technique allows quite small changes to be seen without the figures being confused by individual freak years.

The maps

For the maps a higher standard of locatability is needed, and the numerous views entitled 'View in Hampshire' etc. were discarded. For each period 1,000 locatable landscapes were randomly selected and the British ones plotted. A typographic distinction is made between those which represent places which, at the map's scale, represent points – e.g. views of towns, and those which represent areas e.g. View on the South Downs, or View on the River Tyne.

The London area is plotted separately.

Appendix 2

Rules of the Royal Academy Summer Exhibition

Main historical events and rule changes[1]

1769   First exhibition in Pall Mall, with 136 works, 129 by 'professional artists'. No limit on the number of works per artist. Selection by a Hanging Committee (the Keeper, the Secretary and three Academicians).

1779   Exhibition moved to Somerset House.

1800   Limit imposed of eight pictures and eight drawings per artist.

1820   Ban imposed on 'mere transcriptions of the objects of natural history'.

1837   Exhibition moved to the National Gallery.

1853   Engravers first admitted as full Academicians.

1869   Exhibition moved to Burlington House.

1903   Limit changed to six works for members (RAs and ARAs) and three for other exhibitors.

1914   Ban imposed on works over ten years old. (Very few ever had been).

Present-day rules[2]

a)   Exhibition to be open for twelve weeks.

b)   Works to be chosen by a Selection Committee comprising the President and Council plus four Associates (one painter, one sculptor, one engraver and one architect).

1 From S.C. Hutchinson, *The History of the Royal Academy 1768–1968*, London, Chapman & Hall, 1968.

2 From Royal Academy of Arts, *The Laws of the Royal Academy of Arts in London 1768–1968*, London, 1968.

c) Members may submit six works, non-members three, none of which have been previously on public exhibition in London.
d) Deceased members, works may be admitted for one year after death.
e) Hanging Committee shall comprise five painters or engravers, one sculptor, one architect plus the four Associates from the Selection Committee.

Appendix 3

Counties and areas: statistical information and definition

Bedfordshire – The historic county plus the few unlocatable views on the Great Ouse.

Total number of pictures exhibited	106	(41st)
Weighted index[1]	117	(41st)
Pictures per square mile	0.25	(31st)
Pictures per 1,000 population[2]	0.68	(29th)

Histogram: Figure 12a, p. 42

Berkshire – The historic county, with the northern border strictly along the Thames.

Total number of pictures exhibited	779	(15th)
Weighted index[1]	854	(13th)
Pictures per square mile	1.18	(7th)
Pictures per 1,000 population[2]	3.33	(6th)

Histogram: Figure 59, p. 115

Buckinghamshire – The historic county, with the Thames as southern boundary plus the few unlocatable views in the Chilterns.

Total number of pictures exhibited	309	(29th)
Weighted index[1]	377	(26th)
Pictures per square mile	0.5	(19th)
Pictures per 1,000 population[2]	1.93	(12th)

Histogram: Figure 58, p. 114

Cambridgeshire – The historic county, including the Isle of Ely but excluding Huntingdonshire and the Soke of Peterborough.

Total number of pictures exhibited	178	(36th)

Weighted index[1]   166   (36th)
Pictures per square mile   0.2   (32nd=)
Pictures per 1,000 population[2]   0.87   (26th)
Histogram: Figure 89, p. 153

Cheshire – The historic county, bordering along the Mersey to the north. Numerous unlocatable views on the Dee are included but the few on the Mersey are not.

Total number of pictures exhibited   161   (37th)
Weighted index[1]   163   (37th)
Pictures per square mile   0.15   (38th)
Pictures per 1,000 population[2]   0.2   (40th)
Histogram: Figure 43, p. 93

Cornwall – The historic county including the Isles of Scilly, plus unlocatable views on the Tamar.

Total number of pictures exhibited   1738   (7th)
Weighted index[1]   1515   (8th)
Pictures per square mile   1.12   (8th)
Pictures per 1,000 population[2]   4.7   (4th)
Graph: Figure 77, p. 140

Cumbria – The modern county, including the historic counties of Cumberland and Westmorland and the district of Furness, formerly in Lancashire. Most pictures were of the Lake District which bordered all three counties.

Cumberland
Total number of pictures exhibited   688   (18th)
Weighted index[1]   780   (14th)
Pictures per square mile   0.51   (17th=)
Pictures per 1,000 population[2]   2.92   (8th)

Westmorland
Total number of pictures exhibited   461   (22nd)
Weighted index[1]   511   (22nd)
Pictures per square mile   0.65   (13th)
Pictures per 1,000 population[2]   7.95   (1st)
Graph for Cumbria: Figure 18, p. 52

Derbyshire – The historic county, plus the frequent unlocatable views on the Dove or in Dovedale, and the few of the Peak District, but not the few on the Trent.

Total number of pictures exhibited   375   (25th)
Weighted index[1]   403   (23rd)

Pictures per square mile   0.39   (22nd)
Pictures per 1,000 population[2]   0.65   (30th=)
Histogram: Figure 25, p. 64

Devon – The historic county, excluding unlocated views on the Tamar,
  and those on Exmoor.
Total number of pictures exhibited   1617   (8th)
Weighted index[1]   1758   (7th)
Pictures per square mile   0.67   (11th=)
Pictures per 1,000 population[2]   2.66   (10th)
Graph: Figure 39, p. 87

Dorset – The historic county, thus excluding the Bournemouth area.
Total number of pictures exhibited   737   (16th)
Weighted index[1]   634   (18th)
Pictures per square mile   0.64   (14th)
Pictures per 1,000 population[2]   3.21   (7th)
Graph: Figure 82, p. 146

Durham – The historic county between Tyne and Tees. Unlocated views
  on the Tees are included, but those on the Tyne are not.
Total number of pictures exhibited   299   (30th)
Weighted index[1]   294   (31st)
Pictures per square mile   0.29   (29th=)
Pictures per 1,000 population[2]   0.25   (29th)
Histogram: Figure 104, p. 178

Essex – The historic county, less unlocatable views on the Stour. Several
  places now perceived as part of London, including the Royal Docks are
  east of the River Lea and hence classed as Essex.
Total number of pictures exhibited   934   (11th)
Weighted index[1]   871   (12th)
Pictures per square mile   0.57   (15th=)
Pictures per 1,000 population[2]   0.8   (27th)
Graph: Figure 102, p. 176

Gloucestershire – The historic county, including views of Bristol, and
  unlocatable views on the Cotswolds or 'near Tewkesbury', but not
  those on the Wye.
Total number of pictures exhibited   727   (17th)
Weighted index[1]   644   (17th)
Pictures per square mile   0.51   (17th)
Pictures per 1,000 population[2]   1.01   (23rd)
Graph: Figure 84, p. 148

Hampshire – The historic county but excluding the Isle of Wight. Unlocatable views in the New Forest are included as are those referring to Spithead.

Total number of pictures exhibited	965	(10th)
Weighted index[1]	1008	(11th)
Pictures per square mile	0.67	(11th=)
Pictures per 1,000 population[2]	1.41	(17th)

Graph: Figure 15, p. 48

Herefordshire – The historic county excluding the many unlocated views on the Wye and the few on the Malverns.

Total number of pictures exhibited	120	(40th)
Weighted index[1]	137	(39th)
Pictures per square mile	0.16	(36th=)
Pictures per 1,000 population[2]	1.2	(20th)

Histogram: Figure 17b, p. 51

Hertfordshire – The historic county, but excluding the few unlocatable views in the Chilterns.

Total number of pictures exhibited	336	(27th)
Weighted index[1]	363	(28th)
Pictures per square mile	0.57	(15th=)
Pictures per 1,000 population[2]	1.45	(15th)

Histogram: Figure 32, p. 75

Huntingdonshire – The historic county.

Total number of pictures exhibited	29	(45th)
Weighted index[1]	29	(45th)
Pictures per square mile	0.06	(44th)
Pictures per 1,000 population[2]	0.51	(32nd=)

Histogram: Figure 88, p. 153

Isle of Wight – The island, less unlocated views in Spithead.

Total number of pictures exhibited	491	(21st)
Weighted index[1]	597	(19th)
Pictures per square mile	4.06	(2nd)
Pictures per 1,000 population[2]	7.24	(2nd)

Histogram: Figure 16, p. 49

Kent – The historic county with its western border along the Ravensbourne river, thus including Greenwich.

Total number of pictures exhibited	2544	(3rd)
Weighted index[1]	2728	(2nd)
Pictures per square mile	1.79	(5th)

Pictures per 1,000 population[2]   2.02   (11th)
Graph: Figure 47, p. 98

Lancashire – The historic county the figures including Furness, although
   the histogram does not. Unlocatable views on the Mersey are included.
Total number of pictures exhibited   405   (24th)
Weighted index[1]   369   (27th)
Pictures per square mile   0.2   (33rd=)
Pictures per 1,000 population[2]   0.08   (43rd)
Histogram: Figure 97, p. 169

Leicestershire – The historic county, including the occasional view in
   Charnwood Forest.
Total number of pictures exhibited   86   (43rd)
Weighted index[1]   83   (43rd)
Pictures per square mile   0.1   (41st=)
Pictures per 1,000 population[2]   0.19   (41st)
Histogram: Figure 12c, p. 43

Lincolnshire – The historic county, including unlocated views in the Fens,
   but not those on the Trent.
Total number of pictures exhibited   238   (33rd)
Weighted index[1]   225   (33rd)
Pictures per square mile   0.08   (43rd)
Pictures per 1,000 population[2]   0.45   (34th=)
Histogram: Figure 98, p. 170

London – The area within the Circle Line plus the Isle of Dogs, Waterloo,
   Lambeth and Millbank. This includes most of those areas long thought
   to be central.
Total number of pictures exhibited   3347   (1st)
Weighted index[1]   2924   (1st)
Pictures per square mile   11.82   (1st)[3]
Pictures per 1,000 population[2]   1.15   (21st)[3]
Graph: Figure 99, p. 171

Middlesex – the historic county less those areas classed as London.
Total number of pictures exhibited   1223   (9th)
Weighted index[1]   1213   (9th)
Pictures per square mile   11.82   (1st)[4]
Pictures per 1,000 population[2]   1.15   (21st)[4]
Graph: Figure 100, p. 172

Norfolk – The historic county, including the few unlocatable views on the
   Waveney, but not those in the Fens or Breckland.
Total number of pictures exhibited   794   (14th)
Weighted index[1]   726   (15th)
Pictures per square mile   0.35   (23rd)
Pictures per 1,000 population[2]   1.58   (14th)
Graph: Figure 56, p. 112

Northamptonshire – The historic county, including the Soke of
   Peterborough.
Total number of pictures exhibited   102   (42nd)
Weighted index[1]   113   (42nd)
Pictures per square mile   0.11   (40th)
Pictures per 1,000 population[2]   0.33   (37th)
Histogram: Figure 12b, p. 42

Northumberland – The historic county including unlocatable views on the
   Tyne but not those on the Tweed.
Total number of pictures exhibited   374   (26th)
Weighted index[1]   390   (25th)
Pictures per square mile   0.19   (35th)
Pictures per 1,000 population[2]   0.65   (30th=)
Histogram: Figure 66, p. 123

Nottinghamshire – The historic county including the few unlocatable
   views on the Trent.
Total number of pictures exhibited   129   (39th)
Weighted index[1]   136   (40th)
Pictures per square mile   0.16   (36th=)
Pictures per 1,000 population[2]   0.26   (38th)
Histogram: Figure 67, p. 124

Oxfordshire – The historic county with the Thames as southern boundary.
   Unlocated views on the Thames and those in the Cotswolds are
   excluded.
Total number of pictures exhibited   569   (19th)
Weighted index[1]   514   (21st)
Pictures per square mile   0.69   (10th)
Pictures per 1,000 population[2]   2.83   (9th)
Histogram: Figure 60, p. 115

Rutland – The historic county.
Total number of pictures exhibited   17   (46th)
Weighted index[1]   18   (46th)

Pictures per square mile   0.12   (39th=)
Pictures per 1,000 population[2]   0.91   (25th)
Histogram: Figure 12d, p. 43

Shropshire – The historic county including the few unlocatable views on
the Severn.
Total number of pictures exhibited   273   (31st)
Weighted index[1]   310   (30th)
Pictures per square mile   0.23   (32nd)
Pictures per 1,000 population[2]   1.3   (19th)
Histogram: Figure 17a, p. 51

Somerset – The historic county, with its north-eastern border along the
Avon. Views in Bristol are excluded but unlocatable views on Exmoor
included.
Total number of pictures exhibited   534   (20th)
Weighted index[1]   530   (20th)
Pictures per square mile   0.33   (24th)
Pictures per 1,000 population[2]   1.04   (22nd)
Graph: Figure 10, p. 38

Staffordshire – The historic county excluding unlocatable views in
Dovedale, but including all those in the Black Country.
Total number of pictures exhibited   151   (38th)
Weighted index[1]   143   (38th)
Pictures per square mile   0.12   (39th=)
Pictures per 1,000 population[2]   0.12   (42nd)
Histogram: Figure 45, p. 95

Suffolk – The historic county, including the many unlocatable views on
the Stour but excluding the few on the Waveney.
Total number of pictures exhibited   851   (13th)
Weighted index[1]   713   (16th)
Pictures per square mile   0.48   (20th)
Pictures per 1,000 population[2]   1.86   (13th)
Graph: Figure 87, p. 152

Surrey – The historic county with its northern border as the Thames
except that riverside views from Vauxhall Bridge to Tower Bridge have
been allocated to London. Unlocatable views on the North Downs are
also excluded.
Total number of pictures exhibited   1809   (6th)
Weighted index[1]   1852   (5th)
Pictures per square mile   2.57   (4th)

Pictures per 1,000 population[2]   0.92   (24th)
Graph: Figure 48, p. 98

Sussex – The historic county, including both West and East Sussex.
  Unlocatable views on the South Downs are included.
Total number of pictures exhibited   2811   (2nd)
Weighted index[1]   2499   (3rd)
Pictures per square mile   1.72   (6th)
Pictures per 1,000 population[2]   4.13   (5th)
Graph: Figure 85, p. 148

Warwickshire – The historic county. Unlocatable views on the Warwick-
  shire Avon are included, as are the few in Arden. Those on the
  Cotswolds are not.
Total number of pictures exhibited   324   (28th)
Weighted index[1]   311   (29th)
Pictures per square mile   0.32   (25th=)
Pictures per 1,000 population[2]   0.35   (36th)
Histogram: Figure 44, p. 94

Wiltshire – The historic county. Unlocatable views on Salisbury Plain are
  included but not those on the Cotswolds.
Total number of pictures exhibited   417   (23rd)
Weighted index[1]   392   (24th)
Pictures per square mile   0.29   (29th=)
Pictures per 1,000 population[2]   1.43   (16th)
Histogram: Figure 81, p. 145

Worcestershire – The historic county, including Dudley. The unlocatable
  views on the Malverns are included, but not those in the Black
  Country, or on the Severn.
Total number of pictures exhibited   199   (35th)
Weighted index[1]   219   (34th)
Pictures per square mile   0.31   (27th)
Pictures per 1,000 population[2]   0.45   (34th=)
Histogram: Figure 29, p. 69

Yorkshire – The historic county. Unlocatable views on the Tees are
  excluded, but those on the Pennines included.
Total number of pictures exhibited   1886   (5th)
Weighted index[1]   1823   (6th)
Pictures per square mile   0.3   (28th)
Pictures per 1,000 population[2]   0.51   (32nd=)
Graph: Figure 103, p. 177

The Channel Islands – For convenience these have been treated as if they formed one English county.

Total number of pictures exhibited	214	(34th)
Weighted index[1]	218	(35th)
Pictures per square mile	2.01	(3rd)

Histogram: Figure 62, p. 118

The Isle of Man – For convenience treated as one English county.

Total number of pictures exhibited	73	(44th)
Weighted index[1]	72	(44th)
Pictures per square mile	0.32	(25th=)

Histogram: Figure 63, p. 119

Wales

The Welsh counties have been rarely used by artists in the titles of Welsh landscapes, the terms North, Mid and South Wales being preferred. The Principality has, therefore, been divided into these three regions, counting each as if it were a county. For graph see Figure 33, p. 76; for histogram see Figure 34, p. 77.

North Wales – includes Anglesey, Merionethshire, Caernarvonshire, Denbighshire and Flint. Unlocatable views on the Dee are excluded.

Total number of pictures exhibited	2034	(4th)
Weighted index[1]	2309	(4th)
Pictures per square mile	0.97	(9th)
Pictures per 1,000 population[2]	5.27	(3rd)

Mid Wales – includes Radnorshire, Montgomeryshire, Brecknockshire and Cardiganshire, excluding unlocatable views on Wye and Severn but including those on the Usk.

Total number of pictures exhibited	267	(32nd)
Weighted index[1]	271	(32nd)
Pictures per square mile	0.1	(41st=)
Pictures per 1,000 population[2]	1.37	(18th)

South Wales – includes Monmouthshire, Glamorgan, Carmarthenshire, and Pembrokeshire, including the many unlocatable views on the Wye, but not those on the Usk.

Total number of pictures exhibited	887	(13th)
Weighted index[1]	1015	(10th)
Pictures per square mile	0.43	(21st)
Pictures per 1,000 population[2]	0.74	(28th)

Scotland

The Scottish counties have scarcely been used by artists in their titles. The graph of Scottish popularity (Figure 69, p. 126) therefore represents the whole of Scotland. Some idea of the breakdown between different areas can be seen in the histogram, Figure 68, p. 125. For this purpose the areas were as follows:

Borders – the present-day regions of Dumfries and Galloway and Borders.
Lowlands – the regions of Lothian and Fife, and the regions of Tayside, Central and Strathclyde as far north as the Highland Boundary Fault.
Highlands – the mainland north of the Highland Boundary Fault excluding the Grampian and Tayside Regions.
Grampian – Grampian and Tayside Regions north of the Highland Boundary Fault.
Island – the northern and Western Isles, and all the islands of the west coast, including Arran and Bute.

Ireland

As in Scotland the Irish counties have scarcely been used, so the histogram of Irish popularity (Figure 70, p. 126) is for the whole island. The histogram uses the following regions:

Dublin – Co. Dublin.
South East – Cos Wicklow, Wexford, Kilkenny, Carlow and Waterford.
South West – Cos Cork, Kerry and Limerick.
West – Cos Clare, Galway and Mayo.
North West – Cos Donegal, Leitrim and Sligo.
Ulster – Present-day Northern Ireland.
Central – The remainder of Ireland.

1 The weighted index alters the actual total to allow for the various total numbers of pictures exhibited in the various periods. Thus counties with a peak in the early years will show a weighted index higher than the crude total, those with a peak in the large exhibitions at the end of the nineteenth century will have a lower weighted index.
2 Census of 1901.
3 Includes Middlesex.
4 Includes London.

Actual number of depictions for each county in each period

| County | Periods | | | | | |
	I	II	III	IV	V	VI
Bedfordshire	6	29	14	24	17	17
Berkshire	31	148	180	186	109	112
Buckinghamshire	18	50	51	95	83	76
Cambridgeshire	1	24	13	36	76	50
Cheshire	1	27	28	38	43	33
Cornwall	5	54	110	509	726	333
Cumbria	72	302	207	196	223	168
Derbyshire	15	83	72	62	72	68
Devon	84	204	410	381	327	224
Dorset	18	45	29	134	321	202
Durham	9	52	46	67	80	68
Essex	18	128	121	135	261	282
Gloucestershire	16	81	51	68	323	180
Hampshire	45	191	105	231	215	190
Herefordshire	˙10	36	22	12	16	26
Hertfordshire	15	95	47	39	69	65
Huntingdonshire	1	3	2	18	13	7
Kent	133	476	594	398	414	551
Lancashire	13	36	42	74	122	116
Leicestershire	1	11	8	28	13	27
Lincolnshire	5	31	14	60	83	50
London (central)	105	365	202	365	1,100	1,202
Middlesex	40	253	183	150	252	348
Norfolk	18	72	88	177	255	204
Northamptonshire	6	34	11	16	22	17
Northumberland	13	49	68	118	82	58
Nottinghamshire	1	21	27	48	16	23
Oxfordshire	18	78	63	103	159	150
Rutland	0	8	1	3	3	3
Shropshire	11	92	38	29	71	33
Somerset	34	74	55	84	185	127
Staffordshire	2	21	26	24	42	41
Suffolk	4	38	58	194	325	244
Surrey	58	229	367	474	323	372
Sussex	20	218	300	587	941	761
Warwickshire	5	66	79	76	54	52
Isle of Wight	17	156	137	64	44	71
Wiltshire	9	75	40	59	132	99
Worcestershire	8	50	28	43	50	23

County	Periods					
	I	II	III	IV	V	VI
Yorkshire	62	233	261	387	601	384
Channel Isles	1	10	58	87	26	30
Isle of Man	0	3	7	36	22	5
South Wales	39	312	138	120	101	189
Mid Wales	4	64	33	50	49	70
North Wales	51	476	589	459	225	247
Wales total	94	852	760	629	375	506
Borders	5	32	30	86	76	37
Lowlands	15	122	118	197	150	81
Grampian	3	28	79	147	88	70
Highlands	8	79	189	462	285	138
Islands	2	13	46	199	100	94
Scotland total	33	274	461	1,091	699	420
Dublin	3	35	16	10	13	10
Wicklow (SE)	1	52	22	10	20	7
Kerry (SW)	6	33	40	18	20	26
Galway (W)	1	4	11	28	35	43
Donegal (NW)	0	1	0	9	9	22
Ulster	1	14	16	8	22	13
Central Ireland	0	0	2	2	1	0
Ireland total	12	139	107	85	120	121

Notes

1 Why study pictures?

1 J.B. Jackson, 'The vernacular landscape', in Edmund C. Penning-Rowsell and David Lowenthal (eds), *Landscape Meanings and Values,* London, Allen & Unwin, 1986, pp. 65–81.
2 A. Farmer, 'Lynton and Lynmouth in art', unpublished PhD thesis in preparation, Polytechnic South West, 1989.
3 D.W. Meinig (ed.), *The Interpretation of Ordinary Landscapes: Geographical Essays*, Oxford, Oxford University Press, 1979, p. 72.
4 R.L. Heathcote, 'The artist as geographer: landscape painting as a source for geographical research', *Proceedings of the Royal Geographical Society of Australasia, South Australia Branch*, vol. 73, 1972, p. 1.
5 M.H. Nicholson and N. Nicholson, *Mountain Gloom and Mountain Glory: The Development of the Aesthetics of the Infinite*, New York, Cornell University Press, 1959.
6 R. Rees, 'The taste for mountain scenery', *History Today*, vol. XXV, May 1975, p. 305.
7 K. Thomas, *Man and the Natural World: Changing Attitudes in England 1500–1800*, London, Allen Lane, 1983.
8 M. Hardie, *Water-colour Painting in Britain, Vol.1 , The Eighteenth Century*, London, Batsford, 1966, p. 56.
9 M. Rosenthal, *British Landscape Painting*, Oxford, Phaidon, 1982, p. 10. See also 'Origins of landscape painting in England', *Burlington Magazine*, vol. 109, 1967, p. 483.
10 H.V.S. Ogden and M.S. Ogden, *English Taste in Landscape in the Seventeenth Century*, Ann Arbor, University of Michigan Press, 1955.
11 See p. 192.
12 C. Harrison, *English Art and Modernism 1900–1939*, Indiana University Press, 1981, p. 17.
13 R.R. Wark (ed.), *Sir Joshua Reynolds: Discourses on Art*, San Marino, Calif., Huntington Library, 1959, Discourse III, p. 51.
14 Sir R.P. Collier, The Presidential Address, *Transactions of the Devonshire Association*, vol. 11, 1879, p. 32.

15 F. Inglis, 'Landscape as popular culture', *Landscape Research*, vol. 12, no. 3, 1987, pp. 20–5.

16 Algernon Graves, *Royal Academy of Arts: A Complete Dictionary from its Foundation in 1769 to 1904*, London, George Bell, 1907. This is brought more up to date by: Royal Academy of Arts, *RA Exhibitors 1905–1970*, London, EP Publishing, 1976–81.

17 J.R. Abbey, *Scenery of Great Britain and Ireland in Aquatint and Lithography 1770–1860*, London, Curwen, 1952, and *Travel in Aquatint and Lithography*, London, Curwen, 1956.

18 Further details concerning both the Royal Academy and Devon figures are in P.J. Howard, 'Changing taste in landscape art', unpublished PhD thesis, University of Exeter, 1984.

19 In one review, wearying of Turner's 'tornadoes of colour', Thackeray was glad to 'plunge into a green shady landscape of Lee or Creswick, and follow a quiet stream babbling beneath whispering trees and chequered with cool shade and golden sunshine'. W.M. Thackeray, 'A pictorial rhapsody', *Fraser's Magazine*, June/July, 1840; also in *Contributions to Punch etc.* ed. W. Jerrold, London, Dent, 1903, p. 285.

20 C.W. Stillman, 'This fair land', in E.H. Zube, R.O. Brush and J.G. Fabos (eds), *Landscape Assessment: Values, Perceptions and Resources*, Dowden, Hutchinson & Ross, 1975, p. 20.

21 The third canto of Byron's *Childe Harold*, dealing with the Rhine, was published in 1816.

22 Geoffrey Grigson, *Britain Observed: The Landscape Through Artists' Eyes*, Oxford, Phaidon, 1975. Monet's rejected submission was *The Thames and the Houses of Parliament*, now in the National Gallery.

23 For a discussion of Morland's problems see John Barrell, *The Dark Side of the Landscape*, Cambridge, Cambridge University Press, 1980.

24 N. Pevsner, *The Englishness of English Art*, London, Architectural Press, 1956.

25 E. Hyams, *Soil and Civilization*, 2nd edn, London, John Murray, 1972.

26 Hokusai, The Great Wave, Victoria and Albert Museum, London.

27 E. Johns, 'The artist and the scientific study of scenery', *The Studio*, vol. 149, 1955, pp. 42–9.

28 R.G. Wheeler, *Man, Nature and Art,* London, Pergamon, 1968.

29 Nicolas Poussin, *Et in Arcadia Ego*, c. 1638, Paris, Louvre.

30 A. Altdorfer, *St George in the Forest*, Munich, Alte Pinakothek.

31 K. Grahame, *The Wind in the Willows*, London, Methuen, 1908.

32 J. Appleton, *The Experience of Landscape*, London, John Wiley, 1975. The theory is discussed in Chapter 2.

33 H. Rousseau, *The Dream*, 1910, Metropolitan Museum, New York.

34 W. Stechow, *Dutch Landscape Painting of the Seventeenth Century*, Oxford, Phaidon, 1966, is particularly valuable because of the close attention and classification of subjects.

35 Constable, J., in a letter to Bishop Fisher of Salisbury, dated 23 October, 1821, and quoted in M. Sturge Henderson, *Constable*, London, Duckworth, 1905, p. 60.

36 D. Lowenthal and H. Prince, 'The English landscape', *Geographical Review*, vol. 54, no. 3, 1964, pp. 309–46, and the same authors' 'English landscape tastes', *Geographical Review*, vol. 55, 1965, pp. 186–227.

2   Landscape studies: a new field

1   Sir F. Younghusband, 'Natural beauty and geographical science',
    Geographical Journal, vol. 56, no. 1, 1920, pp. 1–13.
2   E.W. Gilbert, *British Pioneers in Geography*, Newton Abbot, David &
    Charles, 1972, contains a critique of Cornish's work, pp. 227–59. See also V.
    Cornish, *Scenery and the Sense of Sight*, Cambridge, Cambridge University
    Press, 1935.
3   For example, O.J.R. Howarth, *The Scenic Heritage of England and Wales*.
    London, Pitman, 1937.
4   John Leighly, 'Some comments on contemporary geographic method',
    Annals of the Association of American Geographers, vol. 27, 1937, p. 141.
5   See for example, D.C.D. Pocock (ed.), *Humanistic Geography and
    Literature: Essays on the Experience of Place*, London, Croom Helm, 1981.
6   Landscape evaluation work is reviewed in P. Jacobs, 'Landscape image:
    current approaches to the visual analysis of the landscape', *Town Planning
    Review*, vol. 46, no. 2, 1975, p. 127, and later by P. Dearden, 'Landscape
    assessment: the last decade', *The Canadian Geographer*, vol. 24, 1980,
    p. 316.
7   J. Appleton, *The Experience of Landscape*, London, John Wiley, 1975. See
    also the same author's 'Prospects and refuges revisited', *Landscape Journal*,
    vol. 8, 1984, pp. 91–103.
8   G.H. Orians, 'An ecological and evolutionary approach to landscape
    aesthetics', in E.C. Penning-Rowsell and D. Lowenthal (eds), *Landscape
    Meanings and Values*, London, Allen & Unwin, 1986.
9   P. Shepard, *Man in the Landscape: A Historic View of the Esthetics of
    Nature*, New York, Alfred A. Knopf, 1967.
10 Yi Fu Tuan, *Topophilia: A Study of Environmental Perception, Attitudes and
    Values*, Englewood Cliffs, NJ, Prentice-Hall, 1974.
11 K. Lynch, *The Image of the City*, Cambridge, Mass., MIT Press, 1972. ·
12 B. Goodey, *Images of Place: Essays on Environmental Perception,
    Communications and Education*, University of Birmingham, Centre for
    Urban and Regional Studies, Occasional Paper no. 30, 1974.
13 P. Munton, 'Arabian landscapes and Islam', *Landscape Research*, vol. 13,
    no. 2, 1988, pp. 2–5.
14 K. Thomas, *Man and the Natural World: Changing Attitudes in England
    1500–1800*, London, Allen Lane, 1983.
15 D. Lowenthal and H. Prince, 'English landscape tastes', *Geographical
    Review*, vol. 55, 1965, pp. 186–227.
16 D. Lowenthal, 'The American scene', *Geographical Review*, vol. 58, 1968,
    pp. 61–8, and 'Finding valued landscapes', *Progress in Human Geography*,
    vol. 2, no. 3, 1978, pp. 373–418. Although dealing with attitudes to the past
    rather than to landscape, there is much of relevance also in *The Past is a
    Foreign Country*, Cambridge, Cambridge University Press, 1985.
17 E.H. Zube and D.G. Pitt, 'Cross-cultural perceptions of scenic and heritage
    landscapes', *Landscape Planning*, vol. 8, 1981, pp. 69–87. Cross-cultural
    work is reviewed in R. Kaplan and E.J. Herbert, 'Familiarity and preference:
    a cross-cultural analysis', in J.L. Nasar (ed.), *Environmental Aesthetics:
    Theory, Research and Applications*, Cambridge, Cambridge University Press,
    1988. See also Rachel and Stephen Kaplan, *The Experience of Nature: A
    Psychological Perspective*, Cambridge, Cambridge University Press, 1989.
18 C. Harrison, M. Limb and J. Burgess, 'Recreation 2000: Views of the

country from the city', *Landscape Research*, vol. 11, no. 2, 1986, pp. 19–24.

19 R. Rees, 'Images of the prairie: landscape painting and perception in the western interior of Canada', *The Canadian Geographer*, vol. 20, no. 3, 1976, and 'The prairie: a Canadian artist's view', *Landscape*, vol. 21, no. 2, 1977. B.S. Osborne, 'The iconography of nationhood in Canadian art', in D. Cosgrove and S. Daniels (eds), *The Iconography of Landscape*, Cambridge, Cambridge University Press, 1988, pp. 162–78. V. Vallis, 'Artist and environment: an Australian study', *British Journal of Aesthetics*, vol. 2, 1962, p. 328. J. Watkins, 'Stories of Australian art', essay in exhibition catalogue of the same title, Commonwealth Institute, London, 1988, pp. 13–44.

20 A. Gussow, *A Sense of Place: The Artist and the American Land*, New York, Friends of the Earth, 1971.

21 J.B. Jackson, *Discovering the Vernacular Landscape*, New Haven, Yale University Press, 1985.

22 P. Howard, 'Designing the vernacular landscape', *Landscape Research*, vol. 13, no. 3, 1988, pp. 1–2.

23 F. Inglis, 'Landscape as popular culture', *Landscape Research*, vol. 12, no. 3, 1987, pp. 20–5.

24 M. Rosenthal, 'Approaches to landscape painting', *Landscape Research*, vol. 9, no. 3, 1984, pp. 2–13.

25 R. Williams, *The Country and the City*, London, Chatto & Windus, 1973. J. Barrell, *The Dark Side of the Landscape*, Cambridge, Cambridge University Press, 1980. The material from media studies is reviewed in J. Burgess, 'Landscapes in the living-room: television and landscape research', *Landscape Research*, vol. 12, no. 3, 1987, pp. 1–7. See also several essays in Simon Pugh (ed.), *Reading Landscape: Country–City–Capital*, Manchester, Manchester University Press, 1990.

26 D.H. Solkin, *Richard Wilson: The Landscape of Reaction*, London, Tate Gallery Publications, 1982.

27 D. Cosgrove, *Social Formation and Symbolic Landscape*, London, Croom Helm, 1984. S. Daniels, 'The implications of industry: Turner and Leeds', *Turner Studies*, vol. 6, no. 1, 1986, pp. 10–17. D. Cosgrove and S. Daniels (eds), *The Iconography of Landscape*, Cambridge, Cambridge University Press, 1988.

28 E. Relph, *Place and Placelessness*, London, Pion, 1976.

29 T. Griffiths, *Beechworth: An Australian Country Town and its Past*, Melbourne, Greenhouse Publications, 1987.

30 S. Clifford, 'Common Ground: promoting the value of local places', *Landscape Research*, vol. 12, no. 1, 1987, pp. 2–4.

31 J. Jakle, *The Visual Elements of Landscape*, Amherst, Mass., University of Massachusetts Press, 1987.

32 E. Relph, op. cit., p. 51.

33 K. Craik, 'Psychological reflections on landscape', in E.C. Penning-Rowsell and D. Lowenthal (eds), *Landscape Meanings and Values*, London, Allen & Unwin, 1986. S. Kaplan and R. Kaplan (eds), *Humanscape: Environments for People*, Belmont, Calif., Duxbury, 1978. J.L. Nasar (ed.) *Environmental Aesthetics: Theory, Research and Applications*, Cambridge, Cambridge University Press, 1988.

34 B. Goodey, 'Spotting, squatting, sitting, or setting: some public images of landscapes', in E.C. Penning-Rowsell and D. Lowenthal, op. cit., pp. 82–101. D.W. Meinig, 'Ten versions of the same scene' in D.W. Meinig (ed.), *The Interpretation of Ordinary Landscapes: Geographical Essays*, Oxford, Oxford University Press, 1979.

35 J. Jakle, op. cit. D. Cosgrove, 1984, op. cit.
36 G. Cox, '"Reading" Nature: reflections on ideological persistence and the politics of the countryside', *Landscape Research*, vol. 13, no. 3, 1988, pp. 24–34.
37 K. Thomas, op. cit.
38 E. Relph, *Rational Landscapes and Humanistic Geography*, London, Croom Helm, 1982.
39 K. Lynch, *What Time is this Place?*, Amherst, Mass., MIT Press, 1972.
40 D. Lowenthal, *The Past is a Foreign Country*, Cambridge, Cambridge University Press, 1985.
41 National Gallery of Scotland, *The Discovery of Scotland*, Exhibition Catalogue, Edinburgh, 1978. John Murdoch (ed.), *The Lake District: A Sort of National Property*, Victoria and Albert Museum, 1986. E. Moir, *The Discovery of Britain: The English Tourists 1540–1840*, London, Routledge & Kegan Paul, 1964. R. Rees, 'The taste for mountain scenery', *History Today*, vol. 25, 1975, p. 305. J. Zaring, 'The Romantic face of Wales', *Annals of the Association of American Geographers*, vol. 67, no. 3, September 1977.
42 K. Thomas, op. cit.
43 G. Grigson, *Britain Observed: The Landscape through Artists' Eyes*, Oxford, Phaidon, 1975.
44 M. Jacobs and M. Warner, *The Phaidon Companion to Art and Artists in the British Isles*, Oxford, Phaidon, 1980.
45 M. Rosenthal, *British Landscape Painting*, Oxford, Phaidon, 1982.
46 See particularly Tate Gallery, *Landscape in Britain c.1750–1830*, Exhibition Catalogue, 1973, and Arts Council, *Changing Nature: British Landscape Painting 1850–1950*, Exhibition Catalogue, 1983.
47 J.G. Links, *Townscape Painting and Drawing*, London, Batsford, 1972, but see also Arts Council, *Cityscape 1910–1939, Urban Themes in American, German and British Art*, Exhibition Catalogue, 1977.
        On country houses see J. Harris, *The Artist and the Country House*, London, Sotheby Parke Bernet, 1979, and John Steegman, 'The Artist and the Country House', *Country Life*, n.d.
48 A.H. Holcomb, 'Bridge in the middle distance – symbolic elements in Romantic landscape', *Art Quarterly*, vol. 37, 1974, pp. 31–58.
49 G. Grigson, 'Symbols of continuity – church towers in the landscape', *Country Life*, no. 160, 2 December 1976.
50 B.M. Stafford, 'Rude Sublime: the taste for Nature's Colossi during the late 18th and early 19th centuries', *Gazette des Beaux-Arts*, vol. 87, 1976, p. 113. Further work is forthcoming from S. Smiles.
51 G.P. Landow, 'The rainbow: a problematic image', in U.C. Knoepflmacher and G.B. Tennyson, *Nature and the Victorian Imagination*, Berkeley, University of California Press, 1977, pp. 341–69.
52 D. Davies, 'The evocative symbolism of trees', and S. Daniels, 'The political iconography of woodland in later Georgian England', both in D. Cosgrove and S. Daniels (eds), op. cit., pp. 32–42.
53 G. Sheldon, 'Devonshire scenery depicted in English prose literature', *Transactions of the Devonshire Association*, vol. 63, 1931, p. 283.
54 D.C.D. Pocock, *Humanistic Geography and Literature: Essays on the Experience of Place*, London, Croom Helm, 1981.
55 M. Drabble, *A Writer's Britain: Landscape in Literature*, London, Thames & Hudson, 1979. D. Eagle and H. Carnell (eds), *The Oxford Literary Guide to the British Isles*, Oxford, Clarendon Press, 1977. J. Freeman, *Literature and Locality: The Literary Topography of Britain and Ireland*, London, Cassell, 1963.

56 A. Higson, 'Space, place, spectacle', *Screen*, vol. 25, nos 4–5, 1984. See also the same author's 'The landscapes of television' and J.R. Gold, 'Blueprints, false utopias and the Siren's song: "Equinox" and the future city', both in *Landscape Research*, vol. 12, no. 3, 1987, pp. 8–13, 26–30.

57 R.W. Hepburn, 'Aesthetic appreciation of Nature', *British Journal of Aesthetics*, vol. 3, 1963, p. 197.

58 E. Relph, op. cit., 1976, p. 51 *et seq.*

59 Jerome K. Jerome, *Three Men in a Boat*, Dent, 1889, Penguin edition, 1957, p. 159.

60 John Burke, *Musical Landscapes*, Exeter, Webb & Bower, 1983. The radio series was broadcast in the autumn of 1988.

61 V. Cornish, *The Scenery of Sidmouth*, Cambridge, Cambridge University Press, 1935.

62 Anon., 'The moorlands and glens of Cornwall', *Art Journal*, 1883, p. 314.

63 H.V.S. Ogden and M.S. Ogden, *English Taste in Landscape in the Seventeenth Century*, Ann Arbor, University of Michigan Press, 1955, p. 91.

64 J. Barrell, op. cit., p. 20. M. Rosenthal, op. cit., p. 96. A. Martin, 'Content and culture in Victorian painting: attitudes to landscape', unpublished M.Phil. thesis, University College, London, 1988.

65 H.V.S. Ogden and M.S. Ogden, op. cit.

66 J.B. Harley, 'Maps, knowledge and power', in D. Cosgrove and S. Daniels (eds), op. cit., pp. 277–312.

67 T. Risdon, *The Chorographical Description of & Survey of the County of Devon*, London, 1811, from an original manuscript of *c.* 1630.

68 C. Fiennes, *Through England on a Side Saddle*, 1695, and quoted in R.P. Chope, *Early Tours in Devon and Cornwall*, Newton Abbot, David & Charles, 2nd edn., 1967, pp. 111–37, which includes the west country sections of ten tours up to 1796.

69 See E.W. Manwaring, *Italian Landscape in Eighteenth Century England*, London, Frank Cass, 1925.

3 Classical landscape 1770–1790

1 H.V.S. Ogden and M.S. Ogden, *English Taste in Landscape in the Seventeenth Century*, Ann Arbor, University of Michigan Press, 1955.

2 The survival of pictures is dependent on many factors. Some of these vary spatially. Some county and regional museums, for example, make strenuous efforts to collect local work. In other areas either there is no museum, or no such policy is in force.

3 For work exhibited there see: A. Graves, *The Society of Artists of Great Britain, 1760–1791, The Free Society of Artists, 1761–1783, A Complete Dictionary of Contributors and Their Work from the Foundations of the Societies to 1791*, London, G. Bell, 1907.

4 For these roots see: K. Clark, *Landscape into Art*, London, John Murray, 1949; E. Manwaring, *Italian Landscape in Eighteenth Century England*, London, Frank Cass, 1925; L. Herrman, *British Landscape Painting of the Eighteenth Century*, London, Faber & Faber, 1973.

5 For example, D. Clifford, *A History of Garden Design*, New York, Praeger, 1966.

6 A. Burgess, *The Grand Tour*, Elek, London, 1957.

7 W. Thornbury, *The Life of J.M.W. Turner, R.A.,* London, Chatto & Windus, 1877, p. 143, quoting from the autobiography of Cyrus Redding.

8   I am indebted for the identification of the foreground to S. Smiles, in a personal communication, yet to be published.

9   The *coulisse* is the side screen in a picture, forming the same role as the wings of a stage. A *repoussoir* is a figure or object in the foreground of a picture leading the eye towards an important feature.

10 See D. Thomas, 'Claude Lorrain and the English Landscape', *The Connoisseur*, vol. 172, December 1969.

11 J. Swete, 'Picturesque sketches of Devon', unpublished MS, 20 vols, Devon Record Office. The Watcombe reference is vol. 2, p. 82, and the Axmouth reference in vol. 9. p. 152.

12 J. Appleton, *The Experience of Landscape*, London, John Wiley, 1975.

13 For information on this school see G. Briganti, *The View Painters of Europe*, Oxford, Phaidon, 1970.

14 Most notably by Tobias Smollett in 1765, quoted in H. Massingham and P. Massingham, *The Englishman Abroad*, London, Phoenix House, 1967, p. 43.

15 Sidney C. Hutchinson, *The History of the Royal Academy, 1768–1968*, London, Chapman & Hall, 1968, p. 22.

16 ibid, p. 78.

17 ibid, p. 22.

18 Such tours are discussed in P. Anderson, *Over the Alps: In the Steps of Boswell, Beckford and Byron*, London, Rupert Hart-Davies, 1969.

19 M. Hardie, *Water-Colour Painting in Britain, Vol. 1, The Eighteenth Century*, London, Batsford, 1966, p. 137. Also see F.W. Hawcroft, 'Grand Tour sketchbooks of John Robert Cozens', *Gazette des Beaux-Arts*, vol. 91, 1978, p. 99.

20 John Rothenstein, *An Introduction to English Painting*, London, Cassell, 1933.

21 G. Grigson, *Britain Observed: The Landscape through Artists' Eyes*, Oxford, Phaidon, 1975, p. 13.

22 J. Swete, op. cit., vol. 13, p. 3.

23 R.R. Wark (ed.), *Sir Joshua Reynolds: Discourses on Art*, San Marino, Calif., Huntington Library, 1959, Discourse III, p. 51.

24 K. Clark, op. cit., p. 34.

25 Richmond Hill was 'that favourite national scene of ours . . . [which] nature had graciously submitted to be aristocratically groomed'. From an anonymous review of Cropsey's *Richmond Hill*, *Art Journal*, 1863, p. 102.

26 John Barrell, *The Dark Side of the Landscape*, Cambridge University Press, 1980.

27 L. Herrman, op. cit. and John Hayes, 'British patrons and landscape painting: 3) The response to nature in the eighteenth century', *Apollo*, June 1966, pp. 444–51.

28 Celia Fiennes, *Through England on a Side Saddle*, 1695, and Daniel Defoe, *A Tour through Great Britain by a Gentleman*, 1724, both quoted in R.P. Chope (ed.), *Early Tours in Devon and Cornwall*, Newton Abbot, David & Charles, 2nd edn. 1967, pp. 111–37 and pp. 145–78.

29 Tiverton was seen in 1801 as 'handsome' and a 'renovated phoenix from its own ashes'. H.C.S. Cruwys, 'C. Dibdin's account of travelling in North Devon, 1801', *Devon & Cornwall Notes and Queries*, vol. 22, 1956, p. 123.

30 Van de Velde, *Plymouth*, Plymouth, Plymouth Municipal Museum.

31 Jan Siberechts 'Landscape with View of Henley on Thames', 1691, Coll'n Lord Middleton.

32 See P.H. Hulton, 'Drawings of England in the seventeenth century by W. Schellinks, J. Esselens and L. Doomer' *The Walpole Society*, vol. XXXV, 1955.

33   J.M.W. Turner, *Exeter*. Steel line engraving by T. Jeavons, 1829, from *Picturesque Views in England and Wales*.

34   R. Rees, 'Historical links between cartography and art', *Geographical Review*, vol. 70, 1980, pp. 60–78.

35   From 1820 onwards the Royal Academy imposed a ban on 'mere transcripts of the objects of natural history'.

36   W. Gilpin, *Observations on the Western Parts of England Relative Chiefly to Picturesque Beauty*, London, 1798. Reprinted Richmond Publishing 1973, sect. XVII, p. 174.

37   J. Swete, op. cit., vol. 1, p. 202.

38   D. Birch, 'Development of panorama painting', *The Artist*, December 1950, p. 93.

39   Daniel Defoe, 1724, quoted in R.S. Chope, op. cit., pp. 145–78.

40   See B.M. Stafford, 'Rude Sublime: the taste for Nature's colossi during the late 18th and early 19th centuries, *Gazette des Beaux-Arts*, vol. 87, 1976, p. 113.

41   H. Berry, 'Canaletto's England', *History Today*, vol. 31, 1981, pp. 46–50.

42   L. Herrman, op. cit.

43   M. Jacobs and M. Warner, op. cit. p. SE32.

44   Charlotte Seddon, 'The Image of Charlecote', unpublished dissertation, Exeter College of Art and Design, 1988.

45   D.P. Clifford, *Watercolours of the Norwich School*, London, Cory, Adams & Mackay, 1968.

46   J. Greig (ed.), *The Farington Diary*, London, Hutchinson, 1922, vol. VI, entry for 15 October 1810.

47   Richard Wilson, 'Croome Court', 1758, Coll'n the Earl of Coventry. Thomas Gainsborough, 'Mr and Mrs Andrews', National Gallery.

48   John Swete on his tours around Devon was only refused entry once, whether the family was in residence or not.

49   Society of the Dilettanti, founded in 1732, was originally a gentleman's dining society, but came to devote itself to the Fine Arts especially in connection with the Grand Tour.

50   See p. 71.

51   See p. 195.

52   C. Seddon, op. cit.

53   J. Appleton has discussed this need in J. Appleton, (ed   ), *The Aesthetics of Landscape*, Rural Planning Service, Landscape Research Group, 1979. For the problem of conquering space in landscape painting see C. Gould, *Space in Landscape*, The National Gallery, 1974.

54   R.J. Gemmett, 'Beckford's Fonthill: the landscape as art', *Gazette des Beaux-Arts*, vol. 80, 1972, pp. 335–56.

55   Celia Fiennes, *Through England on a Side Saddle*, 1695, quoted in R.P. Chope (ed.), *Early Tours in Devon and Cornwall*, Newton Abbot, David & Charles, 1967, pp. 111–37.

56   Dr. Richard Pococke, *Travels through England*, 1750, quoted in R.P. Chope, op. cit., pp. 178–215.

57   ibid.

58   W. Thornbury, *The Life of J.M.W. Turner R.A.*, London, Chatto & Windus, 1877, pp. 142 *et seq.*

59   R. Ayton, *A Voyage round Great Britain Undertaken in the Year 1813, and Commencing from the Land's End, Cornwall*, London, 1814, Reprinted Tate Gallery, 1978. (Engravings by William Daniell). vol. 8, p. 33.

60   W. Gilpin, op. cit., p. 215.

61 see p. 72.
62 E. Burke, *A Philosophical Enquiry into the Origins of our Ideas on the Sublime and the Beautiful*, London, 1759, is the clearest early account of these ideas. They are well summarized in J. Appleton, op. cit., 1975. See also Tate Gallery, *Gordale Scar: An Essay in the Sublime*, Exhibition Catalogue, 1983.
63 J. Swete, Picturesque sketches of Devon, 1795, vol. 4, pp. 22–3.
64 J. Greig (ed,), *The Farington Diary*, London, Hutchinson, 1922, vol. VI, entry for 3 November 1810.
65 J. Swete op. cit., vol. 1, p. 150.
66 Dr William Stukeley, *Itinerarium Curiosum*, 1724, quoted in R.P. Chope, op. cit., pp. 137–45.
67 See B.M. Stafford, op. cit.
68 R. Rosenblum, 'Abstract Sublime', in H. Geldzahler, *New York Painting and Sculpture, 1940–1970*, London, Pall Mall, 1969.
69 See E.H.H. Archibald, *Dictionary of Sea Painters*, Antique Collectors' Club, 1980.
70 James L. Clifford, *Johnson's Trip to Devon in 1762*, New York, The Grolier Club. 1970.
71 One writer remarked, 'What ungainly objects are these triumphs of naval architecture', J.E.R, 'Leaves from a sketcher's notebook', *Magazine of Art*, 1879, p. 408.
72 See also J. Hunt, 'A Regency View of the Isle of Wight', *The Connoisseur*, vol. 201, no. 807, 1979, pp. 12–15.
73 F.D. Klingender, *Art and the Industrial Revolution*, London, Curwen, 1947.
74 Sir George Beaumont. See M. Jacobs and M. Warner, op. cit., p. MD9.
75 F.D. Klingender, op. cit., p. 54.
76 ibid., p. 9.
77 M. Jacobs and M. Warner, op. cit., p. WA3.
78 M. Woodall (ed.), *The Letters of Thomas Gainsborough*, London, Cupid Press, 1961, p. 123. Letter is dated 8 July 1779.
79 W. Gilpin, op. cit., p. 173. The view was near Barnstaple.
80 J. Swete, op. cit., vol. 20, 1801, pp. 80 and 90.
81 All quoted in R.P. Chope op. cit.: Fiennes on p. 111, Defoe on p. 146, Shaw on pp. 218 and 232.
82 M. Woodall, op. cit., p. 91, letter to Mr Harvey of 22 May 1788.
83 W. Stechow, *Dutch Landscape Painting of the Seventeenth Century*, Oxford, Phaidon, 1966.
84 K. Clark, 'On Painting of English landscape', *Proceedings of the British Academy*, 1936, p. 187.

4 The Picturesque Period 1790–1830

1 C. Hussey, *The Picturesque; Studies in a Point of View*, London, Frank Cass., 1927. See also Malcolm Andrews, *The Search for the Picturesque: Landscape Aesthetics and Tourism in Britain, 1760–1800*, London, Scolar Press, 1989.
2 E. Burke, *A Philosophical Enquiry into the Origins of our Ideas on the Sublime and the Beautiful*, London, 1759, reprinted Menston, Scolar, 1970.
3 W. Gilpin, *Remarks on Forest Scenery*, London, 1791.
4 J. Appleton, *The Experience of Landscape*, London, John Wiley, 1975, p. 31.
5 W. Jackson, *Thirty Letters on Various Subjects*, London, 1784, Letter VI.

6   This question of appropriation is discussed by Fred Inglis, 'Landscape as popular culture', *Landscape Research*, vol. 12, no. 3, pp. 20–5.

7   W. Gilpin, *Observations on the Western Parts of England Relative Chiefly to Picturesque Beauty*, London, 1798, reprinted Richmond Publishing 1973, p. 172.

8   ibid., p. 236.

9   K. Clark 'On painting of English landscape', *Proceedings of the British Academy*, 1936, p. 192.

10 ibid., p. 186.

11 J. Swete, 'Picturesque Sketches of Devon', unpublished MS, 20 vols, Devon Record Office, 1792, vol. 6, p. 160.

12 William Gilpin, op. cit., p. 258.

13 J. Swete., op. cit., vol. 11, p. 15.

14 W.G. Maton, *Observations on the Western Counties of England*, 1794–6, quoted in R.P. Chope, *Early Tours in Devon and Cornwall*, Newton Abbot, David & Charles, 1967, pp. 233–78.

15 H.C.S. Cruwys, 'C. Dibdin's, Account of travelling in North Devon, 1801', quoted in *Devon & Cornwall Notes and Queries*, vol. 22, 1956, p. 123.

16 For a description of the Alpine tours of the time see P. Anderson, *Over the Alps: in the Steps of Boswell, Beckford and Byron*, London, Hart-Davis, 1969.

17 Invented in 1813 by Seenefelder. See M. Twyman, *Lithography, 1800–1850*, Oxford, Oxford University Press, 1970, p. 35.

18 T. Fawcett, *The Rise of English Provincial Art, Artists, Patrons and Institutions outside London, 1800–1830*, Oxford, Clarendon Press, 1974, ch. 1.

19 For details of the business side of artistic life see S. Smiles, 'Plymouth and Exeter as Centres of Art, 1820–1865', unpublished PhD thesis, University of Cambridge, 1982.

20 See E. Shanes, *Turner's Rivers, Harbours and Coasts*, London, Chatto & Windus, 1981, pp. 5–12.

21 Richard Ayton, *A Voyage round Great Britain Undertaken in the Summer of the year 1813 and Commencing from the Land's End, Cornwall, with a series of Views drawn and engraved by William Daniell R.A.*, London, 1814, Facsimile Tate Gallery, 1978.

22 J. Greig (ed.), *The Farington Diary*, 2nd edn, Hutchinson, 1922.

23 ibid., entry for 13 September 1809.

24 ibid., entry for 23 September 1809.

25 One example is J. Hunt, 'A Regency view of the Isle of Wight', *The Connoisseur*, vol. 201, no. 807, May 1979, pp. 12–15.

26 J. Swete, op. cit., vol. 8, p. 69. The five were Lydford, Becky Falls, Canonteign, Brent and Chudleigh.

27 J. Greig, op. cit. Entry for 3 November 1810.

28 W. Gilpin, *Observations on the River Wye and Several Parts of South Wales etc. Relative Chiefly to Picturesque Beauty*, London, 1782.

29 Much later Alfred East, PRBA, ARA, wrote 'Tintern and the Wye as a sketching ground', *The Studio*, vol. 50, 1910, p. 141.

30 J. Greig, op. cit., entry for 9 September 1803. See also M. Andrews, op.cit.

31 S. Hodges, 'Artists' Haunts II: Raglan Castle and the Wye', *Magazine of Art*, 1878, pp. 85–90, when from Monmouth to Tintern cost 10 shillings. Hodges also was pleased that 'the ruins [of Tintern] are not kept in such a painful state of neatness as some ruins are.'

32 J.A. Blaikie, 'The Dart III: Buckfastleigh to New Bridge', *Magazine of Art*,

1885, p. 398 – 'If the Dart is without its Tintern, it is in no respects second to the Wye in the changeless charms of nature.'

33 J. Appleton, op. cit., pp. 86–7.

34 Swete regards Kent's Cavern, near Torquay, as 'nothing comparable to those in the peak of Derbyshire', op. cit., vol. 2, p. 111. For a later appreciation see Edward Bradbury, 'Sketching grounds: the Peak', *Magazine of Art*, 1879, pp. 173 and 277.

35 Mrs S.C. Hall, 'A Day at Chatsworth', *Art Journal*, 1852, pp. 28–32.

36 E. Bradbury, op. cit., pp. 173 and 278.

37 Thomas R. Macquoid, 'Bolton Abbey and the Bolton Woods', *Magazine of Art*, 1879, pp. 112–15.

38 J. Swete, op. cit., vol. 4, p. 110.

39 ibid., vol. 8, p. 115.

40 ibid., vol. 1, p. 40.

41 ibid., vol. 20, p. 147.

42 The interest was largely over by the time of a series of articles in the *Art Journal* of 1887, by D. Hannay and D. MacWhirter, 'Sir Walter Scott's country', pp. 1, 49, 109 and 232.

43 C. Wood, *Victorian Panorama: Paintings of Victorian Life*, London, Faber & Faber, 1976, p. 81.

44 W.G. Maton, *Observations on the Western Counties of England*, 1794–1796, quoted in R.P. Chope, op. cit., pp. 233–78.

45 Don Manuel Alvarez Espriella, *Letters from England*, 1802. Entry for 23 April, quoted in R.P. Chope, op. cit., pp. 298–310. Widely held to be by Robert Southey.

46 T.G. Bonney, 'Canterbury Cathedral', *Magazine of Art*, 1882, pp. 360–6.

47 John Swete, op. cit., vol. 7, p. 131.

48 W.C. Lefroy, 'The ruined abbeys of Yorkshire', *The Portfolio*, 1882, p. 1.

49 W.Gilpin, *Observations on the Western Parts of England, Relative Chiefly to Picturesque Beauty*, London, 1798, reprinted Richmond Publishing, 1973, sect. XIX.

50 R.J. Gemmett, 'Beckford's Fonthill: the landscape as art', *Gazette des Beaux-Arts*, vol. 80, 1972, pp. 335–356.

51 J. Swete, op. cit., vol. 9, p. 120. The reference is to Uvedale Price, whose ideas were formulated in *An Essay on the Picturesque*, London, 1798.

52 J. Swete, op. cit., vol. 13, p. 97, and vol. 18, pp. 115ff.

53 ibid., vol. 17, p. 160. He was, however, disgusted with their hewing down trees merely to allow light into the servants' hall.

54 Rev. S. Shaw, *A Tour to the West of England*, 1788, reproduced in R.P. Chope, op. cit., pp. 215–33.

55 J. Swete, op. cit., vol. 15, p. 131 (Moretonhampstead) and p. 161, (Chagford).

56 ibid., vol. 14, p. 77. Swete complains that one of his pictures 'needs gypsies but there are none in Devon.'

57 For the holiday habits of the century see S. Margetson, *Leisure and Pleasure in the Nineteenth Century*, London, Cassell, 1969.

58 J. Swete, op. cit., vol. 2, p. 40.

59 A.B. Granville, *Spas of England and Principal Sea-Bathing Places*, 1841, reprinted Bath, Adams & Dart, 1971, p. 475.

60 Wallis's Library at Sidmouth, or Banfield's of Ilfracombe, for example.

61 J. Greig, op. cit., entry for 10 October 1809. Only two years later Turner was to make an oil sketch of the same estuary at low water.

62 W. Gilpin, op. cit., sect. XX, p. 199.
63 See Walmesley, *Okehampton Castle, Devonshire*, 1810, no. 1818 in J.V. Somers-Cocks, *Devon Topographical Prints. 1660–1870, a Catalogue and Guide*, Exeter, Devon Library Services, 1977.
64 See, for example, H. Prince, 'Art and agrarian change', in D. Cosgrove and S. Daniels, *The Iconography of Landscape*, Cambridge, Cambridge University Press, 1988, pp. 98–118.
65 J. Swete, op. cit., vol. 8, p. 164.
66 ibid., vol. 10, p. 128.
67 F.D. Klingender, *Art and the Industrial Revolution*, London, Curwen, 1947, p. 93.
68 John Swete, op. cit. vol. 13, p. 197.
69 ibid., vol. 9, p. 152.
70 Although Farington enjoyed 'old houses of picturesque forms and colours' in Exeter, he was aware that this was an idiosyncratic taste. J. Greig, op. cit. Entry for 26 October 1810.
71 M.C. Gillington, 'Salisbury Hall', *Magazine of Art*, 1889, p. 45.
72 M. Hope-Nicholson, *Mountain Gloom and Mountain Glory*, New York, Cornell University Press, 1959, and R. Rees, 'The taste for mountain scenery', *History Today*, May, 1975, vol. 25. p. 305.
73 J. Swete, op. cit., vol. 1, p. 160. The valley was believed to 'derive its form from the Deluge'.

5   The Romantic Period 1830–1870

1   From an anonymous review of Henry Twining, *The Elements of Picturesque Scenery*, Longman, *c.* 1852, published in *Art Journal*, 1852, p. 35.
2   P. Fuller, 'The geography of Mother Nature', in D. Cosgrove and S. Daniels (eds), *The Iconography of Landscape*, Cambridge, Cambridge University Press, 1988, pp. 11–31.
3   D. Cosgrove, 'John Ruskin and the geographical imagination', *Geographical Review*, vol. 69, 1979, pp. 43–62.
4   Professor Ansted, 'Science and art: I – The representation of water', *Art Journal*, 1863, pp. 13–15, and subsequent articles on Plains, Tablelands, Hills and Valleys; Mountains; Clouds, Air and Atmospheric Meteors in their relation to the Picturesque; and On the general relation of physical geography and geology to the progress of landscape art in various countries.
5   P. Quennell, *Romantic England: Writing and Painting 1717–1851*, New York, Macmillan, 1970.
6   See, for example, W. Gaunt, *Bandits in a Landscape: A Study of Romantic Painting from Caravaggio to Delacroix*, New York, Studio, 1937.
7   S. Hodges, 'Artists' haunts VIII: Lynton and Lynmouth', *Magazine of Art*, 1878, p. 225.
8   S. Hodges, 'Nooks and corners of the Devonshire coast – Dartmouth and the Dart', *Magazine of Art*, 1879, p. 50.
9   From an anonymous review of *The Lake Country* by E. Lynn Linton (Smith Elder, *c.* 1865) published in *Art Journal*, 1865, pp. 46–7.
10 See Fig 77, p. 140.
11 W.M. Thackeray, *Little Travels and Roadside Sketches*, in *The Prose Works of William Makepeace Thackeray – Denis Duval etc.*, edited by W. Jerrold, London, Dent, 1903, p. 410.

12 Carl Gustav Carus, *The King of Saxony's Journey through England and Wales in the Year 1844*, translated by S.C. Davidson, 1846. Carus was a painter of the German Romantic School.

13 R. Lister (ed.), *The Letters of Samuel Palmer*, Oxford, Clarendon Press, 1974, p. 720, quoting a letter to Julia Richmond, of January 1865.

14 Newhaven, Scotland, was photographed by David Octavius Hill, and Whitby by Frank Meadow Sutcliffe.

15 The anonymous reviewer of J.H. Bennett's *Winter in the South of Europe*, in 1866, thought 'all Germany, Lombardy, Venetia and Piedmont will for many reasons be intolerable this autumn (should even peace be maintained)' so there may be political reasons for this change. *Nature & Art*, 1866, p. 78.

16 E. Malins, *Samuel Palmer's Italian Honeymoon*, Oxford, Oxford University Press, 1968, pp. 42ff.

17 H.N. Humphreys, *Rome and its Surrounding Scenery*, London, 1840, p. 1.

18 *Art Journal*, 1851, p. 225.

19 C.T. Dent, 'Fine art and mountaineering', *Art Journal*, 1896, p. 270.

20 D. Robertson, 'Mid Victorians among the Alps', in U.C. Knoepflmacher and G.B. Tennyson (eds), *Nature and the Victorian Imagination*, Berkeley, University of California Press, 1977, pp. 113–36.

21 W.M. Thackeray, *The Kickleburys on the Rhine*, London, 1851 and R. Doyle, *The Foreign Tour of Brown, Jones and Robinson*, 2nd edn, London, Routledge, 1904. Original edition *c.* 1855. See also 'Art rambles in Belgium', *Art Journal*, 1865, pp. 209–12 for the London–Antwerp route.

22 From an anonymous review of *Dieppe, the Route by Newhaven* by C. Booth, in *Art Journal*, 1865, p. 292.

23 W.M. Thackeray, *Notes of a Journey from Cornhill to Grand Cairo*, London, 1845, p. 62.

24 Thomas Wright, *Art Journal*, 1851, p. 35. In 1885 J. Penderel-Brodhurst could write 'Elizabethan is, pictorially speaking, the perfection of English domestic architecture', *Magazine of Art*, 1885, p. 24.

25 H.D. Rodee, 'France and England, Some mid-Victorian views of one another's painting', *Gazette des Beaux-Arts*, vol. 91, 1977, p. 39.

26 W.B. Pope (ed.), *The Diary of Benjamin Robert Haydon*, Harvard University Press, Cambridge, Mass., 1960–3, vol. III, p. 396.

27 See S. Hodges, 'Artists' haunts VIII: Lynton and Lynmouth', *Magazine of Art*, 1878, p. 225

28 R. Lister (ed.), op. cit., p. 694, in a letter of July 1864.

29 A.H. Palmer, *The Life and Letters of Samuel Palmer*, Eric & Stevens, London, 1972, p. 55.

30 J.L.W. Page, 'The Rivers of Devon', *The Portfolio*, 1893, p. 7.

31 J.L.W. Page, 'Dartmoor', *The Portfolio*, 1889, p. 67.

32 See D. Bell, *The Artist in Wales*, London, Harrap, 1957.

33 The Usk was Birket Foster's favourite. See J.D., 'A walk in South Wales', *Art Journal*, 1864, p. 133–6, illustrated by Birket Foster, Abergavenny, Crickhowell and Brecon were the main sites.

34 Discussed on p. 182. See R. Lister, op. cit., p. 746. Letter dated September 1866.

35 Walter Crane, *An Artist's Reminiscences*, London, 1907, p. 5.

36 C. Wood, *The Pre-Raphaelites*, London, Weidenfeld & Nicolson, 1981, p. 22.

37 This was the beginning of a major invasion of the Wealden area by artists, which became the archetype of many types of scene later sought elsewhere.

See P. Brandon, 'Wealden nature and the role of London in the nineteenth-century artistic imagination', *Journal of Historical Geography*, vol. 10, 1984, pp. 53–74.

38 R. Ayton, *A Voyage round Great Britain Undertaken in the Summer of the Year 1813, and Commencing from the Land's End, Cornwall*, London, 1814, Tate Gallery, 1978, p. 48.

39 Marmaduke Langdale, *View of Tintagel*, Royal Academy, 1865, awarded the Turner Gold medal in 1866.

40 Robert Hunt's *Popular Romances of the West of England* was reviewed in the *Art Journal*, 1865, p. 291, which journal also reviewed in the same year *Fairy legends and Traditions of the South of Ireland* by T.C. Croker and *The Romance of London* by John Timbs.

41 Walter H. Tregellas, 'Artists' haunts I: Cornwall, the cliffs', *Magazine of Art*, 1878, pp. 8 and 141.

42 Murray, J., *A Handbook for Travellers in Devon and Cornwall*, John Murray, 1851. Ayton (op. cit., p. 46) had previously referred to 'another dreary flat three miles in extent called Woolocombe Sands'.

43 C.G. Carus, op. cit., p. 198.

44 C.C. Loomis 'The Arctic Sublime' and D. Robertson, 'Mid-Victorians among the Alps', both in Knoepflmacher and Tennyson, op. cit.

45 Jay Appleton, *The Experience of Landscape*, London, John Wiley, 1975, pp. 105–6.

46 C.G. Carus, op. cit., p. 200.

47 W. Crane, op. cit., p. 11.

48 J. Staley, *The Pre-Raphaelite Landscape*, Oxford University Press, Oxford, 1973, p. 115.

49 A map of the distribution of all the 6,000 pictures in the Devon study shows the least popular areas to be those of the north west and the South Hams, where the hills are all of a level, and which represent the sub-Eocene wave-cut platform. Figure 109 in P.J. Howard, 'Changing taste in landscape art', unpublished PhD thesis, University of Exeter, 1984.

50 J. Penderel-Brodhurst, 'An old English town – Tewkesbury', *Magazine of Art*, 1887, pp. 348–54.

51 E. Bradbury, 'Hardwick Hall', *Magazine of Art*, 1887, pp. 247–52.

52 F.D. Klingender, op. cit., p. 159.

53 For Arran's attractions see E.A. Taylor, 'The Island of Arran as a sketching ground', *The Studio*, vol. 59, 1913, p. 206.

54 T. Pringle, 'The privation of history: Landseer, Victoria and the Highland myth', in S. Daniels and D. Cosgrove (eds), op. cit., pp. 142–61.

55 T.S. Cooper, *My Life*, vol. 1, London, 1890, p. 328.

56 G.M.Trevelyan, *Illustrated English Social History*, vol. 4, Harmondsworth, Penguin, 1964, p. 111.

57 P. Brandon, op. cit.

58 D. Hannay, 'The lower Medway', *Magazine of Art*, 1886, pp. 20–7.

6   The Heroic Period 1870–1910

1 H.D. Rodee, 'The "Dreary Landscape" as a background for scenes of rural poverty in Victorian paintings', *Art Journal*, vol. XXXVI, no. 4, 1977, pp. 307–13.

2 A phenomenon studied in M. Jacobs, *The Good and Simple Life*, Oxford, Phaidon, 1985.

3   *The Diary of Albert Goodwin RWS, 1883–1927*, Published privately 1934, copy in Bodleian Library.
4   This innocence has been stressed by F. Inglis, 'Landscape as popular culture', *Landscape Research*, vol. 12. no. 3, 1987, pp. 20–5.
5   R.L. Stevenson, 'Fontainebleau: village communities of painters', *Magazine of Art*, 1884, pp. 265–72, 340–5, 359–66, describing 'the great *alfresco* school of art of modern France'. Also see K. de Mattos, 'Apple-Tree Corner', *Magazine of Art*, 1886, pp. 508–13, describing Sevray-sur-Vallais which 'to the uninitiated looks no more than a bit of woodland, but it is always bristling with camp-stools, easels, and figures, feverishly or meditatively at work'. Also M. Talneyr, 'The Forest of Fontainebleau: Winter', *Magazine of Art*, 1888, pp. 38–42, 153–8 and 273–6, where the forest is likened to the New Forest in being favoured by artists.
6   The photographs of Emerson perhaps represent this at its most obvious. See Sainsbury Centre for Visual Art, *Life and Landscape, P.H. Emerson, Art and Photography in East Anglia, 1885–1900*, Exhibition Catalogue, 1986.
7   Typical of the time was H. Blackburn, *Artists and Arabs*, London, Low, Son & Marston, 1868.
8   Anonymous review of David Gorrie, *Summers and Winters in the Orkneys*, (Hodder, 1868), in *Art Journal*, 1868, p. 164.
9   J. Fortescue, 'Exmoor', *Magazine of Art*, 1888, p. 34.
10 H. Hunt, 'Lady Hilda's town', *Art Journal*, 1885, p. 33.
11 J. Craig Annan took photographs for the local board concerned with health.
12 R. G. Wheeler, *Man, Nature and Art*, London, Pergamon, 1968.
13 See Sainsbury Centre for Visual Art, op. cit.
14 S. Baring-Gould, *The Book of Devon*, London, Methuen, 1899, for example, uses watercolour illustrations by Collier for the Dartmoor scenes and monochrome photographs for all others.
15 P. Brandon, 'Wealden nature and the role of London in the nineteenth-century artistic imagination', *Journal of Historical Geography*, vol. 10, 1984, pp. 53–74.
16 J.A. Blaikie, 'On Dartmoor', *Art Journal*, 1885, p. 203.
17 J.L.W. Page, 'Dartmoor', *The Portfolio*, 1889, p. 32.
18 J. Swete, 'Picturesque sketches of Devon, unpublished MS, 20 vols, Devon Record Office, vol. 15, p. 173.
19 ibid., vol. 17, p. 3.
20 John Leland, 1534–43, quoted in R.P. Chope, *Early Tours in Devon and Cornwall*, Newton Abbot, David & Charles, 1967, p. 62.
21 *Art Journal*, 1850, p. 162.
22 J. Swete, op. cit., vol. 12, p. 105.
23 Daniel Defoe, *A Tour through Great Britain by a Gentleman*, 1724, quoted in R.P. Chope, op. cit., p. 176.
24 Marshall, W., *The Rural Economy of the West of England, 1796*, quoted in R.P. Chope, op. cit., p. 296.
25 J.L.W. Page, 'The Highlands of West Somerset', *The Portfolio*, 1890, p. 37.
26 See P. Brandon, op. cit.
27 Review of *The County of Surrey*, London, Cassell, 1865, in *Art Journal*, 1865, p. 260.
28 Strictly the areas around Reigate. *Art Journal*, 1892, p. 301.
29 W. Gilpin, *Remarks on Forest Scenery*, London, 1791.
30 See note 5.
31 M. Garrett-Fawcett, 'The New Forest', *Magazine of Art*, 1885, pp. 1–8 and 45–52. She also condemns the 'hideous parallelograms of Scotch firs',

although indiscriminate felling had already been stopped in 1871.

32 Arthur Tomson, 'Studland', *Art Journal*, 1903, pp. 232–4.

33 S. Colvin, 'East Suffolk memories', *Magazine of Art*, vol. 8, 1885, pp. 221–8 and 265–72.

34 From a critique of W. Roelan's picture *In the Marshes*, in *Magazine of Art*, 1884, p. 149.

35 See G.C. Davies 'The Norfolk Broads', *Art Journal*, 1886, p. 193, and H.F. Wilson, 'The meres of East Anglia', *The Portfolio*, 1887, p. 190.

36 For the role of the new patrons see A. Martin, 'Content and culture in Victorian painting: attitudes to landscape', unpublished M. Phil. dissertation, University College London, 1988, p. 196 *et seq.*

37 F. Watt, 'The rapid Spey', *Magazine of Art*, 1886, p. 359.

38 Burnham Beeches had been conserved in 1879, by the City of London, and acted as a local New Forest. See M. Garrett-Fawcett, 'Burnham Beeches', *Magazine of Art*, 1885, pp. 485–92.

39 'Backwaters of the Thames', *Art Journal*, 1883, p. 145, and Professor A.J. Church, 'The Thames at Oxford', *The Portfolio*, 1884, p. 25.

40 See 'Little-known sketching grounds: Bedford to Lynn', *Art Journal*, 1881, p. 9.

41 G. Grigson, *Britain Observed*, Oxford, Phaidon, 1975, p. 201.

42 M. Jacobs, op. cit.

43 See Alice Meynell, 'Newlyn', *Art Journal*, 1889, pp. 97 and 137.

44 H.E. Butler, 'Polperro', *Art Journal*, 1910, p. 205.

45 Henry Scott Tuke, 'A day in Falmouth harbour', *The Studio*, vol. III, 1894, p. 76. Tuke was an important painter of the harbour, not infrequently depicting young lads bathing from boats.

46 L. Wassermann, 'Some fisher folk', *Art Journal*, 1887, p. 57.

47 *Art Journal*, 1880, p. 346.

48 E. Bradbury, 'Jersey', *Magazine of Art*, 1881, pp. 513–17.

49 Anon., 'Sark', *Magazine of Art*, 1878, pp. 120–3, recommends as subjects 'the tillers of the soil and the "toilers of the sea" who, with their wives and families . . . form its primitive population'.

50 W.H. Tregellas, 'Artists' haunts: I, Cornwall, the Cliffs, Land's End', *Magazine of Art*, 1878, pp. 8–11, states that the Scilly Isles do not afford good sketching ground.

51 All quotes from, E. Bradbury, 'Manxland', *Magazine of Art*, vol. 4, 1881, pp. 54–7.

52 W.G. Maton, *Observations on the Western Counties of England*, 1794–6, quoted in R.P. Chope, op. cit., p. 276.

53 R. Ayton, *A Voyage round Great Britain Undertaken in the Summer of the Year 1813, and Commencing from the Land's End, Cornwall*, London, 1814, reprinted Tate Gallery 1978, p. 41.

54 W.W. Fenn, 'Favourite sketching grounds: Clovelly', *Magazine of Art*, 1880, p. 87.

55 Rev. W. Harrison, 'Clovelly', *Art Journal*, 1896, pp. 321–5.

56 P.V. Bradshaw, 'My favourite sketching grounds, II, Clovelly', *The Artist*, vol. 48, 1954, p. 45. *The Artist* had a largely amateur readership.

57 A. Watson, 'After the Herring', *Magazine of Art*, 1882, pp. 405–11 and 454–60.

58 R.J. Charleton, 'Cullercoats', *Magazine of Art*, 1886, pp. 456–62.

59 A. Watson, 'The coaly Tyne', *Magazine of Art*, 1883, pp. 114–21.

60 H.E. Ward, 'Out of doors in Surrey', *Magazine of Art*, 1882, pp. 287–94.

61 All quotes from Anon. 'Favourite sketching grounds: Surrey commons',

Magazine of Art, 1879, pp. 52–6.

62 G. Allen, 'Wootton House', *Magazine of Art*, 1887, pp. 145–50.

63 J. Fortescue, op. cit., p. 31.

64 J.L.W. Page, 'The rivers of Devon, Dartmouth and the Dart', *The Portfolio*, 1893, p. 30.

65 These included: P.G. Hamerton, 'A painter's camp in the Highlands and thoughts about art', reviewed in *Art Journal*, 1863, p. 60; R.Walker, 'The Clyde and the Western Highlands', *Art Journal*, 1891, p. 161; D.S. Graham, 'By the salmon pools of Tay', *Art Journal*, 1894, p. 233; J. MacWhirter, 'Glen Affaric', *Art Journal*, 1897, p. 73; H. MacMillan, 'The source of the Tay', *Art Journal*, 1899, p. 151, and the same author's 'Rothiemurchus', *Art Journal*, 1902, p. 7.

66 G.P.J. Hood, 'The fisher-folks' homes', *Magazine of Art*, 1882, p. 36.

7 The Vernacular Period 1910–1950

1 C. Harrison, *English Art and Modernism, 1900–39*, Bloomington and London, Indiana University Press and Allen Lane, 1981, p. 17.

2 Denys Val Baker, *The Timeless Land, The Creative Spirit in Cornwall*, Bath, Adams & Dart, 1973.

3 See, for example, John Sheail, *Rural Conservation in Inter-war Britain*, Oxford, Clarendon Press, 1981.

4 For example A.G. Street was one of the most popular writers and radio broadcasters of the day offering in books such as *Country Calendar*, London, Eyre & Spottiswoode, 1935, a view of farming which stressed its continuity and righteousness.

5 C. Williams-Ellis, *England and the Octopus*, London, Geoffrey Bles, 1928, and C. Williams-Ellis (ed.), *Britain and the Beast*, London, Dent, 1937.

6 Very little work has as yet been done on the impact of the flood of photographic books of the period, except for Ian Jeffrey, 'The culture of connotation and after: some notes on landscape photography in Britain since 1900', in *Undercut*, nos. 7/8, 1983, pp. 62–8.

7 See C.S. Law and E.H. Zube, 'Effects of photographic composition on landscape perception, *Landscape Research*, vol. 8, no. 1, 1983, pp. 22–3.

8 K. Clark, *Landscape into Art*, London, John Murray, 1949, p. 222.

9 For the details of sites associated with artists in the French Riviera and Paris, see B. Whelpton, *Painters' Provence*, London, Johnson, 1970, and the same author's *Painters' Paris*, London, Johnson, 1970.

10 See A. Paterson, 'Evesham', *The Studio*, vol. 14, p. 87.

11 F. Rutter 'The art of Robert P. Bevan', *The Studio*, vol. 91, 1926, p. 110.

12 John Gold, 'Blueprints: false utopias and the Siren's song: "Equinox" and the future city', *Landscape Research*, vol. 12, no. 3, 1987, pp. 26–30.

13 Sydney C. Hutchinson, *The History of the Royal Academy, 1768–1968*, London, Chapman & Hall, 1968, p. 159.

14 Albert Goodwin, *The Diary of Albert Goodwin R.W.S., 1893–1927*, published privately 1934, p. 319.

15 R. Ayton, *A Voyage round Great Britain Undertaken in the Summer of the Year 1813, and Commencing from the Land's End, Cornwall*, London, 1814, reprinted Tate Gallery 1978, p. 44.

16 Anon., 'Rye: its artistic resources', *Art Journal*, 1881, p. 97.

17 See E.L. Seeley, 'Christchurch, Hants', *Art Journal*, 1890, p. 93.

18 By V.C. Boyle, in *Transactions of the Devonshire Association*, vol. 83, 1951, p. 212.

19 R. Ayton, op. cit., p. 46.

20 Albert Goodwin, op. cit., p. 418.

21 *A Handbook for Travellers in Devon and Cornwall*, 3rd edn, London, John Murray, 1856.

22 See Arthur Tomson, 'Dorchester', *Art Journal*, 1901, p. 231, and C. Holland, 'The work of Frederick Whitehead, a painter of Thomas Hardy's Wessex', *The Studio*, vol. 32, 1905, p. 105.

23 R. Ayton, op. cit., vol. VIII, p. 10.

24 W.H. Hudson, *A Shepherd's Life*, London, Methuen, 1910, p. 2.

25 ibid., p. 2.

26 W.G. Maton, quoted in R.P. Chope, *Early Tours in Devon and Cornwall*, Newton Abbot, David & Charles, 1967, p. 233.

27 F. Watt, 'The Wiltshire Avon', *Art Journal*, 1888, p. 293.

28 W.W. Fenn, 'Favourite sketching grounds: Lulworth Cove, Dorsetshire', *Magazine of Art*, 1879, pp. 212–16.

29 C.R. Ashbee, 'The Guild of Handicraft at Chipping Camden', *Art Journal*. 1903, pp. 147–52.

30 Batsford published The British Heritage Series in the 1930s which was most successful in publicizing the contemporary view of the attractive, e.g. H. Batsford and C. Fry, *The English Cottage*, London, Batsford, 1938.

31 W.W. Fenn, 'The South Downs as a sketching ground', *Magazine of Art*, 1883, pp. 207–11. He continues by praising stubble burning as offering painterly fumes and suggesting the 'noble tasks of husbandry'.

32 This book is, however, indebted to Philpotts if only because it has been written in what was once his study.

33 Stephen Daniels is currently working on 'Constable's *Haywain*: the making of a cultural icon'.

34 G.D. Leslie and F.A. Eaton. 'John Constable R.A.', *Art Journal*, 1903, pp. 5–9.

35 F. Rutter, op. cit.

36 A. Tomson, 'Studland', *Art Journal*, 1903, pp. 232–4.

37 J. Hine, 'A plea for the Picturesque in Devonshire towns', *Transactions of the Devonshire Association*, 1877, vol. 9, p. 156.

38 S.P.B. Mais and T. Stephenson, *Lovely Britain*, London, Odhams, 1934, p. 79.

39 John Betjeman, *John Piper*, London, Penguin, 1944, p. 10.

40 Edward Bawden, quoted in Douglas Percy Bliss, *Edward Bawden*, Godalming, Pendomer Press, 1979, p. 32.

41 Though the movement known as Neue Sachlichkeit in Germany, including photographers such as Renger-Patzch, may have influenced both Americans and British.

42 In 1884 a series of articles in the *Art Journal* had listed the sketching grounds within the cab radius as: the river from the Pool to Westminster; the Tower; Hyde Park and Kensington Gardens; St James's Park; Chelsea Hospital and Battersea Park; Regent's Park and the Inns of Court.

43 Mr and Mrs S.C. Hall, *Ireland: A Week at Killarney*, George Virtue, 1850. Reviewed in *Art Journal*, 1850, pp. 253–6.

44 S.C. Hall, 'A week at Killarney', *Art Journal*, 1865, pp. 118–20, in which a large influx of summer visitors is forecast because of the exhibition.

45 For example, Charles Wilkinson, 'Mid the Hills of Kerry', *Art Journal*, 1903, pp. 137–41.

8   The Formal Period 1950–1980

1   For a discussion of the reaction of English artists to modernism see
    C. Harrison, *English Art and Modernism, 1900–1939*, Bloomington and
    London, Indiana University Press and Allen Lane, 1981.
2   W. Barron, *The Camden Town Group*, London, Scolar, 1979.
3   See E. Jussim and E. Lindquist-Cock, *Landscape as Photograph*, New
    Haven, Yale University Press, 1985 for a discussion of the various ways of
    seeing landscape through the lens.
4   M. Haworth-Booth, in Gordon Fraser Gallery, *The Land – Twentieth
    Century Landscape Photographs*, Exhibition Catalogue, 1975, p. 11.
5   J. Jakle, *The Visual Elements of Landscape*, Amherst, University of
    Massachusetts Press, 1987.
6   J.R. Gold, 'Blueprints: false utopias and the Siren's song: "Equinox" and the
    future city', *Landscape Research*, vol. 12, no. 3, 1987, pp. 26–30.
7   See D.W. Meinig, 'Symbolic landscapes: some idealizations of American
    communities', in D.W. Meinig (ed.), *The Interpretation of Ordinary
    Landscapes: Geographical Essays*, Oxford, Oxford University Press, 1979.
8   See R. Rosenblum, 'Abstract Sublime', in H. Geldzahler, *New York Painting
    and Sculpture, 1940–1970*, London, Pall Mall, 1969.
9   B. Stonehouse, *The Aerofilms Book of Britain from the Air*, London,
    Weidenfeld & Nicolson, 1982.
10 A. Higson, 'The landscapes of television', *Landscape Research*, vol. 12,
    no. 3, 1987, p. 12.
11 I. Jeffrey, 'The culture of connotation, and after: some notes on landscape
    photography in Britain since 1900', *Undercut*, nos. 7/8, 1983, pp. 62–8.
12 B. Jarvis, 'The next best thing to being there: the environmental rhetoric of
    advertising', *Landscape Research*, vol. 12, no. 3, pp. 14–19.
13 From an anonymous review of S. Moody, *The Palm Tree* (London, Nelson,
    c. 1864), *Art Journal*, 1864, p. 92.
14 J. Williamson, *Decoding Advertisements: Ideology and Meaning in
    Advertising*, London, Marion Boyars, 1978, and S. Pettit, 'Nature in
    Advertising', unpublished dissertation, Exeter College of Art and Design,
    1988.
15 F.D. Klingender, *Art and the Industrial Revolution*, London, Curwen, 1947,
    p. 9.
16 See M.S. Young, 'American realists of the 1930s', *Apollo*, March 1981,
    vol. CXIII, no. 229.
17 See G.S. Whittet, 'Painting industrial Britain,' *The Studio*, vol. 151, 1956,
    p. 106, and G.L. Peters and B.L. Anderson, 'Industrial landscapes: past
    views and stages of recognition', *Professional Geographer*, vol. 28, no. 4,
    1976, pp. 341–8.
18 V. Cornish, 'Harmonies of scenery: an outline of aesthetic geography',
    Geography, vol. 14, 1928, pp. 275–83 and 383–94.
19 W.G. Hoskins in a television documentary on *The Making of the Cornish
    Landscape*, 1983.
20 M. Creighton, 'Hoghton Tower', *Magazine of Art*, 1887, pp. 19–24.
21 P. Theroux, *The Kingdom by the Sea*, London, Hamish Hamilton, 1983.
22 For a general survey of London see D. Piper, *Artists' London*, London,
    Weidenfeld & Nicolson, 1982.
23 J. Penderel-Brodhurst, 'Round about West Drayton', *Magazine of Art*, 1887,
    pp. 73–7.
24 R. Hewison, *The Heritage Industry*, London, Methuen, 1987.

25 An interest recommended in E. Johns, 'The Artist and the scientific study of scenery', *The Studio*, vol. 149, 1955, pp. 42–9.

26 R. Jefferies, 'New facts in landscape', *Magazine of Art*, 1882, p. 470.

27 To be seen at the Beaford Centre, Beaford, Devon.

28 J.E.R. 'Leaves from a sketcher's notebook', *Magazine of Art*, 1879, p. 243. The landscape was around Harwich.

29 R. Ingrams and J. Piper, *Piper's Places: John Piper in England and Wales*, London, Chatto & Windus, 1983, p. 105.

30 For example D. Hill, *In Turner's Footsteps: Through the Hills and Dales of Northern England*, London, John Murray, 1984.

31 R.St J. Tyrwhitt, 'Craven and the Dales', *Magazine of Art*, 1883, pp. 409–15.

32 S. Daniels, 'Constable's *Haywain*: the making of a cultural icon', in preparation.

9   Processes and possibilities

1   D.P. Bliss, *Edward Bawden*, Godalming, Pendomer Press, 1979, p. 73.

2   D. Meinig, *The Interpretation of Ordinary Landscapes: Geographical Essays*, Oxford, Oxford University Press, 1979, p. 175.

3   T. Griffiths, *Beechworth: an Australian country town and its past*, Melbourne, Greenhouse Publications, 1987.

4   D. Lowenthal, 'Finding valued landscapes', *Progress in Human Geography*, vol. 2, no. 3, 1978, p. 376.

5   J. Greig (ed.), *The Farington Diary*, entries for 13 September 1809 (Bishop Fisher) and 23 September 1809, (John Swete).

6   University of Manchester, *Landscape Evaluation*, University of Manchester, 1976, p. 3.38.

7   R. Lister (ed.), *The Letters of Samuel Palmer*, Oxford, Clarendon Press, 1974, p. 720.

8   H. Vizetelly, *Glances Back through Seventy Years*, London, Kegan Paul, 1893, p. 366ff.

9   A. Goodwin, *The Diary of Albert Goodwin R.W.S., 1883–1927*, private, 1934, p. 319.

10 T. Pringle, 'The privation of history: Landseer, Victoria and the Highland Myth', in D. Cosgrove and S. Daniels (eds), *The Iconography of Landscape*, Cambridge, Cambridge University Press, 1988, pp. 142–61.

11 G. Grigson, *Britain Observed: The Landscape through Artists' Eyes*, Oxford, Phaidon, 1975, p. 197.

12 P.F. Brandon, 'Wealden nature and the role of London in the nineteenth-century artistic imagination', *Journal of Historical Geography*, vol. 10, 1984, pp. 53–74.

13 J.L.W. Page, 'The rivers of Devon', *The Portfolio*, 1893, p. 36.

14 R. Mabey, S.Clifford and A. King (eds), *Second Nature*, London, Jonathan Cape, 1984, and A. King and S. Clifford, *Holding Your Ground: An Action Guide to Local Conservation*, London, Wildwood House, 1987.

15 W.J. Loftie, 'Guildford', *Magazine of Art*, 1886, pp. 265–71.

16 E. Moir, *The Discovery of Britain: The English Tourists 1540–1840*, London, Routledge & Kegan Paul, 1964.

17 J.A. Blaikie, 'The Dart: Totnes to Buckfastleigh', *Magazine of Art*, 1885, p. 398.

18 W. Crane, *An Artist's Reminiscences*, London, private, 1907, p. 220.

19 B. Goodey. 'Turned out nice again . . . disaster averted in

Northamptonshire', *Landscape Research*, vol. 13, no. 1, 1988, pp. 14–18.
20 J. Greig, op. cit., entry for 16 July 1807.
21 R.Lister (ed.), op. cit., p. 720, letter dated January 1865.
22 In a review of Royal Academy picture no. 154, *A Devonshire Mill*, by Frederick Lee. *Art Journal*, 1855, p. 173.
23 S. Smiles, 'Plymouth and Exeter as Centres of Art, 1820–1865', unpublished PhD thesis, University of Cambridge, 1981, p. 122.
24 J. Jakle, *The Visual Elements of Landscape*, Amherst, University of Massachusetts Press, 1987.
25 F.G. Bernáldez, J.P. Ruiz, J. Benayas and R.P. Abelló, 'Real landscapes versus photographed landscapes: preference dimensions', *Landscape Research*, vol. 13, no. 1, 1988, pp. 10–11.
26 See p. 19.
27 C. Harrison, M. Limb and J. Burgess, 'Recreation 2000, views of the country from the city', *Landscape Research*, vol. 11, no. 2, 1986, pp. 19–24.
28 W.W. Fenn, 'The love of landscape', *Art Journal*, 1882, p. 197.
29 E. Verhaeren, 'The Island of Marcken', *Magazine of Art*, 1896, p. 413.
30 R.L. Heathcote, 'The artist as geographer: landscape painting as a source for geographical research', *Proceedings of the Royal Geographical Society of Australasia, South Australia Branch*, vol. 73, 1972, p. 19.
31 Quoted in K. Clark, *Landscape into Art*, London, John Murray, 1949, p. 34.
32 G. Grigson, op. cit., p. 34.
33 J. Swete. 'Picturesque Sketches of Devon', unpublished MS, 20 vols, Devon Record Office, vol. 2, p. 179.
34 C.G. Carus, *The King of Saxony's Journey through England and Wales in the Year 1844*, S.C. Davidson, 1846, p. 203.
35 J.A. Blaikie, 'The Dart: Galmpton to Totnes', *Magazine of Art*, 1885, p. 320.
36 S. Hodges, 'Nooks and corners of the Devonshire coast: Dartmouth and the Dart', *Magazine of Art*, vol. 2, 1879, p. 54.
37 J.L.W. Page, 'The rivers of Devon: Dartmouth and the Dart', *The Portfolio*, 1893, p. 30.
38 C.G. Carus, op. cit., p. 216.
39 ibid., p. 218.
40 S. Hodges, 'Artists' haunts VIII: Lynton and Lynmouth', *Magazine of Art*, 1878, p. 225.
41 V. Vallis 'Artist and environment: an Australian study', *British Journal of Aesthetics*, vol. 2, 1962, p. 329.
42 ibid., p. 329
43 J.L.W. Page, op. cit., p. 8.
44 Mrs S.C. Hall, 'A day at Chatsworth', *Art Journal*, 1852, p. 28.
45 D. Hannay, 'The lower Medway', *Magazine of Art*, 1886, pp. 20–7.
46 S.P.B. Mais, *Lovely Britain*, London, Odhams, 1934, p. 84.
47 Yeend King 'A round in France', *Magazine of Art*, 1885, pp. 116–20.
48 From a letter of 1851, quoted in H. Massingham and P. Massingham, *The Englishman Abroad*, London, Phoenix House, 1962, p. 78.
49 D. Meinig, op. cit., p. 164.
50 E. Relph, *Place and Placelessness*, London, Pion, 1976.
51 J.B. Jackson, *Discovering the Vernacular Landscape*, New Haven, Yale University Press, 1985.

Bibliography

Sources used for original perceptions

Anderson, P., *Over the Alps: in the Steps of Boswell, Beckford and Byron*, London, Rupert Hart-Davis, 1969.

Anon. 'The moorlands and glens of Cornwall', *Art Journal*, 1883, p. 314.

Ayton, Richard, *A Voyage round Great Britain Undertaken in the Summer of the Year 1918*, and Commencing from the Land's End, Cornwall, London, 1814, reprinted Tate Gallery 1978. (Engravings by William Daniell.)

Blaikie, J.A., 'The Dart III: Buckfastleigh to New Bridge', *Magazine of Art*, 1885, pp. 397–401.

Bonney, T.G., 'Canterbury Cathedral', *Magazine of Art*, 1882, pp. 360–6.

Bradbury, Edward, 'Sketching grounds: the Peak', *Magazine of Art*, 1878, pp. 173 and 278.

Clifford, James L., *Johnson's Trip to Devon in 1762*, New York, Grolier Club, 1970.

Cruwys, H.C.S., 'C. Dibdin's account of travelling in North Devon, 1801', *Devon & Cornwall Notes and Queries*, vol. 22, 1956, p. 123.

Defoe, Daniel, *A Tour through Great Britain by a Gentleman*, 1724.

East, Alfred, 'Tintern and the Wye as a sketching ground', *The Studio*, vol. 50, 1910, p. 141.

Espriella, Don Manuel Alvarez, *Letters from England*, 1802, in R.P. Chope (ed.), *Early Tours in Devon and Cornwall*, Newton Abbot, David & Charles, 2nd edn, 1967, p. 298–310. Widely held to be by Robert Southey.

Fiennes, Celia, *Through England on a Side Saddle*, 1695, in R.P Chope, (ed.), *Early Tours in Devon & Cornwall*, Newton Abbot, David & Charles, 2nd edn, 1967, pp. 111–37.

Gillington, M.C., 'Salisbury Hall', *Magazine of Art*, 1889, p. 45.

Gilpin, William, *Observations on the River Wye and Several Parts of South Wales etc. Relative Chiefly to Picturesque Beauty*, Richmond, Surrey, Richmond Publishing, 1782.

—— *Remarks on Forest Scenery*, London, 1791.

—— *Observations on the Western Parts of England Relative Chiefly to Picturesque Beauty*, London, 1798, Reprinted Richmond Publishing, 1973.

Grahame, Kenneth, *The Wind in the Willows*, London, Methuen, 1908.

Granville, A.B., *Spas of England and Principal Sea-Bathing Places*, 1841, reprinted Bath, Adams & Dart, 1971, p. 475.

Greig, J. (ed.), *The Farington Diary*, London, Hutchinson, 1922.

Hall, Mrs S.C. 'A day at Chatsworth', *Art Journal*, 1852, pp. 28–32.

Hannay, D. and MacWhirter D., 'Sir Walter Scott's country', series in *Art Journal*, 1887, pp. 1, 49, 109 and 232.

Hodges, Sydney, 'Artists' haunts II: Raglan Castle and the Wye', *Magazine of Art*, 1878, pp. 85–90.

J.E.R., 'Leaves from a sketcher's notebook', *Magazine of Art*, 1879, p. 408.

Jerome, Jerome K., *Three Men in a Boat*, Dent, 1889. Penguin edition 1957.

Lefroy, W.C., 'The ruined abbeys of Yorkshire', *The Portfolio*, 1882.

Macquoid, Thomas R., 'Bolton Abbey and the Bolton woods', *Magazine of Art*, 1879, pp. 112–15.

Massingham, H. and Massingham, P., *The Englishman Abroad*, London, Phoenix House, 1967.

Maton, W.G., *Observations on the Western Counties of England*, 1794–6, in R.P. Chope (ed.), *Early Tours in Devon and Cornwall*, Newton Abbot, David & Charles, 1967, pp. 233–78.

Pococke, Dr Richard, *Travels through England*, 1750, in R.P. Chope (ed.), *Early Tours in Devon and Cornwall*, Newton Abbot, David & Charles, 2nd edn, 1967, pp. 178–215.

Risdon, Tristram. *The Chorographical Description of & Survey of the County of Devon*, London, 1811, from an original manuscript of *c.* 1630.

Shaw, Rev. S., *A Tour to the West of England*, 1788, reprinted in R.P. Chope (ed.), *Early Tours in Devon and Cornwall*, Newton Abbot, David & Charles, 2nd edn, 1967, pp. 215–33.

Stukeley, Dr William, *Itinerarium Curiosum*, 1724, in R.P. Chope (ed.), *Early Tours in Devon and Cornwall*, Newton Abbot, David & Charles, 2nd edn, 1967, pp. 215–33.

Swete, John 'Picturesque sketches of Devon', unpublished MS, 20 vols, (of which 3 are missing), Devon Record Office.

Thackeray, William M., 'A pictorial rhapsody', *Fraser's Magazine*, June/July, 1840.

Woodall, Mary (ed.), *The Letters of Thomas Gainsborough*, London, Cupid Press, 1961.

Secondary sources

Abbey, J.R., *Scenery of Great Britain and Ireland in Aquatint and Lithography 1770–1860*, London, Curwen, 1952.

—— *Travel in Aquatint and Lithography*, London, Curwen, 1956.

Andrews, Malcolm, *The Search for the Picturesque: Landscape Aesthetics and Tourism in Britain 1760–1800*, London, Scolar Press, 1989.

Appleton, Jay, *The Experience of Landscape*, London, John Wiley, 1975.

—— (ed.), *The Aesthetics of Landscape*, Rural Planning Service, Landscape Research Group, 1979.

—— 'Prospects and refuges revisited', *Landscape Journal*, vol. 8, 1984, pp. 91–103.

Archibald, E.H.H., *Dictionary of Sea Painters*, Woodbridge, Suffolk, Antique Collectors' Club, 1980.

Arts Council, *Cityscape 1910–1939, Urban Themes in American, German and British Art*, Exhibition Catalogue, 1977.

—— *Changing Nature: British Landscape Painting 1850–1950*, Exhibition Catalogue, 1983.

Barrell, John, *The Dark Side of the Landscape*, Cambridge, Cambridge University Press, 1980.

Berry, H., 'Canaletto's England', *History Today*, vol. 31, 1981, pp. 46–50.

Birch, D., 'Development of panorama painting', *The Artist*, December, vol. 44, 1950, p. 93.

Bourassa, Steven C., 'Toward a theory of landscape aesthetics', *Landscape and Urban Planning*, vol. 15, 1988, pp. 241–52.

Briganti, G., *The View Painters of Europe*, Oxford, Phaidon, 1970.

Burgess, A., *The Grand Tour*, Elek, London, 1957.

Burgess, Jacquelin, 'Landscapes in the living-room: television and landscape research', *Landscape Research*, vol. 12, no. 3, 1987, pp. 1–7.

Burke, Edmund, *A Philosophical Enquiry into the Origins of our Ideas on the Sublime and the Beautiful*, London, 1759, reprinted Menston, Scolar Press, 1970.

Burke, John, *Musical Landscapes*, Exeter, Webb & Bower, 1983.

Clark, Kenneth, 'On painting of English landscape', *Proceedings of the British Academy*, 1936.

—— *Landscape into Art*, London, John Murray, 1949.

Clifford, D.P., *Watercolours of the Norwich School*, London, Cory, Adams & Mackay, 1968.

Clifford, Derek, *A History of Garden Design*, New York, Praeger, 1966.

Clifford, Susan, 'Common Ground: promoting the value of local places', *Landscape Research*, vol. 12, no. 1, 1987, pp. 2–4.

Collier, Sir R.P., The Presidential Address, *Transactions of the Devonshire Association*, vol. 11, 1879, p. 32.

Commonwealth Institute, *Stories of Australian Art*, Exhibition Catalogue, London, 1988.

Cornish, Vaughan, *Scenery and the Sense of Sight*, Cambridge, Cambridge University Press, 1935.

—— *The Scenery of Sidmouth*, Cambridge, Cambridge University Press, 1935.

Cosgrove, Denis, *Social Formation and Symbolic Landscape*, London, Croom Helm, 1984.

Cosgrove, Denis and Daniels, S. (eds), *The Iconography of Landscape*, Cambridge, Cambridge University Press, 1988.

Cox, Graham, '"Reading" nature: reflections on ideological persistence and the politics of the countryside', *Landscape Research*, vol. 13, no. 3, 1988, pp. 24–34.

Craik, Kenneth, 'Psychological reflections on landscape', in E.C. Penning-Rowsell and D. Lowenthal (eds), *Landscape Meanings and Values*, London, Allen & Unwin, 1986.

Daniels, Stephen, 'The implications of industry: Turner and Leeds', *Turner Studies*, vol. 6, no. 1, 1986, pp. 10–17.

—— 'The political iconography of woodland in later Georgian England', in D. Cosgrove and S. Daniels (eds), *The Iconography of Landscape*, Cambridge, Cambridge University Press, 1988, pp. 43–82.

Davies, D., 'The evocative symbolism of trees', in D. Cosgrove and S. Daniels (eds), *The Iconography of Landscape*. Cambridge, Cambridge University Press, 1988, pp. 32–42.

Dearden, P., 'Landscape assessment: the last decade', *The Canadian Geographer*, vol. 24, 1980, p. 316.

Drabble, Margaret, *A Writer's Britain: Landscape in Literature*, London, Thames & Hudson, 1979.

Eagle, D. and Carnell, H. (eds), *The Oxford Literary Guide to the British Isles*, Oxford, Clarendon Press, 1977.

Farmer, Andrew, 'Lynton and Lynmouth in art', PhD thesis in preparation, Polytechnic South West, 1989.

Fawcett, T., *The Rise of English Provincial Art, Artists, Patrons and Institutions outside London 1800–1830*, Oxford, Oxford University Press, 1974.

Freeman, John, *Literature and Locality: The Literary Topography of Britain and Ireland*, London, Cassell, 1963.

Gemmett, R.J., 'Beckford's Fonthill: the landscape as art', *Gazette des Beaux-Arts*, vol. 80, 1972, pp. 335–56.

Gilbert, E.W., *British Pioneers in Geography*, Newton Abbot, David & Charles, 1972, contains a critique of Vaughan Cornish's work, pp. 227–59.

Gold, John R., 'Blueprints, false utopias and the Siren's song: "Equinox" and the future city', *Landscape Research*, 1987, vol. 12, no. 3, pp. 26–30.

Goodey, Brian, *Images of Place: Essays on Environmental Perception, Communications and Education*, University of Birmingham, Centre for Urban and Regional Studies, Occasional Paper no. 30, 1974.

—— 'Spotting, squatting, sitting, or setting: some public images of landscapes', in E.C. Penning-Rowsell and D. Lowenthal (eds), *Landscape Meanings and Values*, London, Allen & Unwin, 1986, pp. 82–101.

Gould, C., *Space in Landscape*, London, The National Gallery, 1974.

Graves, Algernon, *Royal Academy of Arts: A Complete Dictionary from its Foundation in 1769 to 1904*, London, George Bell, 1907.

Griffiths, Tom, *Beechworth: An Australian Country Town and its Past*, Melbourne, Greenhouse Publications, 1987.

Grigson, Geoffrey, *Britain Observed: The Landscape through Artists' Eyes*, Oxford, Phaidon, 1975.

—— 'Symbols of continuity – church towers in the landscape', *Country Life*, No. 160, 2 December 1976.

Gussow, A., *A Sense of Place: The Artist and the American Land*, New York, Friends of the Earth, 1971.

Hardie, Martin, *Water-Colour Painting in Britain, Vol. 1, The Eighteenth Century*, London, Batsford, 1966.

Harley, J.B., 'Maps, knowledge and power', in D. Cosgrove and S. Daniels (eds), *The Iconography of Landscape*, Cambridge, Cambridge University Press, 1988.

Harris, J., *The Artist and the Country House*, London, Sotheby Parke Bernet, 1979.

Harrison, Carolyn, Limb, M. and Burgess, J., 'Recreation 2000: views of the country from the city', *Landscape Research*, vol. 11, no. 2, 1986, pp. 19–24.

Harrison, Charles, *English Art and Modernism 1900–1939*, Bloomington, Indiana University Press, 1981.

Hawcroft, F.W., 'Grand Tour sketchbooks of John Robert Cozens', *Gazette des Beaux-Arts*, vol. 91, 1978, p. 99.

Hayes, John, 'British patrons and landscape painting: (3) the response to nature in the eighteenth century', *Apollo*, June 1966, pp. 444–51.

Heathcote, R.L., 'The artist as geographer: landscape painting as a source for geographical research', *Proceedings of the Royal Geographical Society of Australasia, South Australia Branch*, vol. 73, 1972.

Hepburn, R.W., 'Aesthetic appreciation of Nature', *British Journal of Aesthetics*, vol. 3, 1963, p. 197.

Herrman, Luke, *British Landscape Painting of the Eighteenth Century*, London, Faber & Faber, 1973.

Higson, Andrew, 'Space, place, spectacle', *Screen*, 1984, vol. 25, nos. 4–5.
—— 'The landscapes of television', *Landscape Research*, 1987, vol. 12, no. 3, pp. 8–13.
Holcomb, A.H., 'Bridge in the middle distance – symbolic elements in Romantic landscape', *Art Quarterly*, 1974, vol. 37, no. 1, pp. 31–58.
Hope-Nicholson, M., *Mountain Gloom and Mountain Glory*, New York, Cornell University Press, 1959.
Howard, Peter J., 'The use of art works in landscape studies', *Landscape Research*, vol. 4, no. 3, 1979, pp. 10–12.
—— 'Changing taste in landscape art', unpublished PhD thesis, University of Exeter, 1983.
—— 'Change in the landscape perceptions of artists', *Landscape Research*, vol. 9, no. 3, 1984, pp. 41–4.
—— 'Painters' preferred places', *Journal of Historical Geography*, vol. 11, no. 2, 1985, pp. 138–54.
—— 'Designing the vernacular landscape', *Landscape Research*, vol. 13, no. 3, 1988, pp. 1–2.
Hulton, P.H., 'Drawings of England in the seventeenth century by W. Schellinks, J. Esselens and L. Doomer', *The Walpole Society*, vol. XXXV, 1955.
Hunt, J., 'A Regency view of the Isle of Wight', *The Connoisseur*, vol. 201, no. 807, 1979, pp. 12–15.
Hussey, Christopher, *The Picturesque: Studies in a Point of View*, London, Frank Cass, 1927.
Hutchinson, Sidney C., *The History of the Royal Academy, 1768–1968*, London, Chapman & Hall, 1968.
Hyams, Edward, *Soil and Civilization*, 2nd edn, London, John Murray, 1972.
Inglis, Fred., 'Landscape as popular culture', *Landscape Research*, vol. 12, no. 3, 1987, p. 20–5.
Jackson, John B., *Discovering the Vernacular Landscape*, New Haven, Yale University Press, 1985.
—— 'The vernacular landscape', in Edmund C. Penning-Rowsell and David Lowenthal (eds), *Landscape Meanings and Values*, London, Allen & Unwin, 1986, pp. 65–81.
Jackson, William, *Thirty Letters on Various Subjects*, London, 1784.
Jacobs, M. and Warner, M., *The Phaidon Companion to Art and Artists in the British Isles*, Oxford, Phaidon, 1980.
Jacobs, P., 'Landscape image: current approaches to the visual analysis of the landscape', *Town Planning Review*, vol. 46, no. 2, 1975, p. 127.
Jakle, John, *The Visual Elements of Landscape*, Amherst, University of Massachusetts Press, 1987.
Johns, Ewart, 'The artist and the scientific study of scenery', *The Studio*, vol. 149, 1955, pp. 42–9.
Kaplan, Rachel and Herbert, E.J., 'Familiarity and preference: a cross-cultural analysis', in J.L. Nasar (ed.), *Environmental Aesthetics: Theory, Research & Applications*, Cambridge, Cambridge University Press, 1988.
Kaplan, S. and Kaplan, R. (eds), *Humanscape: environments for people*, Belmont, Calif., Duxbury, 1978.
Klingender, F.D., *Art and the Industrial Revolution*, London, Curwen, 1947.
Landow, G.P., 'The rainbow: a problematic image', in U.C. Knoepflmacher and G.B. Tennyson, *Nature and the Victorian Imagination*, Berkeley, University of California Press, 1977, pp. 341–69.
Links, J.G., *Townscape Painting and Drawing*, London, Batsford, 1972.

Lowenthal, David, 'The American scene', *Geographical Review*, vol. 58, 1968, pp. 61–8.

—— 'Finding valued landscapes', *Progress in Human Geography*, vol. 2, no. 3, 1978, pp. 373–418.

—— *The Past is a Foreign Country*, Cambridge, Cambridge University Press, 1985.

Lowenthal, David and Prince, Hugh, 'The English landscape', *Geographical Review*, vol. 54, 1964, pp. 309–46.

—— 'English landscape tastes', *Geographical Review*, vol. 55, 1965, pp. 186–227.

Lynch, Kevin, *The Image of the City*, Cambridge, Mass., MIT Press, 1972.

—— *What Time is this Place?*, Cambridge, Mass., MIT Press, 1972.

Manwaring, E.W., *Italian Landscape in Eighteenth Century England*, London, Frank Cass, 1925.

Margetson, S., *Leisure and Pleasure in the Nineteenth century*, London, Cassell, 1969.

Martin, Alison, 'Content and culture in Victorian painting: attitudes to landscape', unpublished M.Phil. thesis, University College, London, 1988.

Meinig, Donald W., (ed.), *The Interpretation of Ordinary Landscapes: Geographical Essays*, Oxford, Oxford University Press, 1979.

Moir, E., *The Discovery of Britain: The English Tourists 1540–1840*, London, Routledge & Kegan Paul, 1964.

Munton, Paul, 'Arabian landscapes and Islam', *Landscape Research*, vol. 13, no. 2, 1988, pp. 2–5.

Murdoch, John (ed.), *The Lake District: A Sort of National Property*, Victoria and Albert Museum, 1986.

Nasar, Jack L. (ed.), *Environmental Aesthetics: Theory, Research & Applications*, Cambridge, Cambridge University Press, 1988.

National Gallery of Scotland, *The Discovery of Scotland*, Exhibition Catalogue, Edinburgh, 1978.

Nicholson, M.H. and Nicholson, N., *Mountain Gloom and Mountain Glory: The Development of the Aesthetics of the Infinite*, New York, Cornell University Press, 1959.

Ogden, H.V.S. and Ogden, M.S., *English Taste in Landscape in the Seventeenth Century*, Ann Arbor, University of Michigan Press, 1955.

Orians, Gordon H., 'An ecological and evolutionary approach to landscape aesthetics', in E.C. Penning-Rowsell and D. Lowenthal (eds), *Landscape Meanings and Values*, London, Allen & Unwin, 1986, pp. 3–22.

Osborne, B.S., 'The iconography of nationhood in Canadian art', in D. Cosgrove and S. Daniels (eds), *The Iconography of Landscape*, Cambridge, Cambridge University Press, 1988, pp. 162–78.

Pevsner, Nicholas, *The Englishness of English Art*, London, Architectural Press, 1956.

Pocock, Douglas C.D. (ed.), *Humanistic Geography and Literature: Essays on the Experience of Place*, London, Croom Helm, 1981.

Price, Uvedale, *An Essay on the Picturesque*, London, 1798.

Prince, Hugh, 'Art and agrarian change', in D. Cosgrove and S. Daniels (eds), *The Iconography of Landscape*, Cambridge, Cambridge University Press, 1988, pp. 98–118.

Rees, Ronald, 'The taste for mountain scenery', *History Today*, vol. XXV, May 1975, p. 305.

—— 'Images of the prairie: landscape painting and perception in the western interior of Canada', *The Canadian Geographer*, vol. 20, no. 3, 1976.

—— 'The prairie: a Canadian artist's view', *Landscape*, vol. 21, no. 2, 1977.

—— 'Historical links between cartography and art', *Geographical Review*, vol. 70, 1980, pp. 60–78.

Relph, Edward, *Place and Placelessness*, London, Pion, 1976.

—— *Rational Landscapes and Humanistic Geography*, London, Croom Helm, 1982.

Rosenblum, R., 'Abstract Sublime' in H. Geldzahler, *New York Painting and Sculpture, 1940–1970*, London, Pall Mall, 1969.

Rosenthal, Michael, *British Landscape Painting*, Oxford, Phaidon, 1982.

—— 'Approaches to landscape painting', *Landscape Research*, vol. 9, no. 3, 1984, pp. 2–13.

Rothenstein, John, *An Introduction to English Painting*, London, Cassell, 1933.

Royal Academy of Arts, *RA Exhibitors 1905–1970*, London, EP Publishing, 1976–81.

Shanes, Eric, *Turner's Rivers, Harbours and Coasts*, London, Chatto & Windus, 1981.

Sheldon, Gilbert, 'Devonshire scenery depicted in English prose literature', *Transactions of the Devonshire Association*, vol. 63, 1931, p. 283.

Shepard, P., *Man in the Landscape: A Historic View of the Esthetics of Nature*, New York, Alfred A. Knopf, 1967.

Smiles, Sam, 'Plymouth and Exeter as centres of art, 1820–1865', unpublished PhD thesis, University of Cambridge, 1982.

Solkin, D.H., *Richard Wilson: The Landscape of Reaction*, London, Tate Gallery Publications, 1982.

Somers-Cocks, J.V., *Devon Topographical Prints. 1660–1870, a Catalogue and Guide*, Exeter, Devon Library Services, 1977.

Stafford, B.M., 'Rude Sublime: the taste for Nature's colossi during the late 18th and early 19th centuries', *Gazette des Beaux-Arts*, vol. 87, 1976, p. 113.

Stechow, W., *Dutch Landscape Painting of the Seventeenth Century*, Oxford, Phaidon, 1966.

Steegman, John, *The Artist and the Country House*, Country Life, n.d.

Stillman, C.W., 'This fair land', in E.H. Zube, R.O. Brush and J.G. Fabos (eds), *Landscape Assessment: Values Perceptions and Resources*, Stroudsburg, Pennsylvania, Dowden, Hutchinson & Ross, 1975, pp. 18–30.

Tate Gallery, *Landscape in Britain c. 1750–1830*, Exhibition catalogue, 1973.

—— *Gordale Scar: An Essay in the Sublime*, Exhibition Catalogue, 1983.

Thomas, D., 'Claude Lorrain and the English landscape', *The Connoisseur*, vol. 172, December 1969.

Thomas, Keith, *Man and the Natural World: Changing Attitudes in England 1500–1800*, London, Allen Lane, 1983.

Thornbury, Walter, *The Life of J.M.W. Turner, R.A.*, London, Chatto & Windus, 1877.

Tuan, Yi fu, *Topophilia: A Study of Environmental Perception, Attitudes and Values*, Englewood Cliffs, NJ, Prentice-Hall, 1974.

Twyman, Martin, *Lithography, 1800–1850*, Oxford, Oxford University Press, 1970.

Vallis, Val, 'Artist and environment: an Australian study', *British Journal of Aesthetics*, vol. 2, 1962, p. 328.

Wark, R.R. (ed.), *Sir Joshua Reynolds: Discourses on Art*, San Marino, Calif., Huntington Library, 1959.

Wheeler, R.G., *Man, Nature and Art*, London, Pergamon, 1968.

Williams, Raymond, *The Country and the City*, London, Chatto & Windus, 1973.

Wood, Christopher, *Victorian Panorama: Paintings of Victorian Life*, London, Faber & Faber, 1976.

Younghusband, Sir Francis, 'Natural beauty and geographical science', *Geographical Journal*, vol. 56, no. 1, 1920, pp. 1–13.

Zaring, Jane, 'The Romantic face of Wales', *Annals of the Association of American Geographers*, vol. 67, no. 3, September 1977.

Zube, E.H., R.O. Brush and J.G. Fabos (eds), *Landscape Assessment: Values Perceptions and Resources*, Dowden, Hutchinson & Ross, 1975.

Zube, E.H. and Pitt, D.G., 'Cross-cultural perceptions of scenic and heritage landscapes', *Landscape Planning*, vol. 8, Stroudsburg, Pennsylvania, 1981, pp. 69–87.

Index